50
50 BOOKS
THE BEST OF
INDIAN FICTION

50 WRITERS
50 BOOKS

THE BEST OF
INDIAN FICTION

Edited by
Pradeep Sebastian
and **Chandra Siddan**

HarperCollins *Publishers* India

First published in India in 2013 by Collins
An imprint of HarperCollins *Publishers* India

This edition published in India by
HarperCollins *Publishers* in 2017
Building 10, Tower A, 4th Floor, DLF Cyber II,
Gurugram Haryana - 122002, India
www.harpercollins.co.in

10 9

P-ISBN: 978-93-5029-428-4
P-ISBN: 978-93-5029-476-5

Typeset in 12/15 Perpetua Regular at
SÜRYA

Printed and bound at
MicroPrints India, New Delhi

To the memory of our teacher and friend,
T.G. Vaidyanathan

CONTENTS

INTRODUCTION:
NEW, TIMELESS

What hubris to think that here we have the definitive list of the fifty best books of India! The audacity of such a claim! Whose fifty best and whose notion of India? As argued by fifty different writers, *50 Writers, 50 Books: The Best of Indian Fiction* is a collective, subjective view of the Indian literary map. What we have here is a cloud that was raised when authors, literary critics and scholars of various Indian literatures were asked what books in any given Indian language, including English, could be argued to belong in such a short list. It is the first of a kind: fifty essays commissioned from writers who felt so passionately about their favourite work of fiction that they leaped to the task of representing it here. Not all of these essays may convince or convince equally; some very humbly and modestly focus on what the work offers without making any worldly claims for it to be an 'Indian classic' or 'one of the top fifty'. But each of these essayists, several being novelists themselves, is fashioning their argument in a sarcophagus of their love of this book, not really caring who else will be at this party. And who can resist the beauty of such passionate claims?

One cannot but sit up and take notice when Abhijit Gupta calls

Nabarun Bhattacharya's *Harbart* 'a Molotov cocktail hurled at the heart of the literary establishment', or when Siddharth Chowdhury celebrates Upamanyu Chatterjee as 'a bona fide homegrown rockstar', or when Anita Roy quotes David Godwin's description of *The God of Small Things* as 'a shot of heroin in the arm'. They are all celebrating moments of rupture in literary history.

Many of the essayists are overwhelmed by the task of representing their favourite. Here is Sampurna Chattarji on *The Trotter-Nama*: 'My exhilaration at the prospect of communicating just one small fraction of what Allan Sealy's magnificent debut novel meant for Indian fiction in English — what it encompassed, extolled, lampooned, what it revelled in, what it did for literature — is immediately followed by despair. It cannot be done.' And Pico Iyer makes this apology in his essay on *A Fine Balance*: 'To anyone who has not read the book, much of this may sound extravagant; to many who have, it will only seem inadequate.' Such sincere humility renders their arguments all the more seductive.

And the diversity of tone and content are a joy unto themselves: the irresistible charm of Amitava Kumar's defence of the heroine's choice in *A Suitable Boy*, or the exuberance of Nilanjana Roy's celebration of Desani's torrential logorrhea in *All About H. Hatterr*, or the nonchalance of Ashwin Kumar on Ananthamurthy's obsession with authenticity, or the belligerence of Hartosh Singh Bal on Raja Rao's place above Booker prize-winners. While some essays provide scholarly context (P. Radhika: *Sharapanjara*; Ashutosh Potdar: *Dhag*), others stay breathlessly personal (Mita Kapur: *Pinjar*). A few offer a literary socio-historical context so wide that it provides a profound understanding of our post-colonial condition (Pankaj Mishra: *The Guide*) and others zoom into a problematic moment (Ben Conisbee Baer: *Hansuli Banker Upakatha*). Some are all plot (Meghnad Desai: *Gujarat No Nath*), some focus on the concept (Rimi Chatterjee: *Aranyer Adhikar*). While some meditate intensely on the work alone

(Kalyan Raman: *Thanneer*; Anjum Hasan: *The Shadow Lines*), for a few others it is more about the author, a looming presence who gives the book its meaning (S. Theodore Baskaran: *Karukku*; Vijay Nair: *Sunlight on a Broken Column*; Aamer Hussein: *River of Fire*).

Despite the diversity of the voices, the passion of all the essays is strongly connected, it turns out, to the issue of modernity, both the novel's perspective on it as well as that of the essayist who is speaking for it. Clearly something important is at stake. Because when we say books we mean novels (and in a few cases short story collections) and we are conscious that when dealing with the Indian novel we are engaging with India's social history seen through the filter of plot and characters and therefore, inevitably, we are dealing with India's relationship to modernity as well as its discontent with it.

Because it was with this genre that we saw the birth of the free agent, the man or woman who made their own choice, successfully or not, and questioned their destiny. Talking of *Durgeshnandini*, arguably the first Indian novel, Arunava Sinha points out: 'Chattopadhyay tore off the tyranny of the gods, of predestination and of divine will, on storytelling . . . it was *Durgeshnandini* that showed the way in terms of investing characters with free will and the power to choose.'

The protagonists of these books are not idealized legendary heroes and virtuous heroines who get their just deserts but characters that spill over their cultural containers and derail themselves spectacularly into the unquantifiable space of freedom, whether in Tagore's *Ghare Baire* or Ashokamitran's *Thanneer* or Arundhati Roy's *The God of Small Things*. And it is from that space that a modern self-desiring love, justice and a unique space of its own could be accessed, irrespective of the deficits of its circumstances: poverty, caste, class, language, tribal identity, untouchability, sexual orientation and gender difference.

Even when modernity is not the subject in any way, by its very form the work is by default modern, since the novel is a modern genre. Arunava Sinha recounts a charming urban legend about the writing of *Durgeshnandini*: 'When Chattopadhyay gathered his friends in a room to read the novel to them, they were thunderstruck by its use of the language, which miraculously echoed both the cadences of regular speech and the exalted register of a literary idiom.' Talking of Pudumaippithan's style in *Pudumaippithan Kathaigal*, A.R. Venkatachalapathy says, 'he made a clear rupture with romanticist and idealistic outpourings which were the lot of Tamil writing of the days, and attempted to shock readers with stark portrayals of subaltern life – the life of the mill workers, prostitutes, hotel servers, plantation workers . . .' That an author calls himself 'Pudumaippithan' (meaning 'Crazy about Modernity') shows the degree of investment in it. Venkatachalapathy clarifies that the 'crazy' in the pseudonym is a reference to 'the crazy one' – Shiva, the god of time – pointing to the timeless yet new aspect of modernity.

So is modernity then universally translatable into any culture? We get a clue to that in Chandrahas Choudhury's essay on *Chha Mana Atha Guntha* as he celebrates Fakir Mohan Senapati's style as an 'indigenous modernity that could see the faults and failings of the traditional Indian order without assenting wholesale to the values of Western modernity'. Summarizing another literary scholar Himanshu Mohapatra, he refers to 'how the "links, nudges and dodges" of the narrator produce "an active reader", one who discerns the skeptical and critical awareness required of him as a political subject'. Speaking of Marathi literature before Uddhav Shelke's *Dhag*, Ashutosh Potdar points out a key difference from previous Marathi literature which 'entertained the reader as a spectator and not as a stakeholder'.

Hence it is not surprising that it is as modern subjects ourselves, as stakeholders with something to lose, that we relate to the characters, their choices and the resulting outcomes. We cannot but be elated at the explosion of the consummate modern woman in Bama or the modern man in Birsa. Their recognition of the modern epoch is one that liberates their voices and brings about a sea change in their respective subaltern subjectivities. Tellingly, both protagonists are based on real-life characters, *Karukku* is autobiographical and speaks of the Dalit Christian life in Tamil Nadu and *Aranyer Adhikar* is based on the life of Birsa Munda, a tribal hero and freedom fighter who died in a British jail in Ranchi in 1900. Birsa's modernity is based not just 'on his fight for freedom from the British: it was, and is, the *dikus*, the moneylenders, the landlords, the colliery owners, the hirers of itinerant labour and the corrupt petty officials who were and are their oppressors'. Likewise, Bama's world shows caste oppression and systems of landownership that block the Dalits' access to the sustaining wealth of nature. Both these writers' understanding of these oppressive relations and a demand for justice is quintessentially modern.

Bama's very writing of the book is a liberatory act: 'In 1992 I looked upon myself as a bird with the wings clipped. Now I see myself as a falcon soaring high in the sky.' The autobiographical novel turned out to be a modernist Dalit manifesto: '*Karukku* gave me a new hope, brought in a new sense of responsibility and provided me with clear-sightedness. It made a big impact on those who read it. To those caught up in the tentacles of caste oppression and were being destroyed, to those who have been marginalized, the book gave confidence. The novel gave them optimism to continue their journey, to break the mindset and live with self-esteem and freedom, with their head held high.' Both these voices, Bama's and Mahasweta Devi's rendition of Birsa Munda's story, explode the old and inaugurate the new.

We should also add Shaman of Ismat Chughtai's *Tehri Lakir* to

Bama and Birsa as another arch example of the modern Indian subject. Shaman is the sovereign subject taking full advantage of the freedom from the past offered by modernity. But then, as we see among the essays in this book, there is also a great degree of questioning of that freedom and 'a return' or an attempt to return to nature or regional certainties, as in Karanth's *Marali Mannige* or Vijayan's *The Legends of Khasak*, or Poornachandra Tejaswi's *Carvalho*, all of which are still an engagement with modernity.

Along with such ambivalence towards modernity overlaps the clarifying and confusing presence of nationalism, which was supported by the new popular genre of the novel. As acknowledged by Arunava Sinha writing on *Durgeshnandini*:

> This emergence of free will in the narrative was not just emancipation for characters. This was also an artistic assertion of the emerging nationalist identity that Chattopadhyay was to develop in his subsequent work – the right to decide one's own future instead of giving in to the dictates of the British Raj. Significantly, it was not until the 1857 uprising that India's British rulers actually abandoned their tolerance of local cultural practices and began to dictate aspects of private life as well through laws. The rise of the Indian novel can also be conflated with the reaction to this intrusion, which accelerated the resistance to occupation and loaded ammunition in the barrels of the revolutionaries.

In other words, the British were hoisted on their own petard when the newborn Indian novel took to oppose their presence vociferously. In the essays on *Mrityunjoy*, *Aranyer Adhikar* as well as *Ghare Baire* we see modernity and a violent anti-British nationalism to be one and the same, though the attitudes to that dynamic moment range from critical to the celebratory. Mrityunjoy's rejection of the peaceful Gandhian resistance in order to carry out a violent anti-colonial act is clearly modernist as is Birsa Munda's tribal resistance to the British. But while one is framed critically against the framework of Gandhian nationalism, the other is celebrated independent of it. And there is the more ambivalent take on modernity in *Ghare Bhaire* in which a rich, happy, feudal couple finds a liberation more radical than they would have wished for since modernity, notwithstanding its visionary, timeless and new promises, is anti-feudal as well as anti-colonial. Whereas the modernity presented in *Hansuli Banker Upakatha* is a more difficult one: pro-colonial and anti-caste.

It is perhaps because our modernism is so tied up with nationalism that our disenchantment with one could perhaps also trigger disenchantment with the other. Pankaj Mishra articulates this aptly in his pithy summary of our post-colonial condition while commenting on R.K. Narayan's heroes:

> The early novels with their energetic young men (Swami, Chandran and Krishna), the middle novels with the restless drifters (Srinivas, Sriram) and the later novels, with the men wounded and exiled by the modern world (Jagan, Raman) map out an emotional and intellectual journey that many middle-class people in formerly colonial societies have made: the faint consciousness of individuality and nationality through colonial education; confused anti-colonial assertion; post-colonial sense of inadequacy and failure; unfulfilled private lives; distrust of modernity and individual assertion; and finally in middle or old age, the search for cultural authenticity and renewal in the neglected once great past.

We see this arc in a number of novels other than *The Guide*: O.V. Vijayan's *The Legends of Khasak* shows a disenchanted urban young man Ravi fleeing a promising career in physics and a fellow physicist lover to take refuge in the small village of Khasak. Kala Krishnan

Ramesh's essay contextualizes the book thus: Vijayan, a solid communist himself, was disillusioned by Soviet communism during the writing of this novel and refashioned his hero out of the 'mould of the urban revolutionary come to conscientize the village' and recast him as a 'spiritual wanderer'. Poornachandra Tejaswi's *Carvalho* displays a similar ambivalence to modernity despite the scientific quest for a rare gecko and Shivaram Karanth's *Marali Mannige* shows the return of the grandson from the treacherous city to the grandfather's village farm as the deliverance the family women were waiting for. (The heroine of *A Suitable Boy* is perhaps the first fictional Indian woman to make that centripetal turn, choosing a man her mother chooses when she could have taken a modern romantic risk.) Gone are the high expectations of game-changing, life-altering modernism, one is grateful to return to village life and the arms of the earth, a humble step away from merging with it.

However, in the Sturm und Drang of the Indian urban male's drama of enchantment and disenchantment with the nationalist and the modernist project is the simultaneous margin-to-centre movement of the emerging voices of the subalterns: women, the indigenous people, Dalits and oppressed regional languages – which, by their very emergence, are modern.

But let us zoom back and ask: what is the map that manifests from the engagement of the Indian writer with the modernist project? Three broad categories appear: the perspective of the disenchanted or bored if not maddened cosmopolitan male questioning the track he is on, the outward-bound subaltern female discovering her sexuality, literary voice and sovereignty all at the same time (not surprisingly quite a few women's books are strongly autobiographical) and the eruption of the laughter of the marginalized tribal/Dalit/villager/child of nature.

What we see in this elaborate patchwork canvas is a questioning of the project of progress (a colonial legacy as well as a modernist one) on which several male protagonists have ground to a halt. And we also see the contrapuntal events of the traditionally isolated and now self-actualizing women reaching out for erotic love if not successfully connecting with it, and a celebration of the survival of the subaltern indigenous/Dalit consciousness and of the rural poor, the acknowledgement of their lonely struggles and mourning of the dead.

The cosmopolitan male is lost and falling – or attempting to fall consciously – from the exalted position traditionally saved for him. He is a failure, or an outsider, stuck in a rut and sometimes courts death. We see this dynamic at work in a number of novels mentioned previously as well as in *Kosala, Harbart, A Rag Called Happiness* and *English, August*. Pandurang of *Kosala* who gives up his studies and returns to his rural home run by an oppressive father, Harbart, an orphan communicating with the dead before eventually joining them, the teenaged authorial narrator of *A Rag Called Happiness* and the bored Agastya of *English, August* can all be compared to Holden Caulfield of *The Catcher in the Rye*, their condition being determined by their intelligence combined with a non-heroic sensitive temperament. A fierce authenticity reduces these men/boys into isolated observation posts in an ugly/cruel world from which they broadcast their uncompromising view.

Such connection to failure or base materiality in life, however, can be gold for a writer and Siddharth Chowdhury's *Day Scholar* is proof. Chowdhury, the only one in this book who writes (affectionately on *English, August*) and is written about, could be argued to belong to this world. But the meaning the narrator gains by his position in the underworld of Shokeen Niwas redeems the experience, as well as the people and the place. What is existentially threatening in the other novels becomes the wealth of the budding writer. In *Zero Degree*, however, the narrator-authorial voices are frequently silenced, edited and challenged, leaving behind a non-triumphal trace of their agonies.

The most provocative modernist voice arguing for the beleaguered individual is seen to emerge from the urban modern woman opening her lips for the first time ever, showing how sharply the personal is inevitably political. *Tehri Lakir* by Ismat Chughtai delivers a resounding slap in the face of patriarchal writing by fearlessly narrating its heroine Shaman's uncompromising sexual adventures so much so that it provoked an obscenity case. Similarly, the forbidden love between an upper-caste, upper-class woman with an untouchable in *The God of Small Things* precipitated a legal case for Arundhati Roy. Bama's use of foul language in *Karukku* not only by the characters but by the narrator upended establishmentarian notions of literary language, till now labouring under the rules of upper-caste decorum. The short stories in *The Smell of a Bird* by Kamala Das surprise us with refreshing snapshots of modern women stealing pleasure/pain and exercising choices in the free spaces of the Indian metropolis. And we are delighted not only by the 'stories of those who defy and dare' but 'also of those in whose outward surrender is an astonishing grace' in Ambai's *In a Forest, a Deer*. And Krishna Sobti's *The Heart Has Its Reasons* questions traditional male privilege by depicting a man, his wife and his mistress. All these writers clearly testify to the margins being brought to the centre.

These flamboyantly modern characters are powerful and uncompromising, whether it is the unnamed woman of 'Journey 1' who insists on sitting in the single seat at the front of the bus in an Ambai short story, or Pooru of *Pinjar* who refuses to be co-opted into a family based on abduction, or Triveni's heroine Kaveri, the 'madwoman' of *Sharapanjara*, who protests her silencing in patriarchal society, or Giribala, a rebellious widow in Indira Goswami's *The Moth Eaten Howdah of the Tusker* who defies convention and throws herself at a foreign man risking death. Such strong modern women are all created by women writers with perhaps the exception of Bimala of *Ghare Bhaire* by Tagore and Jamuna of

Thanneer by Ashokamitran. These characters could not afford ambivalence towards the past like Ananthu, the narrator-subject of 'Stallion of the Sun'. For these women the past is too present and their authenticity, if not their very existence, lies on an unequivocal rejection of it.

For many of these characters modernity comes in the shape of love: extramarital, adulterous, inter-caste, inter-racial, unrequited, anti-patriarchal, same-sex, incestuous love. After all it is in this intimate department that modernity revolutionized social relations in India, and a woman or man who chose to pursue his/her own object of desire was clearly, if nothing else, a modern subject. In this project of erotic freedom, Bollywood and other mainstream regional cinemas invested heavily, offering in fantasy what reality denied. But the modern novel, being realistic, tends to be about the impossibility of love. *The Shadow Lines*, *The Moth Eaten Howdah of the Tusker*, *The Wayward Streak*, *The Heart Has Its Reasons*, *Pinjar* and *The God of Small Things* all bitterly enumerate the reasons why this is so. In most of them, if not all, the issue of love is entangled in that of justice. Whether it is the caste system, the Communist Party and the Syrian Christian patriarchy in *The God of Small Things*, the patriarchal order colonizing sexual relations *in Moth Eaten Howdah of the Tusker*, *The Heart Has Its Reasons* and *Tehri Lakir*, or gender violence against the ever-devalued woman in *Pinjar*, it is the unjust environment that denies the expression, the consummation and the expansion of love.

However, Anjum Hasan, writing on *The Shadow Lines*, sees love and justice as belonging to two different registers altogether. 'The contrast between love, which is the most extraordinary subjectivity possible, and justice, which is based on the dream of complete objectivity, mirrors, as I see it, the contrast between the possibilities of fiction and the limitations of "brute fact".' Given the world of brute facts — stamps on passports, national borders and colonial history dividing the lovers – love bears the burden of liberating us from nothing short of the bonds of history. To what degree it manages it would measure the triumph of imagination over the limits of the brute facts.

In the case of *The Guide*, though, something dismissive is being said about love and the individual who may take himself seriously enough to get waylaid by it. Pankaj Mishra points out the lovelessness of Narayan's world and shows how, for Narayan, the excesses of individuality and the delusion of love are simply a part of 'Maya', the immense illusion of existence. It is a harking back to the pre-modern Hindu view of the world that Mishra so well describes: 'It is this religious-seeming acceptingness that gives Narayan's novels their peculiar irony – an irony rooted in not skepticism and disbelief but in faith: an irony that belongs less to the European tradition of the novel than to a Hindu view of the world, in which the conflicts and contradictions of individual men and societies, however acute and compelling, are in the end no more than minor disturbances in the life of an old and serene cosmic order.'

Perhaps the antithesis of *The Guide* is to be found in *A House for Mr Biswas* where a powerful argument for individuality, no matter how humble, is made in the sympathetic account of the protagonist's epic struggle away from the smothering embrace of the extended family and the habits of the past it embodies. The result, though not spectacular, is a triumphant vindication of the modernist impulse towards a heterogeneous individual self-actualization. *The Heart Has Its Reasons*, *Sunlight on a Broken Column* and *Moth Eaten Howdah of the Tusker* all share a similar strong antipathy to the individuality-crushing institution of the joint family.

It is meaningful to read Ashwin Kumar's essay on the *Stallion of the Sun and Other Stories* as an answer to Pankaj Mishra's essay on *The Guide* to reflect upon modernity and its antithesis. While Mishra makes a case for Narayan's (Chekhovian) disdain for the worthless individualities of his heroes and by extension the project of modernity itself, Ashwin Kumar lauds Ananthamurthy's critique of modernity's inability to represent the pre-modern while remaining firmly, if sadly, modern. Commenting on the story 'Stallion of the Sun', about the authenticity-seeking modernist author's feelings of entrapment and isolation from the world of a magical childhood shared with the village idiot, Venkata, Ashwin observes:

> It is a modernist's elegy to a deeply ambiguous past (ambiguous because it is a monument to its own resilience as also the symptom of a degenerate society at the threshold of its own annihilation) and a moment of rupture in the very history of modernist discourse (rupture because here Indian literary modernism meets its own double: the aberrant, degenerate village simpleton transgressing both history and reason – not through an existential encounter with history – but by simply falling through the cracks). No doubt, this is a critique of Ananthamurthy's work but we owe a debt to Ananthamurthy for opening up the possibility for such a critique of Indian modernism and of the social function of writing in India.

In that sense *The Guide* gestures towards *The Chessmaster and His Moves* and *Parsa* (incidentally, all the protagonists here are Brahmin men). While Raju of *The Guide* displays a pathetic attempt at Western individuality before lapsing into gurudom, the other two novels offer quasi-heroic idealized figures, outsiders living life on their own terms. Shivarama Shastry lives in Paris, confused between the is-ness of things and appearance, struggling with the standard binaries of the Hindu Brahmin male world – the normal and the wild, the ascetic and the sensual – when mathematics alone offers the taste of the absolute. And Parsa, the eponymous hero of Gurdial Singh's novel, seeks to overcome the tyranny of caste and class through Sufism. (Parsa refers to Parashurama, the mythical Brahmin who vowed to exterminate all the Kshatriyas.) What mathematics is for Shivarama Shastry, Sufism is for Parsa, a code to live by, a claim for authenticity in a self-chosen heterogeneous space and perhaps a Brahmin's refuge from a fast-changing world.

Compared to the Brahmin male's discomforts with modernity (unless, of course, he is so thoroughly modernized that he does not stumble over his Brahmin identity any more) *Hansuli Banker Upakatha* offers the tribal outsider's problem with it. Compared to *Karukku* and *Rights of the Forest*, which have a manifesto quality about their embrace of modernity, *Hansuli Banker Upakatha* (*The Tale of Hansuli Turn*), first published in 1946, is more ambivalent. In this tale of inter-generational conflict in the tribe of Kahars, a classified 'criminal tribe' in Bengal, a young Kahar chooses to work with the war machine of the colonials against the wishes of the tribal elders. To quote Baer, who also translated this novel by Tarashankar Bandyopadhyay, '*The Tale of Hansuli Turn* approaches a deeply uncomfortable double bind: a suggestion that a certain allegiance with the violence of colonialism and war can also translate into a limited emancipation from the violent strictures of indigenous caste-based oppression.'

Paraja, another take on indigenous life, tells the story of a family in the Paraja tribe living in Orissa, celebrating their life attuned to nature and lamenting its end at the clutches of the forest guards, government officials, moneylenders and landlords. In other words, the tribal's struggle against the British now continues under Indian rule – the native bourgeoisie having stepped into the shoes of the departed colonizers. Like *Paraja* and *Karukku*, *Prithibir Hanhi* (*Laughter of the Earth*) continues the ethnographic celebration of tribal life of the Adi people in Arunachal Pradesh, showing the deep pleasure in a life so close to nature, the key to survival in the face of societal oppression.

The very creation of the Konkani novel *Yug Sanvaar* (*Age of Frenzy*) is a triumphant victory for the language long wiped out of the public sphere by the Portuguese colonizers in Goa. Set in the sixteenth century, *Age of Frenzy* unfolds a wide canvas depicting the impact of the Portuguese colonization on Hindu communities involving banning of idolatry, subsequent conversions and migrations, one even across the seas to witness the inquisitions in Portugal. Among the first of Konkani novels to be written and translated, it is fitting that it unpacks Konkani history from the position of the colonized. *Choubuli and Other Stories* by Vijaydan Detha is likewise groundbreaking for the Rajasthani language which was mainly oral and not recognized as a language till recently. Channelling a world of experiences till now locked away from the literary sphere, Detha's work is richly political while also drawing from traditional oral storytelling practices of Rajasthani women. In the case of both these writers, the newness of the novel was unprecedented in more ways than one.

To look at other modernist perspectives of rural India, Fakir Mohan Senapati's novel *Chha Mana Atha Guntha* (*Six Acres and a Third*), an Oriya tale of a greedy landlord who goes about acquiring the eponymous six acres and a third, is told in a style described by Chandrahas Choudhury as indigenous modernity, a style that combines oral storytelling with a polyphonic rural imagination, accompanied by ironic winks and nudges producing an active critical reader, the modern political subject. Choudhury quotes Jennifer Harford Vargas on how Senapati employs 'underground types of storytelling – mainly oral, ironic, dialogic, and parodic ones – developed by those on the underside of power'. The canvas of the Marathi novel *Dhag* throws open a panorama of pain, jealous maintenance of caste hierarchies by the poor, the attrition of subsistence farming, male depression and female despair. In Kautik, the heroine of the novel, we see that mere dogged survival is an accomplishment and in Mahadev we spot that literary anomaly, the

rural alienated man. But it is not based on the characters that the
novel is modern but rather in the new realist style of *Nav Sahitya*
that Uddhav Shelke helped inaugurate in Maharashtra.

In *Godaan*, however, a different realism is at work. The celebrated
novel by Premchand paints the story of a peasant, Hori, and his
family struggling for survival and dignity in the small village near
Lucknow, of pre-Independence India. The realist depiction of the
rural self-perpetuating systems of exploitation here is undermined
by Gandhian reformist idealism. Likewise in *Marali Mannige*, the
lives of relentlessly labouring powerless women of a subsistence-
farming Kannada Brahmin family can be relieved merely by the
return of the grandson from the city rather than any modernist
liberation he might bring them. After all, in this world modernity is
embodied in the whoring, gambling Laccha (the erring father of
the returning scion), who refused to hold his end of the patriarchal
Brahmin male role. In these two novels we witness a retreat from
modernist promises towards the consolation of local wisdom of
the rural daily quotidian encircled by the mysteries of nature, as
also in *Carvalho* and *The Legends of Khasak*.

While the representation of poverty in the novels set in rural
India protests the unjust social and economic relations that produce
it, the pain and anger intensifies in the urban dystopias of *Thanneer*
and the stories of Pudumaippithan, from the experience of which
conventional bourgeois morality is rejected. In *Day Scholar*, however,
the depiction of underclass existence is excessive, comic and
affectionate, after all it is the bountiful space of writerly material,
the deep well from which the protagonist can draw while remaining
separate. If nothing else, writing saves the writer. In *Poovan Banana
and Other Stories* by Basheer we see the writer engage with ghosts,
those bereft of even bodies, a poverty of sorts. Though the messages
and magical eruptions from the other world only enrich while
subverting the one we live in.

But the sufferings in *A Fine Balance* and *Zero Degree* offer neither hope nor redemption. The humiliations of poverty plumb desperate depths in *Zero Degree*, implicating its multiple narrators as well as the readers in that repetitive misery. And for the characters in *A Fine Balance*, set temporally in the state of Emergency imposed by Indira Gandhi in the mid-1970s, the official Emergency is only a metaphor for a world in which every day is an ongoing emergency, an endless nightmare. Such relentless continuation of pain provokes deep questions for Pico Iyer:

What I remember most, many years on, about my first encounter with the book are questions, so deep they extend far beyond the political circumstances of Mistry's novel: how much do we defer to injustice, and take it to be the unfathomable way of some Fate, even some Divine sense of order? How much do we rise up against it, and die, perhaps, in the struggle? Where does kindness end and weakness begin, and how do we ever begin to find the correct attitude – the right balance of hopefulness and realism – to treat life as a colleague? Can compassion itself at times be a form of hubris?

Such experience goes way past anything that can be called Indian, it is simply human. Likewise in *Zero Degree* the civil war in Rwanda has a deep impact on lives in Tamil Nadu as much as the disappearances in Latin America and the injustices of nature on the planet. As Nirmal Verma says, 'Art is a scream from the artist.'

Besides feminist novels spoken of earlier, the most overtly political modern narratives are perhaps the Dalit novels: the Gujarati *Angaliat*, Tamil *Karukku* and Telugu *Antarani Vasantham* (*Untouchable Spring*). Each of these novels offer a rich social history never heard before, questioning all that was taken for granted in an aesthetic as new as the perspective. Both *Angaliat* by Joseph Macwan and *Untouchable Spring* by Kalyan Rao explore critical perspectives unlocked by the emergence of Ambedkar, an embodiment of modernity especially viewed against the background of Gandhi's nationalist Hindu reformist positions. Manohar Reddy's essay on *Antarani Vasantham* pays particular attention to the politics of conversion, talking about the early nineteenth-century en masse Andhra Dalit conversions to Christianity demonized by Gandhian reformers and dismissed by Marxist historians. Here, finally, we see the modernist project unlinked from the nationalist one as also happens in novels and stories that are set in the backdrop of Partition, India's own poorly acknowledged holocaust: Saadat Hasan Manto's *Dastavez: Manto* (*Collected Stories*), Desani's *All About H. Hatterr* and Salman Rushdie's *Midnight's Children*.

A subject 'too dangerous to be remembered and too difficult to be forgotten', according to Krishna Sobti, Partition renders the project of nation-building very precarious. A complicitous or amnesiac silence on six million deaths is something novelists will not just let lie. As Charumathi Supraja points out, Krishna Sobti refused a Padma Bhushan from the Government of India in 2010, wanting to keep a distance from the establishment, as a writer needs 'a vast sky of freedom'. Saadat Hasan Manto's stories, written in the vast no-man's-land between India and Pakistan, protest the creation of that border, that schism. They erupt from that chasm. His story 'Toba Tek Singh' about the exchange of lunatics between the new countries, based possibly on his experience of incarceration in a lunatic asylum of Lahore, is a bitter laugh of the unconscious in the face of the uplifting, pious, conscious project of building new nations.

As to Desani's Hatterr, he is not Indian at all, even in a pre-Independence Indian sense, being the son of a European father and a Malay mother. Nilanjana Roy points out:

So there you have it: our first bona fide homegrown, school-of-Indian-writing-in-English literary character was not Indian at all. Decades later, writing in partial homage to Desani, Salman Rushdie's Saleem Sinai in *Midnight's Children* would also be half-caste – Anglo-Indian, in his case. Hatterr belonged to the same no-man's-land – territory claimed by three of India's greatest writers, Rushdie, Desani and Saadat Hasan Manto, in works spurred by or written about Independence. And Hatterr, with his permanent logorrhea, his rapid fire, utterly Indian English patter, his frantic capering around a world that includes pukka British clubs and ash-coated fakirs, could belong to Manto's lonely lunatic asylum. In Manto's iconic short story 'Toba Tek Singh', the lunatics occupy the no-man's-land between India and the newly created Pakistan; Hatterr's no-man's-land, between the Orient and the Occident, is wider, but no less lonely.

Allan Sealy, coming years later with *Trotter-Nama*, 'takes wicked delight in jumping up and down on a verbal trampoline, punning, bringing together styles from Anglo-Saracen to 'Hindu-Gingerbread . . .', a space earlier explored by Desani. As Roy says, 'Sealy's *Trotter-Nama* took giant steps in creating a genuinely Indian novel – namely an assimilative, multicultural, polyphonic place.' All these half-caste heroes confronting their own heterogeneity, and wondering why they don't fit, zoom back to expand the canvas of their worlds.

Lest you think the syncretic view of Indian history and culture is a problem suffered by those writing in English, consider *River of Fire* (*Aag ka Darya*, written initially in Urdu and decades later in English by Qurratulain Hyder), which takes an epochal view on Indian history spanning Buddhist, Muslim, British and the post-national eras, and speaks for an expansive view of Indian history and culture. Aamer Hussein's essay on this magnum opus argues its modernity on formal counts – decentred perspectives, epic and mock epic aspects of the ancient genre of *Dastan*, stream of consciousness – as well as in its ambitious thematic preoccupations: 'Instead of espousing nationalist or religious ideologies, Hyder argues for a syncretic reading of Indian culture, which she sees as multivocal and inclusive.' Hyder, herself torn between India and Pakistan like Saadat Hasan Manto, speaks from the chasm in between and questions the notion of the Indian nation.

And in *Zero Degree*, a Tamil novel, the nation that is getting questioned is the Tamil one. The narrators obsess about global genocides, cruelty of nature and the human penchant for self-abuse and repetitive misery, all the while questioning the truisms and parochialisms of the strongly separatist Tamil identity, language and literature.

In *Midnight's Children* the two adversarial characters, Saleem and Shiva, represent respectively the fraying and crumbling nation and the simultaneous fascist attempt to keep it together. The novel is a master counter-narrative to Indian and Pakistani nationalisms, a seismic subcontinental movement in which families and bloodlines are thrown about with no hopes of cohesion, a testimony to the uncontainable liquefaction of life spilling over and under arbitrary political lines drawn in the sand. Lines separating not only India, Pakistan and Bangladesh but also between Hindu and Muslim, rich and poor, the linguistically different and other exponentially diversifying populations of each of these nations. Partition, far from being an unfortunate historical event that people recovered from eventually, continues to be simultaneously coupled with the nationalist project thereby wreaking havoc in perpetuity. So, we face the endlessly relevant question: is it modern to stand apart from these nationalist notions or does being Indian mean also to be Pakistani and Bangladeshi? Or, God forbid, could it mean to be just plain human?

We will let you argue this question. Let this map of Indian

modernity be put to good use, to locate ourselves as stakeholders on this contested ground. It is a living map that changes even as we look afresh, recognize and reconfigure our relation to things as depicted in these literary landmarks. It is important to recognize that not only is the map living but the landscape as well. In this dialogic relationship the project of articulating and claiming, again and again, our sovereignty and free agency is not only timeless and new, it is timely.

THE FAILED ENGLISH NOVELIST

Bankimchandra Chattopadhyay's
Durgeshnandini

ARUNAVA SINHA

In the opening scenes of *Charulata*, Satyajit Ray's filmed version of Rabindranath Tagore's novella *Nashtaneer*, the lonely wife is seen flitting between the empty rooms of the large Calcutta mansion she lives in. During one of the pauses, she goes up to a bookcase, looking for something to read. As she runs her fingers across the spines, she hums under her breath, 'Bankim, Bankim'. The book she picks is *Kapalkundala*, Bankimchandra Chattopadhyay's second novel, a work that reveals how his confidence as a novelist had grown after the near-ecstatic (thirteen editions!) response that his first novel, *Durgeshnandini* (*The Chieftain's Daughter*, 1865) had received on publication.

The scene is Ray's, not Tagore's. But even if he did not pay this tribute personally, Tagore might not have written *Nashtaneer* in 1901 in his spare, sinuous, everyday prose, had it not been for

Chattopadhyay's path-breaking work thirty-six years earlier. In 1865, in one fell swoop, Chattopadhyay broke away from the centuries-old tradition of telling stories in verse, by publishing *Durgeshnandini* in an altogether new linguistic register. An urban legend from the time goes something like this: when Chattopadhyay gathered his friends in a room to read the novel to them, they were thunderstruck by its use of the language, which miraculously echoed both the cadences of regular speech and the exalted register of a literary idiom.

The young man did not respond, for he was distracted. Still concealed behind her companion, the younger of the two women had slowly lowered her veil to gaze steadfastly at him. During their conversation, the traveller's eyes turned in her direction; they could not turn back. He felt that he would never again behold such a miraculously beautiful woman. The young woman's eyes met the young man's. She lowered hers at once. Not receiving a reply, the companion looked at the traveller. Following his eyes, and realizing that the woman accompanying her was also staring at the young man fervently, she whispered in her ear, 'Well? Are you planning to select your own husband in the presence of the Lord?'

Chattopadhyay was already a failed poet and a failed English-language novelist when he wrote *Durgeshnandini*. His volume of poetry had sold all of six copies – though it did include a poem that was to become somewhat famous later. Pressed by the printer to provide an additional poem to fill an empty page, he wrote, in a mixture of contemporary Bengali and broken Sanskrit, the verses starting with the words 'Bande Mataram'. His debut novel in English, *Rajmohan's Wife*, also bombed, despite a not uninteresting storyline. Among other oddities, it had rural Bengali characters displaying unaccountable knowledge of the world, such as a village woman referring to Jericho.

Chastened, Chattopadhyay turned to his mother tongue, perhaps inadvertently becoming the pioneer of speech-as-literary-language. Who knows what might have been, had *Rajmohan's Wife* proved successful. Instead, Chattopadhyay chose to 'infuse the sinewy and resonant energy of Sanskrit', as academician Shirshendu Chakrabarti puts it, into Bengali; in the process practically inventing the medium of the novel in India.

Bimala put her soft hand in the guard's. He was speechless.

'I do not know how to say this,' said Bimala, 'but when you leave after winning the war, will you still remember me?'

G: How could I not remember you?

B: Shall I tell you what I feel?

G: Yes, do.

B: No, I shan't, what will you think of me!

G: No, please tell me — think of me as your servant.

B: I have an irresistible urge to leave this sinful husband of mine and run away with you.

That glance again. The sentry wanted to dance with delight.

Was *Durgeshnandini* really the first Indian novel? Recent scholarship suggests that the mantle could instead be claimed by Hasan Shah's *Nashtar* (*The Surgeon's Knife*), written in Persian in 1790. The novel was translated into English as *The Nautch Girl* by Qurratulain Hyder. No matter; it was *Durgeshnandini* that gave birth to virtually every novel written in India over the next few decades. Read widely in Bengali and translated within a few years into several languages, including English, *Durgeshnandini* made novelists out of generations of writers, who might otherwise have been struggling for a form in which to tell their stories. Undoubtedly this work was influenced by English novels then available in India, though Chattopadhyay went to great lengths to point out that he had not read Sir Walter Scott's *Ivanhoe*, which *Durgeshnandini* is often said to be inspired by.

More importantly perhaps, with this work Chattopadhyay tore off the tyranny of the gods, of predestination and of divine will, on storytelling. The rich tradition of Bengali poetry had till then soaked its tales with devotional rasas, even framing narratives of love and passion within the dictates of divinely approved leela. Despite the earlier publication of *Alaler Gharer Dulal* (*The Spoilt Child*) and *Hutoom Pnyachar Naksha* (*Sketches by an Observant Owl*), both of which wrenched themselves out of the canons of poetic depiction and employed a sort of street prose to document society and its foibles, it was *Durgeshnandini* that showed the way in terms of investing characters with free will and the power to choose.

Throughout the actual events recounted in *Durgeshnandini*, and in the back stories of the principal participants, individuals are seen to make choices. This single act of empowerment for the characters enabled both Chattopadhyay himself and his successors to craft stories that placed humans, rather than overarching destiny, as the prime movers. As he demonstrated with commensurate skill in a novel that spans barely 150 pages of continuous dramatic action, a combination of history, circumstances and propensity propels every individual to the brink, from which they have to chart one path – to the exclusion of others – of their own volition.

This emergence of free will in the narrative was not just for the emancipation for the characters. This was also an artistic assertion of the emerging nationalist identity that Chattopadhyay was to develop in his subsequent work – the right to decide one's own future instead of giving in to the dictates of the British Raj. Significantly, it was not until the 1857 uprising that India's British rulers actually abandoned their tolerance of local cultural practices and began to dictate aspects of private life as well through laws. The rise of the Indian novel can also be conflated with the reaction to this intrusion, which accelerated the resistance to occupation and loaded ammunition in the barrels of the revolutionaries.

The prince's blade flashed like streaks of lightning. When he realized that he could not continue his battle all by himself, he decided to kill as many of the enemy soldiers as he could before dying. With this objective, he positioned himself amidst a phalanx of marauders, gripping his sword with fists of iron and swinging it around his head. He made not the slightest effort to defend himself any more; only showering blows all around. One, two, three — every swing of the sword either felled a Pathan or severed a limb. The enemy's weapons rained blows on the prince from every direction. Now his hands could move no more, blood flowed freely from wounds all over his body, draining his arm of its strength. His head began to spin, his vision became clouded, and the clamour seemed indistinct to his ears.

'Do not kill the prince, the tiger must be caged alive.'

My first engagement with *Durgeshnandini* was not as a regular reader, if it is at all possible to pick up a 'historical romance' — a convenient but not all-encompassing label — more than a hundred years old as a 'regular reader'. I was about to translate it into English, and from the very first sentence I gave up half my brain — the left, possibly — to identifying a suitable register for the English version. This split down the middle lasted all of a single chapter. By the end of it, as 'both the women and the men felt desirous of learning one another's identities, but none wished to be uncivil enough to be the first to enquire', the left brain had been reclaimed.

After all, it is not in every novel that romantic sparks fly in the very first paragraph, while the external world is suitably stormy, followed by moonlight. If, as Jorge Luis Borges said, every writer also chooses his or her literary successors by the very nature of what he or she writes, Chattopadhyay surely chose not only every Indian novelist who came after him but also – dare I say – every scriptwriter of commercial cinema in India. Suspend disbelief for a few minutes, if you will, and imagine what is quaintly referred to as a 'narration' in India's film world taking place inside a movie producer's office in Mumbai.

Against the backdrop of a war between the Pathans and the Mughals in south-west Bengal, goes the story, Jagatsingh, son of Mughal general Mansingh, and Tilottama, the chieftain Virendrasingh's daughter, fall in love at first sight. A fortnight later, Tilottama's companion Bimala – she has another identity as well, which is revealed later – escorts Jagatsingh into the palace secretly to meet the young lady. She inadvertently leaves a window open, allowing the forces of Katalu Khan, Virendrasingh's enemy, into the palace.

Katalu Khan's marauding troops not only occupy the castle and claim its women, they also take away Virendrasingh, Jagatsingh, Bimala and Tilottama. As tradition demands, the last two are to join Katalu Khan's harem, while Virendrasingh is executed – though not before Bimala is revealed to be his second wife Tilottama's (loving) stepmother. Meanwhile, Katalu Khan's daughter Ayesha nurses Jagatsingh back to health, falling in love with him in the process, setting the scene for the eternal love triangle. Unable to reciprocate, Jagatsingh mopes around, convinced that Tilottama has now been defiled, as she is supposed to be a part of Katalu Khan's harem.

Without giving away the rest of the storyline, it is evident that the plot abounds in romance, intrigue, warfare, realpolitik, unbridled passion, a love triangle that is in fact a four-cornered affair, death, murder, tragedy, pathos and a happy – for most, if not for all – ending. This then is the universal set of all the elements that have gone into a century of cinema in India.

The objective here is not to draw a facile comparison, but to demonstrate that Chattopadhyay invented, with economic strokes, a classic narrative for popular consumption, injecting appropriate elements of realistic fantasy and wish-fulfilment without breaking the moral superstructure of life that held – and continues to hold – vast sections of society together. Thus, for instance, *Durgeshnandini* has premarital love – further along the continuum of relationships than real life permitted but not unacceptable by any moral yardstick. It has unrequited love between members of enemy camps, doomed by its very nature but no less fiery in its intensity. It has the repercussions that a life of unbridled passion must necessarily lead to but it also has the opportunity for redemption.

Besides these, if there is one overriding element of their cinema that India's commercial film-makers must tip their hat to Chattopadhyay for, it is the message. In *Durgeshnandini*, there is a breathtaking moment when Ayesha declares her true feelings for Jagatsingh, uttering a line that I have heard middle-aged women repeat with fervour, their years slipping away and their eyes lighting up: 'The prisoner is my beloved.' In those five words, Chattopadhyay conjured up an intent so pure it took the reader's breath away but denied this intent's eventual consummation, so that puritan principles were not brought crashing down. Love is all very well, but propriety is still above all; *roti-and-makhan*, if you will, for middle-class morality, which itself was a product of industrialization and a conservative work ethic imposed by colonizers.

Ray's Charulata spends a few minutes in the afternoon at the window, gazing through her opera glasses at a vendor on the street. Early on in *Durgeshnandini*, Tilottama spends a few minutes at her window in her father's castle, gazing at the river and dreaming of

her new love. And in the very last scene, it is Ayesha's turn to sit at
the window, looking down at the moat surrounding her father's
castle. As in the case of *Charulata*, in *Durgeshnandini* too — the
novel is named not after the valorous hero but after the romantic
heroine — it is the women whose view of the world is depicted with
clarity and tenderness, with moral conviction and artistic richness.

CRAZY ABOUT MODERNITY

Pudumaippithan's *Kathaigal*

A . R . V E N K A T A C H A L A P A T H Y

In the 18 October 1933 issue of *Gandhi*, a nationalist journal, appeared a short article – 'Gulabjan Kadhal', or falling in love with a gulab jamun. It was a humorous polemic on the notion of romantic love, love at first sight. Signed 'Pudumaippithan', it was the debut of arguably the greatest writer of Tamil fiction. The pseudonym, meaning 'the one crazy about the new/modern', was most apt – for nothing captures what Pudumaippithan did to Tamil writing better – and not without irony: 'pithan' ('the crazy one') also refers to Lord Siva. Pudumaippithan's modernity was no rootless wonder – it was deeply imbued by a critical grounding in tradition.

In a brief life of forty-two years and a writing career spanning less than fifteen years, Pudumaippithan (1906–48) wrote short stories, essays, reviews, poems, political biographies, literary translations and an incomplete novel – all this while being squeezed dry by the nascent newspaper industry and the emerging world of Tamil cinema. While the flash of genius is present in every piece of his writing, it is in the short story that Pudumaippithan left his everlasting imprint.

Pudumaippithan's first short story was published in the renaissance journal *Manikkodi*, which heralded a literary modernism in Tamil, in April 1934. More than half of his hundred short stories were published in the first few years of his writing career. Between July 1935, when he joined Ramnath Goenka's Tamil daily *Dinamani*, then edited by the doyen of nationalist editors, T. S. Chokkalingam, and February 1940, when his first book of short stories appeared, he had published another twenty-odd stories. It was from this corpus of about seventy-five stories that Pudumaippithan selected twenty-nine for his first book. However, we do not know if Pudumaippithan himself chose them. He wrote no preface, and there is nothing on record to show what he thought of his book. But we do know from the variorum edition of his collected works that Pudumaippithan revised these stories after their first publication in the journals.

Published in 1940, the book was called *Pudumaippithan Kathaigal* (*Stories of Pudumaippithan*), a title most uninspired, even lazy, from today's perspective. But it was an audacious literary statement, much like his pseudonym, which has a manifesto quality about it. It exuded a supreme self-confidence of the author's own abilities, very much in keeping with his enfant terrible image. No author, least of all a fledgling one with little power in an emerging literary public sphere, had given his own name to his book until then. For Pudumaippithan belonged to the first generation of Tamil writers who tried, unsuccessfully and tragically, to make writing a profession. What was innovative at first became passé later.

Printed on demy octavo, containing 280 pages and priced at two rupees, *Pudumaippithan Kathaigal* was published by Navayuga Prasuralayam Ltd, an offshoot of the Manikkodi group, with clear nationalist leanings and an agenda to educate the reader on contemporary political issues.

The volume was prefaced by a somewhat lengthy foreword by R.S. Desikan, a writer and English teacher at Presidency College, Chennai. It is a celebrated piece that talks about the close association between modern life and the short story. Describing its Western origins, Desikan also elaborates on how Tamil writers had skilfully domesticated it. Against this background, he further states that Pudumaippithan was adept in the 'mysteries of the craft of short story' and sees each story as creating a separate world and lyrical in its stand-alone composition. Interestingly, Desikan invokes the Tamil classical concept of 'akam' and extends its original amorous semantics (drawn from classical Tamil poetry) to include the entire gamut of affect and feeling to analyse the stories. Finally, he ends with the moving words: 'A poetic heart — a heart wilted due to melancholy, a heart that drips with blood by falling on the thorns of life — speaks through these stories.' A more apposite introduction to the debut volume of a precocious writer can hardly be imagined.

The book contained a selection of Pudumaippithan's earliest stories, some relatively short and covering a wide range of themes. He had made a clear rupture with romanticist and idealistic outpourings, which were the lot of Tamil writing of the days, and attempted to shock the readers with stark portrayals of subaltern lives — the lives of mill workers, prostitutes, hotel servers, plantation workers — not to speak of lower-middle-class life in the cities and the unsentimental depiction of rural life.

One of the stories, 'Kavandanum Kamanum' (drawing from Hindu mythology, of a demon who is perennially hungry and the god of lust), begins with the following statement: 'Have you looked around the city of Chennai after eight in the night? If you have, what I describe below will not shock you. Lights that catch the eyes, the civilization that captures the heart. If you want to understand that this is no age of Kali but the age of advertisement you should see the city's nights.' As the tram howls past, it sounds like the triumphant

laugh of the modern yaksha. And then Pudumaippithan cuts to a
dark corner. 'Did you see the wall around the corner? The act of
creation is on. Are they humans or animals? Don't feign politeness
and look away. Your poplin shirt and shell-frame spectacles are but
stolen from what should have been their bread.' And then the story
quickly turns to the streetwalker who accosts a novitiate client
who runs away after thrusting money into her hands. She throws
away the money, swearing at him, saying, 'Did you take me for
a beggar?' And then bends down to search for the coins in
the darkness.

Another celebrated story is 'Ponnagaram'. Set in a working-class
locality adjoining a cotton mill, it talks of Ammalu, a mill worker.
Her husband, a cart man, suffers serious injuries after a drunken
ride, and is moaning in bed for milk gruel. With two more days to
go for wage day, Ammalu goes out to fetch water and espies a man
who has had his eye on her for some time. They disappear into the
darkness. When she emerges a little later she's earned three quarters
of a rupee to make milk gruel. This two-and-a-half-page story,
narrated in the most matter-of-fact manner, with great irony and
sarcasm but no sentiment, ends with the memorable line: 'O Sirs,
who rant about chastity, this is Ponnagaram!'

This brief mapping of his stories may evoke the image of a
'progressive' writer, even a social realist one. However, such labelling
is quite off the mark. As Pudumaippithan himself once remarked,
his writings often have an undercurrent of pessimism, 'a drying up
of hope'. While he was deeply, even violently, critical of the existing
order, he also doubted every emancipatory project. While he wrote
so movingly about caste oppression, he immediately counterposed
the situation with a story about how Dalits themselves beat up a
Brahmin advocate of temple entry.

His stories were not confined to social realism — some variant of
which dominated the writing in the various Indian languages in the

high noon of Indian nationalism. Pudumaippithan wrote fantasy, even pieces that can be called precursors to magic realism and science fiction. And he delighted in rewriting and reinterpreting literary classics and legend and folklore. Some stories are deeply introspective, even philosophical to the extent that they may be called 'stories of ideas'.

Few writers have indulged in as much parody as Pudumaippithan. The stories are experimental in terms of form, content, structure and prose style, and the creative tools that he employed were wit, sarcasm and irony. Digression is a weapon he resorted to frequently. His creative prose blends both literary Tamil and colloquial dialect, and its structure resonates heavily with English prose. His leapfrog style is particularly evident in his early staccato prose which he wielded for realistic depiction and exposition of hypocrisy.

And what did contemporary reviewers think of this collection of short stories? I have traced four contemporary reviews to Pudumaippithan's first book.

These reviews generally reveal the fact that short stories were still somewhat new as a literary genre. *Ooliyan*, the nationalist weekly in which some of Pudumaippithan's early works were published, was generally welcoming of his stories, but took umbrage at a few for their inappropriate content and prose style. K.S. Venkataramani's (the Indian English author of *Kandan, The Patriot* and *Murugan, the Tiller*) *Bharatamani* expressed similar views and again objected to the uneven prose, which was 'akin to stumbling across on an unpaved path'. *Bharatamani* especially expressed incomprehension at his contemplative stories.

These reviews illustrate a general incomprehension of new writing on the part of entrenched literary formations and their reluctance to come to grips with a new kind of prose. Pudumaippithan's bold themes do not seem to have gone down very well and an acute discomfort at his prose style is also evident.

However, the most considered response came from the monthly *Kalaimagal*, which played no small part in the development of Tamil fiction during the 1930s and 1940s. Describing the short story as not mere entertainment, but the depiction of the grotesque truths of life and matters considered even unutterable, *Kalaimagal* identified Pudumaippithan as the expression of a new literary sensibility that had been born in Tamil. 'Even if one feels squeamish at the depiction of life's underside, we have to console ourselves that that's what life is all about.'

Pudumaippithan Kathaigal remains a landmark in modern Tamil writing, seventy years after its first publication — a challenge to young writers. Even though Pudumaippithan published three more collections, *Aaru Kathaigal*, *Kanchanai* and *Aanmai* — the latter two prefaced by his brilliant forewords and *Kanchanai* containing his best and arguably the greatest single collection of Tamil short stories — *Pudumaippithan Kathaigal*, with its uneven mix of brilliance, genius, craft and inspiration, remains the favourite of discerning Tamil readers, without cringing for any concession due to the passage of time.

SENSORY MIRRORS

Kamala Das's *Pakshiyude Manam*

NAVANEETHA MOKKIL MARUTHUR

*A grimy business complex in the city of Calcutta. An anxious, young woman
wanders in search of a textile shop within this crowded maze. Exhausted, she
walks into a vacant shop with the billboard, 'Dying'. No, it is not an absurd
spelling mistake as she first assumes; they are not in the business of dyeing
clothes. She encounters a man with a menacing voice and thick, hairy fingers
who asks her, 'Do you know the smell of death? . . . You do not, right? I will
tell you. Death smells like bird-feathers . . . You will know that, very soon.'*

If the power of fiction lies in its ability to transport us to bewildering
landscapes, where the sureties of reason and order are mercilessly
questioned, Kamala Das's *The Smell of a Bird* is no mean achievement.
This book is strong testimony to Das's skill as a writer to plunge
readers into the emotional undercurrents and erotic dynamics of
middle-class Indian life.

When Das died in June 2009, many of her readers received the
news with a sense of disbelief. Not that I didn't know that she was
ailing for a long time, but her magical ability to string together

real-life performances with provocative writing gave her such a
heroic aura that one felt death would be afraid to come knocking
for her. Her public presence was built on a gleeful irreverence for
social and sexual norms. Many of her writings are set in the milieu
of the privileged Hindu Nair community backdrop in which she
grew up in Kerala. Her conversion to Islam in 1999 and acceptance
of the name Kamala Surayya was a widely debated move in India.
The privileging of the autobiographical voice in her writings
often blurred the boundaries between life and art. The thematics
of transgressive desire and sexuality in *My Story*, one of the
highest-selling Indian memoirs, and her large body of fiction and
poetry have been the central focus in the popular reception of
her work.

She is undoubtedly one of the most well-known twentieth-
century writers from India. Within the field of Indian literature
she is one of the few writers who claims equal ease or unease with
two languages:

The language I speak
Becomes mine, its distortions, its queernesses
All mine, mine alone.

She wrote poetry mainly in English and her short stories were
primarily in Malayalam. She also published autobiographical
writings, essays and novels in both languages. She has won numerous
awards, including the Sahitya Akademi Award in 1985 and was
nominated for the Nobel Prize in Literature in 1984. While she is
known mainly for her poetry and autobiography within national
and international circuits, her popularity with readers from Kerala
is also because of her short stories that appeared in well-circulated
literary journals and magazines under the name 'Madhavikutty'.

Published in 1964, *Pakshiyude Manam* (*The Smell of a Bird*), is one
of Das's early collections of short stories and marks the beginning

of her long and illustrious career as a short-fiction writer. The English translation of some of the stories in this collection appears in the last anthology of writings that Kamala Das compiled before her death, *The Kept Woman and Other Stories*. The nine stories in *Pakshiyude Manam* are all set in metropolitan cities outside Kerala, mainly Calcutta, Bombay and Madras. The public library in Bombay, the banks of the river Hooghly, the botanical gardens in Calcutta — these urban spaces provide the backdrop for the private dramas staged in the stories. Often the women protagonists have recently moved to the city from less urban settings in Kerala. Many of the stories are an ironic statement on the sphere of domesticity; tales of men and women whose marriages grow to lack desire and trust. But these stories are not a simple celebration of transgression and non-monogamy; it captures the fleeting pleasures and seething hurts of romantic connections, both within and outside the family.

'Swathanthrajeevikal' ('Independent Beings') shows the clandestine meeting between a middle-aged, reputed economist and a young woman tortured by her love for this married man; a half-a-day of sex and romance that he pre-arranges in a hotel room close to the airport. This relationship is built on the assumption that they are both independent beings who can walk away from each other without the messiness of tears or complaints. This 'freedom' becomes a burden the woman carries, robbing her of the right to an emotional display. In the end of the encounter as the man smoothly dissolves back into marriage and respectability, she can only pop sleeping pills and fall back to bed, 'this young girl who was said to have a strong sense of discretion was not even brave enough to cry out loud'. This subtle unravelling of the unequal power dynamics within romantic relationships is a repeated thread in the book.

Das exposes the multiple contradictions beneath the placid veneer of middle-class domesticity. In 'Varalakshmipuja', a model wife conducts a grand puja in her decked up house and then requests her husband's lover Vimala not to subject him to any mental pain, 'I do not know if you can love him like I love him. But you should do one thing for me. Do not hurt him. That's my only request to you'. Then she goes off to rest for a while, requesting Vimala to play table tennis with her son. In 'Chathi' ('Betrayal'), a fifty-year-old 'lady doctor' decides to surprise her husband on her birthday and drives back home in the dead of the night after her strenuous medical shift. Basking in the warmth of her long-lived romance with her husband, 'who still has the smile of a sixteen year old', she tiptoes to bed only to encounter the softness of another woman's body. With deft movements and controlled writing, Das captures the tenuousness of human relationships; its knotted tapestry, cutting ironies and effervescent joys.

Most of the stories are set within an upper-middle-class or middle-class setting. The characters' relationships with other class groups are often distant and dismissive; they complain about their new cooks and compare the skills of respective maids. But one of the surprising stories in the collection is 'Kalyani', which blurs the boundary between the respectable wife and the disreputable prostitute. In this story, a married woman, Ammini, a name that connotes upper-caste positioning, is arrested while driving her car in Calcutta and taken to the police station as Kalyani:

'When did you start feeling shy, Kalyani?' one of the policemen asked jeeringly.

'I am not Kalyani,' she sobbed. 'My name is Ammini, I am Mr Menon's wife.'

'Wife!' he replied scornfully and removed the hand-cuffs.

She is disrobed, force-fed alcohol and thrown into a police cell. Hours later when her husband arrives, instead of rescuing her, he is convinced that all the rumours he has heard about her are true. This story unravels the binaries between the wife and the prostitute, two oppositional figures of the sexual canvas of India, and foregrounds the differential treatment meted out to these two categories of women. For a 'Kalyani' respectability and modesty are not an option. In the conclusion, the bewildered Ammini mutters, 'Am I Kalyani?' Kalyani cannot metamorphose back into being Ammini; she can only remain lost within this nightmarish landscape. This story offers a disturbing social commentary on the systemic ways in which women's bodies are elevated or degraded.

There is a deep sense of sympathy that the writer evokes for all the floundering, independent, yet dependent beings she portrays. It is difficult to judge her characters in a moralistic fashion, because Das's aim is to show the hollowness of the rituals of morality. She dwells on the suffering inflicted by individuals who are blind followers of the rules of society. In 'Arunachalathinte Katha' ('Arunachalam's Story'), the protagonist Arunachalam, managing director of a reputed firm in Bombay, looks back on his arid life at the time of his death. His life had been the epitome of self-denial and sexual control; even when his voluptuous secretary threw her throbbing body at him he packed her off home without a second of self-doubt. Yet during the final moments of his life he clings to the memory of that incomplete embrace, 'in the moment of death he felt an intense compassion for his body that would soon be burnt to ash'. With a touch of lightness and incisive humour, Das presents a moving caricature of the 'disciplined man' whose impending death makes him painfully aware of all the untasted pleasures of the body.

In Das's world view, it is the very excesses and messiness of life that make it worth living. Thus the poetess Madhavi, who commits suicide in 'Idanazhikalile Kannadikal' ('The Corridor Mirrors') after an unsuccessful love affair with her husband's boss, is elevated as a character. Her rain-drenched presence and haunting, sensual poetry linger on even after she exits. A line from one of Madhavi's poems, 'When Bats Fly', is the title of the second collection of stories that Das published in 1966. Das's stories are like corridor mirrors; they dwell on the interstices and fractures of day-to-day living. These stories force us to pause and reflect on what is often left unsaid, unseen, unnoticed.

The Smell of a Bird is a significant contribution to Indian literature, because it conveys the ability of fiction to explore the complexities of the drama of living. The final story in the collection, 'Vakilammavan' ('Advocate Uncle'), effectively encapsulates the overarching theme of the whole collection. This story shows a group of middle-class families on a picnic. On the surface it is a humdrum day sprinkled with stilted conversation, samosas and chai. But in the midst of all this, extramarital romances flower, a teenage girl sneaks out to meet her lover, and a precocious thirteen-year-old obsessively asks 'advocate uncle' if she can be his girlfriend. Instead of setting up a neat opposition between tradition and modernity, repression and transgression, Das deftly reveals the cracks and fissures within the fabric of morality itself.

Das's stories have the power to pull the reader into its entangled skeins because she insists that without sensory dramas, life would be completely spiritless. In The Smell of a Bird even death comes with a seductive, visceral power. Only Das's imagination could place us so tantalizingly close to the smell of life and death. This is an overpowering odour that lingers in our mindscapes long after we finish reading the book.

PUTTING THE HEART IN THE HEARTLAND

Vikram Seth's *A Suitable Boy*

AMITAVA KUMAR

The most-discussed fact about *A Suitable Boy*, easily the best-known of Vikram Seth's novels, is its length. It was two feet high in typescript and 1,349 pages long in hardback. The book's 591,552 words (although a *New York Times* profile, in 1993, just prior to the book's publication, estimated the count to be closer to 800,000) mean that it might well be the longest novel ever written in the English language. In the rhymed dedication at the beginning of the book, the author addressed the following words to the reader: 'Buy me before good sense insists/ You'll strain your purse and sprain your wrists.' Seth, who is five foot three, also described the book in an interview as 'a very large novel written by a very small Indian'. Despite its length, the book sold more than a million copies worldwide. In 2009, Seth received an advance of $2.94 million to write a sequel that is likely to be titled *A Suitable Girl*. To my mind, what is most remarkable about *A Suitable Boy* is the way in which this big novel achieves its narrative flow, its ease, its lightness, seemingly defying the downward pull of gravity itself.

The book's length places *A Suitable Boy* in the tradition of panoramic nineteenth-century novels like *Middlemarch* and *War and Peace*. Its ostensible subject, the search for a husband for a young woman, also puts it in line with other, shorter novels of that period, such as Jane Austen's *Pride and Prejudice*.

People with an academic bent of mind might propose that *A Suitable Boy* is an attempt on the part of an Indian to write a capacious novel as voluminous as the Indian nation itself – at the very moment when the coherence of the Indian nation state was unravelling under the threat of separatist struggles and widespread social turmoil. This would explain the novel's setting in the early 1950s when India, under Jawaharlal Nehru, was a newly born country, articulating an idea of itself as an independent nation. The nostalgia present in that return to the past could have much to do with the anxieties and desperation of the period in which the novel was written. It is as if the six million words in the novel and the multiple stories woven together by the novelist's hand were expected to provide a narrative for a nation, whose present was becoming threadbare and its coherent sense of itself, more than a bit frayed at the edges. However, none of the above points provides a compelling reason for actually reading the novel.

A Suitable Boy opens with Mrs Rupa Mehra's search for a suitable husband for her youngest daughter, Lata. Lata is intelligent and well read and, what is more important, she has a mind of her own.

Her rebellious search for a partner of her own choice introduces into the plot other suitors and also the excitement of domestic drama. The broader history of the new nation and the tensions and changes of its divided society provide the backdrop for Lata's search for a suitable boy and give the novel its density and heft. For example, Lata's elder sister Savita gets married into a family that is headed by a political leader, a radical socialist who is the executor of India's laws for the abolition of the feudal system of land-ownership. Through the vicissitudes of the political leader's career, the reader is able to witness the debates around the rights of the landless and the so-called 'untouchables'.

Perhaps more notable than Seth's engagement with historic debates is his focus on the quotidian aspects of national life. The years and the people he chooses to write about are not the most celebrated ones. As Anita Desai remarked in a perceptive review of the book, 'For all the breadth and the scope of the author's intention, there is at the heart of his work a modesty that one would have thought belonged to the miniature, not the epic scale.' This modesty, which one can also view as reticence or reserve, can be viewed simply as a writer's predilection. But a different case can also be made. In *A Suitable Boy*, the relentless pursuit of the ordinary marks an attempt to find the soul of a nation in the vernacular space of the provincial small towns and their familiar, rather conventional inhabitants.

Seth was by no means the first writer to do this. Perhaps the most remarkable entry into the Indian small town, the story and its characters riding the vehicle of English, like so many passengers piled into a sturdy Ambassador of indigenous make, was a book that preceded *A Suitable Boy* by five years, Upamanyu Chatterjee's *English, August*. (As a sample, let me present a few lines taken from the very first page of the novel: 'I've a feeling, August, you're going to get hazaar fucked in Madna.' 'Amazing mix, the English we speak. Hazaar fucked. Urdu and American,' Agastya laughed, 'a thousand fucked, really fucked. I'm sure nowhere else could languages be mixed *and* spoken with such ease.') But the reader is left in no doubt that the language used to describe the heartland (They passed the garages, stalls selling sugar-cane juice, shops. 'Just notice the number of chemists in Madna,' said Bhatia bitterly. 'A clear sign how unhealthy this place is.') is the fashionable lingua franca of the visitor from the metropolis. That single fact is what gives *English, August* its essential dissonance and comic force. But *A Suitable Boy* is different; its comedy is quieter, because its language of entry into the small town was the more intimate tongue of the insider. You couldn't picture the narrator of *English, August* speaking more than a few words of Hindi; the world of *A Suitable Boy* is unimaginable without an easy familiarity with Hindi and Urdu.

The latter world is what I myself had been a citizen of, from birth, and its authenticity was Seth's great gift to me as a beginning writer. The world of Indian writing in English had seemed divided, according to what had taken the shape of a truism, into 'pre-Rushdie' and 'post-Rushdie'; Seth's writing of *A Suitable Boy* told me that Indian writing in English would for a long time be governed by a division between writers who spoke only English and others who were tied to smaller, less valued, or at least commercially less viable, languages and cultures.

Indeed, Seth's novel promotes the belief that it could as easily have been written in those other, vernacular languages. As the literary critic Harish Trivedi has noted, *A Suitable Boy* was 'one of the first new wave Indian novels in English to be translated into Hindi . . . The nineteen, twenty-six or thirty-seven languages worldwide into which some successful recent novels in English have been translated have included remarkably few Indian languages, curiously'. And Seth himself, in his new preface to the Hindi edition, wrote that the translation had returned the novel 'to its source milieu and medium, so that now even some of the characters in it would finally be able to read it'.

Having said that, let's not forget that although our protagonist, nineteen-year-old Lata, is a student of English literature at the university, in Seth's hands the language comes into play in a variety of registers: it is the language at once of the Constituent Assembly, the provincial civil servants, the language Seth uses to present the talk on the streets of Calcutta and also the fictional city of Brahmpur where much of the novel unfolds; it is even the language of discourse in the parlour of a sophisticated courtesan who only speaks in poetic Urdu; English is adequate to the tasks of describing Hindu and Muslim festivals; it is also the language used in the house of an upper-class family in Calcutta where all the family members seem to converse in rhyming verse; without English 'you can't do anything', an illiterate peasant says at one point in the novel, and adds, 'If you talk in English, you are king. The more people you mystify, the more people will respect you;' of course, it is also the language used when one of Lata's suitors, wooing her, takes her to the graveyard in Calcutta where lies buried Walter Savage Landor's 'Rose Aylmer', 'Thackeray's father, and one of Dickens' sons, and the original of Byron's Don Juan'. In one scene in the book, Lata attends a meeting of the Brahmpur Literary Society and discovers what might be called the charm of one kind of Indian English. On such occasions, as when one Dr Makhijani reads his verses to the assembled members, English is being both celebrated and mocked:

Let me recall history of heroes proud,
Mother-milk fed their breasts, who did not bow.
Fought they fiercely, carrying worlds of weight,
Establishing firm foundation of Indian state.

And what of the story itself, the choice that Lata makes? At the university she meets Kabir Durrani, who is her classmate, a cricket player as well as an actor. But while Lata is Hindu, Kabir is a Muslim. He is an unsuitable boy. The person who next comes in the picture is the poet Amit Chatterji, who is a witty and cosmopolitan suitor; but he doesn't win Lata's heart because she fears that he is too self-centred and involved in his writing. At the novel's end, Lata chooses the man her mother had found, the unsophisticated, lower-middle-class suitor Haresh Khanna, who is enterprising and intelligent, his open, direct manner suggesting both vulnerability and ambition. I remember at first being disappointed by this choice, thinking it was less rebellious, less romantic, and then it occurred to me that my mother had probably done the same in her life. There might be little passion and even less excitement involved in Lata's choice, but I could see in the young woman's exercise of judgement a quality of prudent compromise as well as an opting for someone who represented the hard-working and dynamic part of newly independent India. Like everything else in the novel, it felt real.

A TALE FROM AN(OTHER) GUJARAT

Joseph Macwan's *Angaliyat*

RITA KOTHARI

I remember an afternoon in 2003 when I was returning from the district of Anand, an hour's drive from the city of Ahmedabad, where I live. This was one of my visits to Joseph Macwan's house. I had undertaken to translate his novel *Angaliyat*, the first instance of Dalit fiction from Gujarat. A friend had said in jest, 'Ask Josephbhai to translate it into Gujarati first,' thereby betraying his own bias towards the 'standard' Gujarati spoken in cities like Ahmedabad and Vadodara. *Angaliyat* is written in what is called 'the Charotari dialect', shared by Dalits, Rajputs, Patels and other communities living in and around Anand and Petlad in south-central Gujarat. It is a different matter that the famous colonial linguist G.A.Grierson, who compiled the *Linguistic Survey of India* around 1902–03, himself admits that distinctions such as 'language' and 'dialect' did not exist in the Indian linguistic landscape he encountered.

While the hierarchy between a language and dialect is arguably a construct, the fact remains that standard Gujarati and Charotari have a yawning gap, making my task as translator frightening. However, these were not my thoughts while returning in the blazing heat of May after my meeting with the author Josephbhai. What had occurred to me then was that Josephbhai had also translated his orality into a written text, but in ways that the text had not been flattened out. During our meetings, he would point out to the lanes and people who had found their way into his novel, break out into songs and elegies that accompanied the weddings and deaths he had witnessed, the heroism of ordinary people that he so valiantly recorded, if not romanticized. The novel *Angaliyat* shows this vividly. In fact the written word lets people down and befuddles the moral basis of their actions. In the English language of contemporary India, this orality is untranslated despite the physical fact of its publication as *The Stepchild* in 2004 through Oxford University Press.

Before I continue with a personal and lasting relationship with *Angaliyat*, it is important to contextualize briefly the location of *Angaliyat* in Gujarat's tradition of fiction. The nineteenth century witnessed the emergence of the novel form in Gujarat through the publication of *Karan Ghelo* and *Saasu Vahu ni Ladai* (both in 1866). Govardhanram Tripathi's *Saraswati Chandra* brought the nascent efforts of the nineteenth century to a new confidence of a narrative in the twentieth. He played an important role in laying down frameworks and themes for the subsequent generation of writers in Gujarat. The formidable albeit controversial K.M. Munshi forged with his trilogy, *Patanni Prabhuta* (1916), *Gujarat No Nath* (1919) and *Rajadhiraj* (1922), a discourse on sub-nationalism whose 'origins' he saw in the Chalukya rulers. Jhaverchand Meghani shifted attention to the small and local with his *Sorath Taara Vaheta Paani* (1937) and set the example of a 'regional' novel, to be followed by the most

well-known Gujarati novel, *Manvini Bhavai* (1947) by Pannalal
Patel. Based on Gujarat's worst famine (popularly remembered as
chhapaniyo) around 1899–1900, Patel's novel showed humanity
(or lack of it) in times of strife and scarcity in rural Gujarat. *Manvini
Bhavai* remained the solitary example of rural and authentic fiction
for another four decades until *Angaliyat* joined the ranks. Besides
such distinction, *Angaliyat* was also the first Dalit novel, and Joseph
widely acknowledged by then as a master storyteller.

In the years when *Angaliyat* came out and took the Gujarati
literary world by storm, I had little to do with Gujarati literature. I
was beginning my first encounter with English literature as an
undergraduate student. *Angaliyat* had appeared in print in 1987 and
received the Sahitya Akademi Award in 1988. It was mentioned to
me for the first time in the early 1990s by a Dalit Christian named
Peter Macwan who hailed from Petlad and worked as a peon at
St Xavier's College, Ahmedabad, where I taught. He recommended
this to me as a novel about his community of Vankars (weavers) —
one of the scheduled caste communities. It was for him that I read
the novel, although the death of Valji, the silent pain of Teeha, the
charming Bhavaan Bhagat's wisdom moved me beyond measure. I
learnt of the angaliyat society, the Dalit sociology that produced the
novel, and came to know members of the Vankar community. The
title *Angaliyat* is formed through the word 'angali' or finger, and it
refers to a child that goes to the home of his new father through the
remarriage of his mother. Both the tradition of remarrying and the
reality of being marginal are invoked through the story of the
Vankar community in the decades from approximately the 1930s
to 1950s.

Compared to a range of other Dalit groups in Gujarat, the
Vankars are relatively better off. They have had some access to
education, largely through a conversion to Christianity and partially
due to their own success at the profession of weaving, which they

allied with (what was once) the robust textile industry of Gujarat. *Angaliyat* is their first story, and although other Dalit groups in Gujarat may not see it representing their lives, few would deny its symbolic power as a landmark, a rupture in the upper-caste literature of Gujarat. Apart from this historic significance, it is the passion and sweep of this novel that make it almost racy popular fiction reading. Interweaving sharp repartee, songs and an overall sense of drama, Macwan manages to tell a story of pain and suffering without bogging the reader down. The characters are etched with flamboyance; they leap out of the book haunting the reader. Their bases lie in Macwan's own experiences as a Vankar growing up in the decades from benign white colonialism to ruthless post-colonial India. Valji, Teeha, and Bhavaankaka are people from Josephbhai's family and environment. They form continuity with pen-portraits of his previous work *Vyatha Naa Vitak*, which marked Macwan's debut and acclaim in Gujarat's literary world.

Teesalal, popularly called Teeho, is a man of convictions. He stands up to his fellow caste-men and refuses to observe hollow traditions subsequent to the death of his parents. However, he is meticulous in maintaining protocol where his friend Valji is concerned and hosts for Valji and his wife the first ceremonial meal (fuleku) after their marriage. The two weave cloth and sell them at auctions in nearby villages. Valji is warm and committed but politically naïve. Teeho has an astute understanding of the operations of caste and the structures that make Dalits like them vulnerable to the domination of the landowning Patels and Rajputs (called Thakores in the novel). As the novel opens, Teeho and Valji head out of their village with bales of cloth on their shoulders. It is a little surprising for Valji that Teeho should have turned to the neighbouring village of Shilapaar rather than the city. 'Why, are auctions done only in towns? After all our sales are for villages, aren't they? Who but the farmer needs this sackcloth? Keep going. Business and

relations take place where you want them to!' Although Teeho was
avoiding the reference to Methi, a Vankar woman from Shilapaar,
his pragmatic and entrepreneurial sense of business is unmistakably
Gujarati. In fact the Dalit characters in *Angaliyat* are seldom poor, a
departure from Dalit narratives from elsewhere, to which my
attention was drawn by the editor Mini Krishnan. This, of course,
may be true of Vankars and not scavenging castes and other Dalit
groups who have received little opportunity of caste mobility
through education, conversion or affirmative action.

Meanwhile, a pivotal incident follows the sale in Shilapaar. Caste
domination is played out on Methi's body, leading to an open and
historic confrontation between Teeho and the upper castes. A series
of intrigues and plots hatched by the Patel community follow to
avenge the perceived humiliation of a Patel at the hands of a low-
caste man. Macwan gives us an insight into the sociology of the
village that helps sustain power relations cushioned by caste
differences:

> The Patels owned most of the lands, despite the fact that there
> were only twenty-five Patel families in the village. The Thakores
> were their tenants and tilled the lands that belonged to the
> Patels. In economic terms, the Thakores were completely
> dependent upon the Patels and the Patels made full use of the
> fact. The Patels were also the ones providing funds for nationalist
> activities undertaken by the Congress and the Patel mukhi had
> joined in the movement for violating the Salt Law.

Angaliyat casts a pitiless gaze upon the Congress from 1930 to the
1950s. Ineffectual, if not openly unjust to Dalits, Congress came to
be constituted by upper castes, who could translate economic into
social capital. It is the Western Enlightenment, English language
and ideologies of Ambedkar that hold some hope for the Dalits.

The figure of Master is a curious one. He is an organic intellectual, just as Bhavaankaka is a wise old organic philosopher. Both provide critiques of caste and community. Master can speak in flawless English with the district collector and seek protection for Teeha. His English is his step towards an amnesia of caste, so we do not get to know his name, and more importantly, surname, therefore caste. Bhavaankaka on the other hand resorts to riddles and songs to mourn the absence of social anger among Dalits. The 'political' Dalit is formed in the course of the novel, although its inputs come as much from Bhakti as democratic thought of Ambedkar. Bhavaankaka mourns upon seeing the passivity of his community:

In which moment did you create us, my Lord
O potter, on which wheel did you cast the pot?

The webs and vendetta surrounding the Vankars supersede the Englishman's support and Bhavaankaka's wisdom. However, it is important to see the dialogue below as one representing new sites of alliances and self-expression in the village:

'Master rightly says that we are not humans, we're mere cadavers. Even when thorns prick us, we rub dust on ourselves and keep walking. Don't we ever feel hurt? But if we have to fight among ourselves, then we can be more warrior-like than even the Rajputs! . . .'

'So you too Valabhai are influenced by Master?' Dana couldn't help commenting.

'I couldn't make much of what he said about Gandhiji and Babusaheb Hendyakar. The rest is absolutely right, one hundred and one per cent right. I must say, that's bloody education for you!'

Ho . . . ho . . . ho laughed Dano: 'You blundered. It's not babu or Hendyakar. Its Babasahen Ambedkar!'

'Now who's that?'

'You remember that photo on Master's table, with the clothes of a "getliman" — the coat and patloon, and a noose around the neck — that is Ambedkar!'

'Is he a gora sahib?'

'No bhai. Master says he is one of us. Of our caste! He went against Gandhiji for us!'

Angaliyat has sharp political insights and polemics on one hand and passionate relationships between individuals on the other. It misses neither the human nor the political story, and most importantly, reads like an absorbing tale marked with dramatic events and tantalizing endings to each chapter. It is this combination that makes me venture to suggest that audiences interested in Dalit literature as well as those who wish to read a well-written story from contemporary India would find *Angaliyat* worth their time.

This is not to deny those aspects of the novel that may make a discerning reader, especially from Gujarat, question the aesthetics as well as ideology of *Angaliyat*. Although the literary elite hailed *Angaliyat* as an authentic voice from rural Gujarat, it is possible to see the allure of Sanskritization also in the novel. The anxiety around remarriage, a practice that marks, at least in Gujarat, an important line distinguishing pure castes from 'impure', and descriptions that break away from Charotari and are rendered in standard Gujarati have drawn some criticism from Macwan's Dalit contemporaries. However, such tensions contribute to my interest in the novel, which remains an important and well-told story of our times.

FICTION OF NEW VOICES

Uddhav Shelke's *Dhag*

ASHUTOSH POTDAR

When Uddhav Shelke wrote his second novel *Dhag* in 1960, creative writing in Marathi was hanging between a sense of escapism and vociferous nationalism. It offered wish-fulfilment to the post-Independence generation that was living with Nehruvian dreams. There were two scenes that occurred consistently across different forms of writing in Marathi around this period: a newly educated Maharashtrian speaking the Puneri Marathi in 'nasal aspirates' and swallowing a staple of *toop-bhat* (ghee-rice) and an uneducated farmer couple relaxing under a tranquil mango tree after sweating blood in the farm, gulping *kanda-bhakar* (onion-roti). Such 'picturesque' scenes would be complemented with poetic narratives ornamented with ample images of nature to give the effect of a colourful 'reality show'. Besides, writers, through the lenses of self-proclaimed morality of limited privileged groups, would look at medieval fantasies or at *peshvai* to nurture the 'cultural' habits of the newly emerging middle-class Marathi readers. The self-interest of a few was not only distorting society's history, but was also obscuring measures of social preferences of the time. Without being self-reflexive, various forms of creative writing entertained the reader as a spectator but not as stakeholder. Not surprisingly, the majority of readership was urban, rich, middle class, educated or upper caste. Obviously, voices of dissent – of farmers, of women, of adivasis and of the underprivileged across urban and rural environs – were kept at bay.

Marathi literature at this time, however, wasn't just about these stereotypes. It was also an era of transformation and reformation. The newly emerging democratic nation was giving confidence to the never heard voices of the Shelkes. Oppressed classes, outcastes, women and voices of dissent were feeling empowered to participate in the mainstream due to new reforms of the time and socio-political movements led by Bhimrao Ambedkar. With this, a new sense of ownership of nation among the disadvantaged was being established across public spheres, and a large class hitherto at the periphery was now making inroads towards the mainstream. As a result, someone like Uddhav Shelke, an impoverished tailor's son, from a village of the Vidarbha region, particularly known for extreme poverty in Maharashtra, could complete his education at least till matriculation and later become a writer. Shelke's father worked long hours, but he was unsuccessful in his tailoring work. So Shelke had to give up his education to help his father run the house by doing different jobs, such as being compositor and proofreader in printing presses.

It was also the time when the *Pather Panchali* kind of new realism with its thematic grandeur and simplicity had already appeared in the realm of the changed socio-economic and public spheres. Marathi Nav Sahitya was not far from this new realism in questioning the existing romantic, nostalgic and hypothetical real of the Phadke-Khandekar era. The Nav Sahitya of Bhau Padhye, Kamal Desai, Vijay

Tendulkar, Narayan Surve, Bhalchandra Nemade, Arun Kolatkar dedicated itself to self-reflexivity and represented multiple forms of reality seen through layered relationships between the individual and the society. And with *Dhag*, Uddhav Shelke, first among the writers of the Nav Sahitya, inaugurated the new novel trend in Marathi, surprising dogmatists who hitherto had a narrow, dichotomized view of a work of fiction: either as 'showing' of social reality or as a world of ornamented words. *Dhag* represented a work wherein both these aspects of fiction merged seamlessly and without effort.

Dhag is the story of a village woman, Kautik, and her struggle against all odds in life. Set against the background of the innards of village life, *Dhag* unfolds the drama of frustrations of Kautik's life, giving strobe-light glimpses of her three children: Bhima, Nama, Yasoda and her husband Mahadev. The story had its germ in one of Shelke's earlier stories with which he had cut his writing teeth, 'Maay' (Mother), which he had written out of frustration after his mother's accident. Living up to its title *Dhag*, or embers, Shelke represents a village woman's sufferings through Kautik's character, where ashes are blown away by her tears to reveal a scorching, hard reality. When you are inside *Dhag*, you are inside pain; it hits you like a punch in the stomach. *Dhag* ends somewhere in the middle of a visibly devastated Kautik's life, and is pervaded through with an air of melancholia and an acute sense of loss.

One of the most complex characters in Marathi literature, austere Kautik embodies no fixed 'feminine' qualities. Unlike several other Marathi middle-class fictional characters of the time, Shelke's Kautik does not spend unusual time in cooking or gossiping with her husband Mahadev. Mahadev, whose father is a tailor, is a peculiar fellow – moody and an unreliable husband and father. But in spite of Mahadev's recklessness towards his family, Kautik remains steadfast by his side, her feelings revealed in her beautiful language that Bhalchandra Nemade regarded as the *Mahanubhav* style, referring to the thirteenth-century narrative tradition. Kautik announces, 'I'll be where you are. If you cut grass why should I feel ashamed to tie sheaves?' At the same time, she forthrightly alerts him on his imprudence: 'Listen! Are you worrying about work or are you simply . . .' and expresses her 'disbelief, anger and pity' over his slothful attitude.

Repeatedly wounded in her fight against all odds in life, Kautik leads her family that is constantly on the move, managing barely to eke out a semi-decent living through agricultural work. Kautik's heroism lies in the fact that she maintains care and gives scrupulous attention to every detail within the household and rules it with exception and contingency. Through the struggles, the worlds Kautik and her family inhabit are in states of transition, prone to all the awkwardness this entails. While managing the household, strong-jawed Kautik sometimes fails to offer emotional support to the family members. When her children ask for *anarasa* and *papdi* Kautik would thrash them and Ganga, her neighbour and relative, would rush to help them. In another example, as Kautik can't see her young child rolling in bed, she pulls the cloth off his face and shouts, 'Isn't only a boy when he's eating! He puts down two man-sized bhakris, doesn't he?' Also, at the end of the novel, intelligent and sensitive Nama aspires to continue with his education but Kautik asks him to give up on his dreams. The narrative portrays how Bhima, alienating himself from the family, hates his parents and flaunts confidence with brassy sensuality towards his mother. Mahadev reaches a point where he does not have any expectations from his wife or family, asking, 'When were my wife and children dependent on me that they can't do without me now?' Only sometimes does he show 'courage' and warns that 'I don't like anybody talking to me like that. Not even my own father'. But like an avant-garde hero, he becomes strangely detached from his own past and grows acutely lonely. He moves away from his family in frustration, saying, 'I don't know why, but my heart just won't settle here . . . I will go anywhere. Whichever way god takes me.'

The narration in *Dhag* is in the urban form of standard Marathi, while the dialogues are in Varhadi, a dialect of the rural Vidarbha of north Maharashtra. In addition to the colourful language of rural Varhadi that is distinctively Shelkean and a challenging read for today's native Marathi reader, its moving style and acuity of social observation leave the reader teary-eyed. What is highly attractive for me is Shelke's ability to cut through the peculiarities of social relations, which remained his speciality in his later novels also, though not as nuanced and reflective as in *Dhag*. The complexities of language also carry regional and caste references, offering, in Shanta Gokhale's words, 'sociological nuances'. Further, as Gokhale has rightly observed, the nuances 'would make sense only to those who know the caste hierarchy'.

Though Kautik's narrative is set against the tightly woven gregarious neighbourhood, Shelke exposes crevices existing within the village system. Carrying no burden of belonging to the village network, Shelke presents his nuanced understanding of the innards of village life, especially the family system and caste hierarchies. When Namadev suggests seeking help from Kautik's siblings, she ruggedly dismisses the suggestion, saying that 'nobody cares for anybody. There's nothing like blood brother and sister-in-law' because 'they're all good time kin'. At one point, in pursuit of bread and butter, tough and courageous Kautik challenges caste hierarchies: 'What's the shame in it? Human beings have to be ashamed of only two things – thieving and slutting. What shame is there in working for the belly?'

The novel peels layers off of the people living in a village without making any moral judgement. Shelke narrates multiple facets of poverty as they exist and lets things reverberate with their own implications and pros and cons. While poignantly narrating the cruelties of adverse conditions, Shelke empathizes with wretched human conditions, but he does not exhibit blind sympathy towards them. On Lakshmi Pooja day, after facing trauma at the weekly market while buying Diwali clothes for Bhima and Nama, Mahadev manages to get marigold flowers and mango leaves. Nama and Bhima string them into garlands to hang up in the verandah and over the kitchen doors. But Mahadev stops them from hanging one in front of the gods. Answering Bhima's question of why they cannot if 'Janya's hung one before Sitakaki's gods', Mahadev clarifies that 'their gods and ours are different'.

In this way, Shelke lays bare the vanity, selfishness, jealousy of either a rich or poor character. He effectively depicts the complex relations between balutedars fraught with caste discrimination and conflict, even as they are bound inextricably in a web of codependence. Kisna Mali (Gardener) comes to ask Mahadev if Bhima would come for cattle-grazing. Upset over Kisna's offer, Mahadev dismisses it, saying, 'Hell! You got to think before you speak. Think of our caste and all. Or you think because we're poor we'll do any work for the belly?' In another incident, when Bhima is grazing cattle, Bakhadya's son-in-law beats him up, because Bhima's animals trampled upon his embankment. Bhima complains to his mother, 'I was telling the sister-fucker again and again; you want to hit me, use your hands, not your chappals. I'm getting polluted. I'm tailor by caste.'

I am reading *Dhag* in the post-*Dhag* phase when the villages featured in *Dhag* have now left behind those 'common crossovers, vests, knot-blouses'. Ten years ago, it would take hours to reach our village from the district headquarters. But now, the adjoining super-highway takes us to the district headquarters in less than an hour. Villages have televisions and cellphones, though not water and electricity. Farmers do not own oxen, buffaloes and bullock carts, as the cost of maintaining them has gone up. They are selling buffaloes and oxen in order to mechanize the farming.

Also, Uddhav Shelke's balutedars as portrayed in *Dhag* no longer have any stake in the village system. Decamping from villages, many of them have become service providers at a factory set up in the nearby industrial zone, as this work offers much more than what they could have earned by providing services in their village. Therefore they prefer gatekeeping or packaging or sweeping at a factory to ploughing, sowing, tailoring or pottery work. Several are selling their lands to pay their increasing agricultural loans as the government and private companies are offering whopping prices for their lands. They sell and migrate to a dinghy apartment on rent on the outskirts of a nearby small town or a city and accept newer hierarchies.

Not only Uddhav Shelke's *Dhag* narrative, but also the narratives of change of the post-*Dhag* phase have now become familiar from the gruelling writings of several Marathi novelists of the well-received Marathi genre of *grameen* (rural) or *pradeshik* (regional) *sahitya* (literature). In fact, *Dhag* is considered to be a major 'regional' Marathi novel. But by 'regional' I do not refer to human beings who speak in a specific regional register or a dialect that can be classified like insects or that entire populations can confidently be labelled as 'good' or 'bad'. The pradeshik does not depend only on a geographical location. Rather, it is about local social systems, village networks, and ways of life, sensibilities and sociolinguistic identity. However, many novels written in the tradition of the grameen sahitya are parochial and overwhelm the reader with hefty details of village life, nostalgic images of childhood lakes and rivers and glorifying the so-called innocence of a villager.

Shelke's *Dhag*, on the contrary, while writing within the iconic Marathi realistic tradition of representing human life, allows an entry into the social structure and architecture of human habitations, nuances of vertically and horizontally arranged people's lives within the caste and class system. It breaks away from the established forms of Marathi realism by not assuming any correlation with ideological dogmas, romantic sentimentalism or lamenting soporifically over reality. Taking us beyond the depiction of 'beauty' of nature or eroticizing rusticity, *Dhag* embodies all essence of human life: greed, politics, power, goodness and suffering. Without laying down any adjudged programme for fiction, it fascinates with its skills in creating fiction. After *Dhag*, Uddhav Shelke wrote nearly 100 titles that include novels, plays, essays and literature for children before he died in 1992. But *Dhag* stands apart, in flesh and blood, with its haunting beauty even fifty years after its publication. As a narrative of suffering, *Dhag* possesses a lasting quality that outlives the tastes and changes of any time.

The English translations of quotes from *Dhag* used in this essay are taken from Shanta Gokhale's wonderful English translation of the novel, *Embers*. Translated from the Marathi original, edited by Mini Krishnan and published by Macmillan India Limited in 2001, *Embers* is, unfortunately, no longer available in the market. But Shanta Gokhale gave me her own copy of the translation. I am thankful for her help.

I am grateful to Madhura Lohokare and Malavika Menon for carefully reading the article and giving me suggestions.

THREE FORBIDDEN LOVE STORIES

Indira Goswami's
The Moth Eaten Howdah of the Tusker

ARUNI   KASHYAP

It is needless to say that *The Moth Eaten Howdah of the Tusker* is a classic modern Indian novel, joining the ranks of *Prothom Protisruti* by Ashapoorna Devi, *Naalukettu* by M.T. Vasudevan Nair or *Godaan* by Premchand. But little do people know that it is also the most unusual book within Indira Goswami's entire oeuvre. When first published in 1981, it appeared in print in a serialized version in the now defunct *Prakash*, a literary magazine published by the Publication Board of Assam. During its publication, it is said to have caused quite a stir for its unflattering depiction of the plight of women in a Sattra — socio-religious institutions of the Mahapurusha Dharma, a monotheistic religion founded and propagated by Srimanta Sankardeva in the fifteenth century. Initially they functioned as centres of egalitarian learning, to spread the message of the Bhakti

movement that had swept India during that period. But on the eve
of Independence, they had deteriorated into feudal institutions
with the Sattradhikars owning vast tracts of land and its inhabitants,
especially women circumscribed by evil and merciless customs in
the name of tradition.

The main theme of the book – the plight of widows – isn't an
alien subject for Indira Goswami. Her family is from the Amranga
Sattra in Kamrup. Thus she has an insider's knowledge of the plight
of women in these glorified structures. The freedom of women in
these shrines was so limited that many women over the centuries
are said to have died without even seeing the main gate of their own
households. Child marriage was rampant and people who couldn't
marry off their daughters before puberty were socially ostracized,
penalized with expensive Vedic rituals. Indira Goswami was a widow
herself, and she had deconstructed the hype around Vrindavan
in her novel *The Blue Necked Braja*, in which she describes the
hapless world of widows who, jilted by their families, go to spend
the rest of their life in the holy city in the hope of achieving
salvation.

What makes *The Moth Eaten Howdah of the Tusker* different from the
rest of her corpus is not its exceptional position in modern Assamese
or Indian literature, or even its themes, but because it is the only
novel where the author is completely absent in the narrative. Indira
Goswami's life, especially after the publication of her frank
autobiography, has been an open book; ever since its publication it
has been used to draw strong parallels with the novels she has
written. Be it *The Chenab's Current*, *The Blue Necked Braja* or *The Rusted
Sword*, all her novels share parallels with huge chunks of *An Unfinished
Autobiography*, a book far ahead of its time. A reading of any of her
novels demands familiarity with her autobiography, blurring the
lines between fact and fiction; in many interviews she has said that
she does not like to 'imagine' plots. She often wrote about incidents

that had taken place in her own life. In *The Moth Eaten Howdah of the Tusker*, Indira Goswami depicts an Assamese village on the banks of River Jogolia just on the eve of Independence. '1947./Indranath got up' are the first lines of the book.

Though the novel follows the life of three widows, it is basically preoccupied with obsolete 'traditions' and their clash with impending modernity which leaves behind a trail of devastation. From the beginning, the description of the village and the life in the shrine is not even remotely flattering – the first scene of the novel opens at Bolo's place, where several men, including the central character Indranath, have gathered to play cards, something they indulge in till after midnight, which is their daily ritual. He is the heir apparent of the Sattra as well as the position of Sattradhikar; a man of ideals and progressive thinking, constrained by the limitations prescribed by cruel traditions. As he leaves Bolo's house and walks back to his village, he smells betel leaves being roasted to be consumed with opium. When he looks at the betel-leaf creepers hanging empty from the betel-nut trees, he feels as if the hanging twigs look like intestines – a strong statement suggesting the endemic nature of opium addiction in Assam at that time. A sense of decadence pervades the opening mood of the novel, which continues to intensify as the story progresses until things start falling apart, similar to how it is described in the classic Nigerian novel *Things Fall Apart* by Chinua Achebe. If Bolo's character denotes stagnation and an unproductive life in the village, opium addiction points towards self-indulgence.

This hopeless situation does not end soon – as soon as Indranath reaches home, he faces his widowed Pehi (father's younger sister) who has been living in their house for years, with the vague hope that her in-laws will send someone to take her back. Of the three main women characters, Indranath's aunt Durga is the oldest and weakest. She jealously sticks to tradition, never sceptical of the injustice that customs and traditions have meted out to her, or to women like her. A helpless woman, her only dream is to immerse the ashes of her husband in the sea off the coast of Orissa's Puri, a sacred place for Hindus. She believes that doing so will pave the path to heaven for her. At her mother's house, she sits beside the fire for most of the day, with her health gradually failing her. Goswami describes her body as blackened by the smoke from the fire, her figure almost resembling a living skeleton due to continuously losing weight over the years. Durga's condition evokes deep pity, suffocating the atmosphere in the novel.

Amidst this choking atmosphere enters Giribala, Indranath's younger sister, who has just lost her husband. An exceptionally brave, stubborn character, she is like a fresh breeze in the narrative. She shows hope, and makes an effort to break away from the tradition. When she builds up a relationship with Mark, the British Christian monk who comes to transcribe ancient manuscripts at the Sattra, Indranath is almost ready to do something that has never taken place in any Sattra before – give the final nod to that relationship. When women crowd the house to gloat over the plight of the freshly widowed Giribala, she doesn't turn up in front of them nor participate in the discussion about her husband's escapades with low-caste women and whether one of his paramours have been impregnated by him. She doesn't respect him or the customs that choke her. In a conventional situation, she would have cried her heart out, while the women of the neighbourhood shared the information they knew about her dead husband, and pitied her. But Giribala does not behave according to their expectations. She storms out of the room and lashes out at them, 'You all came to see me, right? Haven't you seen me now? Get lost now, get lost!'

Giribala and Mark's relationship is paralleled by two other love stories – the pure, unrequited and forbidden love of Indranath for Elimon, and Soru Gosani's (the widow of Indranath's uncle) sexual desire for Muhidhor, the Brahmin caretaker she has hired to moderate her transactions and immovable possessions. Elimon, the daughter of the village Brahmin, has already started menstruating and her midwife begs Indranath to marry her so that she isn't excommunicated or married off to someone unworthy. An extremely beautiful girl, Indranath develops strong feelings for her. But he is unable to take a decision – Gosains being higher in the caste rung than Brahmins, his decision to marry her might create a huge stir.

Indranath hardly ever talks; it is his meticulously mapped internal monologue that brings his character alive – throughout the novel, he isn't able to make a decision, while troubles saddle his shoulder one by one. Towards the latter part, Soru Gosani, who becomes deeply dependent on Muhidhor's help and develops strong sexual feelings for him, is cheated by the man who has been living in her compound as her employee for years. He is caught by the villagers while trying to escape with cash, gold ornaments and documents forging the transfer of most of Soru Gosani's land to himself. With her dreams to live at least with the support of Muhidhor for the rest of her widowhood shattered, she faints and falls to the floor.

Soru Gosani's hopes, coupled with the warm relationship between Giribala and Mark, are like a fresh breeze in the story, but just like Soru Gosani, Giribala's love story also reaches its doom. Just a day before she was to return to her in-laws' place, she enters Mark's room on a rainy night and throws herself at him, expressing her love for him, stating firmly that she would rather die than go back to her in-laws. Mark does not yield, and before he can say anything, people barge into the room to take her away. Giribala immolates herself, while Mark is left to burn in his unrequited desire for the first woman who touched the core of his heart. But what about Indranath? Could he marry Elimon?

Though the novel dwells with the domestic life of the characters

THREE FORBIDDEN LOVE STORIES

and their internal turmoil, a huge chunk is also about unfolding history. While most people in the villages are wasting away in their opium addiction, the communists begin to rise and start spreading awareness on farmer's rights in Assam. To top it all, a new act of the government that would limit the amount of land that a person could hold causes the feudal Gosain to be on red alert. Inspired by the teachings of the old-timer communists, the farmers start to assert their rights by encroaching upon the land they have been cultivating for ages. From the margins, the physical size of the shrine also starts to erode away with this rampant encroachment, along with its former prestige in a newly independent India.

Indira Goswami does not show any hope at all in the narrative. Except for Giribala, who is shown to be a rebel until the moment she dies, no one in the novel makes a concrete effort to combat the evils in the society. Though we learn about the goings-on in Soru Gosani's and Indranath's minds through their interior monologue, their thoughts are held captive in their minds like caged lions, without translating into actions with positive consequences for their own lives. Indranath's death at the hands of rebellious peasants is the final erasure of the possibility of hope in the novel. On a visit to resolve a land dispute, Indranath is killed by a mob of peasants, who thought he had come to assert his claim over the land, when he had gone with the motive of giving it away.

A few chapters before the final hope of the novel, Indranath is wiped out and Giribala talks to Mark Sahab about a dream while they go looking for research materials. The entire area around the Sattra is on red alert as Indranath's pet elephant Jagannath is on a rampage. Giribala says she believes that if Jagannath can be controlled and brought back home without killing anyone, everything will be all right. But just like the moth eaten howdah – an exquisitely crafted chair that is placed on the back of an elephant for the comfort of the people sitting on it – the institution of the Sattra and its obsolete traditions have weakened the insides of the socio-religious institution. Just as Jagannath leaves a trail of blood and bones in his wake, freeing himself from the shackles that tied him to the trees, only to die at the hands of the government shooter, Indranath and Giribala also have to die because they aren't fit to live in a society that so jealously guards tradition, curtailing freedom, free thought and banning pure love. Later, in 1981, in the Epilogue, Goswami brings back the symbol of the howdah – the symbol of the Sattra's prestige – which was crushed to pieces by Jagannath a few days before he was killed. 'The howdah was moth eaten,' one of the characters who had lifted it up on the back of the elephant says, as if sharing a mystery.

The howdah also had two long iron nails underneath that held it firm on the elephant's back – below the exquisite sculpture, blood would stream out of the mute elephant's back, while people sat on it. Perhaps that is also the reason why the pet elephant went on a rampage across the villages when an era was crumbling, bowing its head to welcome a new age.

'SIR, THE RANK AND FILE IS ENTITLED TO KNOW.'

G. V. Desani's *All About H. Hatterr*

NILANJANA S. ROY

There are literate, widely read book-lovers in this world who have not read *All About H. Hatterr*. I know of their existence, I have even met some, but the thought that they exist is chilling. It's like meeting people who have never read *Tristram Shandy* or *Gormenghast*, or found themselves hallucinating, as Hatterr fans do, about swamis and multiple exclamation marks.

This has nothing to do with literary snobbery. G. V. Desani's 1948 classic appears with dreary regularity on lists of books you must absolutely, positively read in order to be considered truly literary, and his astonishing hero has influenced writers from I. Allan Sealy to Salman Rushdie. But the real reason for anyone to read *Hatterr* has to do with a quality rarely cited in critical texts — never again will anyone write a book with such exuberance.

Desani, for instance, didn't. His next work was the mystical *Hali*;

and then he retreated into the comfortable life of the author-recluse. And in 2000, in the blurred newsprint of the obituary section of an Indian newspaper, next to the *Antim Ardas* and *In Fond Remembrance* notices, a brief postage stamp-sized picture of a blurred young Desani alongside two brief lines informed us of his death. By then the image of Desani the writer had blurred along the edges as well, and *All About H. Hatterr* had plunged into the obscurity of the remainder bin from which it would need (and receive) repeated rescues from its fans in the publishing and literary world.

Hatterr fans are a lonely breed today. We know not just the famous lines – 'Damme, this is the Oriental scene for you!' Sir, I identify it (the novel) as a *gesture*. Sir, the rank and file is entitled to know.' – but all the lovely obscure bits about swamis who trade in second-hand clothes stolen off their disciples and the fact that Desani managed to fit thirteen exclamation marks into one paragraph. There is something slightly deranged about us, and a tendency (as you will have noticed) to digress, that we share with H. Hatterr Esquire.

'The Issue: The following answers the question: Who is H. Hatterr?' unleashes Desani's torrential prose, and his unmatched ability to beguile you into trickster territory, holding your attention for three pages until he answers the question – sort of – on the fourth. Hatterr, born a year after Independence, was an early example of the only kind of Indian protagonist the Indian novel in English could possibly have: a man on the margins, a hero who belonged to two worlds and to neither. 'Biologically, I am fifty-fifty of the species,' writes Hatterr, introducing us to his European Christian father and his Malay Oriental mother and swiftly kicking them offstage as he does so.

So there you have it: our first bona fide, home-grown, school-of-Indian-writing-in-English literary character was not Indian at all. Decades later, writing in partial homage to Desani, Salman Rushdie's

Saleem Sinai in *Midnight's Children* would also be half-caste – Anglo-Indian, in his case. Hatterr belonged to the same no-man's-land, a territory claimed by three of India's greatest writers – Rushdie, Desani and Saadat Hasan Manto – in works spurred by or written about Independence. And Hatterr, with his permanent logorrhea, his rapid-fire, utterly Indian English patter, his frantic capering around a world that includes pukka British clubs and ash-coated fakirs, could belong to Manto's lonely lunatic asylum. In Manto's iconic short story 'Toba Tek Singh', the lunatics occupy the no-man's-land between India and the newly created Pakistan; Hatterr's no-man's-land, between the Orient and the Occident, is wider but no less lonely.

Readers tend to miss the isolation of Hatterr on first reading: the man proceeds from swami to circus act to charlatan fakir with frenetic speed and an unstoppable energy calculated to short-circuit introspection. But it's there in *All About H. Hatterr*, Desani's introduction, showcased as the familiar loneliness of a writer without an audience, a voice rendered loquacious by the fear that he might be talking only to himself.

'Planning a rest, I submitted the manuscript to a typist place, to be typed, three copies please. It came back the same week. The rejection slip pronounced it "Nonsense". Besides, the lady said, it wasn't the sort of nonsense young girls in the office ought to see. I apologized, postscripting me a mere slave of the critics. Then I passed it elsewhere. And he referred it to a well-known psychiatrist friend of his (at a clinic). The doctor posted it, with an invitation to me to meet him – professionally. It was hawked around, three copies please, and finally kept by a very kind person. She typed a quarter and returned it. Her brother, a clergyman, was coming to stay in the house. Chance might lead him to the manuscript. I apologized again . . .'

This is still the voice of Desani, in character as Desani-the-author, not the voice of Hatterr himself. 'In all my experience,' T. S. Eliot wrote famously of the book, 'I have not quite met anything like it.' (The closest parallel to Hatterr's voice might come not from Eliot, Burgess or Joyce or even Laurence Sterne, but from John Kennedy O'Toole's *Confederacy of Dunces*.)

Here is a small sample, from a conversation between Baw Saw and The Sheikh: 'I learnt of the ways of the Occidental people from my master Angus . . . And I possess the *Etiquette-Garter,* the *Honi*! Soot quay *Malay-pence*! Soot quay *Malay-pence*! I am the Sheik of the London County Council, the *'Ell See See*! Behold, I am wearing my *'Ell See See*! Know, this is the source, the device and the secret of my prosperity! With this neck-wear, this mystic material, I am a burrasahib! A man! I am Eaten! I am Westmoreland! I am Shrewsbury! I am 'Arrow! I am Charter's House! I am Rugby-Football! I am Gun Co. Winchester! I am all-in-all! And CLC besides! With the aid of this neck-wear, I have helped others, given countless concrete lessons of pukka Occidental wisdom to the needy, as I myself once was! Verily, O beloved, I am a burrasahib! Listen to me and fathom the world! Pay the fees, and see the world! *Ek dum, och aye! Och aye!*'

Exactly ten years before Hatterr, Raja Rao had published *Kanthapura*, struggling, as he wrote in the introduction: 'One has to convey in a language that is not one's own the spirit that is one's own.' In the same decade, Mulk Raj Anand had struggled with the 'unleavened bread' dilemma in his works, from *Untouchable* to *Across the Black Waters*: the complexities of conveying Indian speech, Indian ways of thought, in a language that was at once ours and alien. (Anand often came off sounding like Kipling in reverse, but he did try.) R.K. Narayan, from 1935 when *Swami and Friends* was published to 1948 when *Mr Sampath* came out, had found an easy Indian English that still seems neither forced nor dated. But even in the 1940s, after more than a century of writing in English, most

Indian writers struggled to loosen their tongues, to find their own voice. Hatterr invented his own: a mongrel hybrid that transliterated Indian phrases, borrowed and mauled Greek and Latin tags, mocked English-English, and turned language into a three-ring circus, shifting from juggler to trapeze artist to clown.

It's been over six decades, and *All About H. Hatterr* has dated – in exactly the same way that *Tristram Shandy* or Burgess's *Enderby* quartet has dated, the way any great classic should date. Desani resisted literary ossification – in a brief encounter with a Betty Bloomsbohemia ('the Virtuosa with knobs on') in his introduction, he writes: 'As for the arbitrary choice of words and constructions you mentioned. Not intended by me to invite analysis. They are there because, I think, they are natural to H. Hatterr. But, Madam! Whoever asked a cultivated mind such as yours to submit your intellectual acumen or emotions to this H. Hatterr mind? Suppose you quote me as saying, the book's simple laughing matter? Jot this down, too. I never was involved in the struggle for newer forms of expression, Neo-morality, or any such *thing!* What do you take me for? A busybody?'

But despite his (and Hatterr's) best efforts, the book invited analysis. Saul Bellow found that Desani was one of the few writers he could read while he worked on his own novel. Allan Sealy's *Trotter-Nama* – another classic that bounces dangerously in and out of existence like *Hatterr*, revived by one generation, forgotten by the next – romps down the yellow brick road Desani had built for Indian writers back in 1948. 'I learnt a trick or two from him,' Rushdie said once of Desani, and perhaps, more than the linguistic exuberance, what Indian writers received from Hatterr was permission. The book opens with a 'Warning!' and a conversation between an Indian middleman and the author. 'Sir,' says the middleman, 'if you do not identify your composition a novel, how then do we itemize it? Sir, the rank and file is entitled to know.' 'Sir,' says the author, 'I identify it as a gesture. Sir, the rank and file is entitled to know.' But there is, the middleman explains, no immediate demand for gestures. There is, however, immediate demand for novels, and the author gives in.

Or perhaps not. Desani's 'novel' is really a breathless, joyful performance, a gesture stretched across 316 pages, and perhaps that is why it remains unforgettable, despite its periodic descents into oblivion. Over the last few decades, Hatterr revivals have depended on the largesse of Western critics and publishers rather than the growing maturity and changing tastes of the Indian reader. And since the West has its own set of classics and India is reluctant to claim any story that is not a success story, *All About H. Hatterr* remains not so much lost as not yet quite found. Damme, that's the Occidental-Oriental scene for you.

A SAGA OF A FRENZIED AGE

Mahabaleshwar Sail's *Yug Sanvaar*

VIDYA PAI

Around twelve years ago when I was doing the rounds of publishers' offices with my translation of a Konkani novel, the first hurdle I encountered was a singular lack of knowledge. Here I was, an unknown translator, trying to place an unknown book by an unknown writer, but the problem was that no one had heard of Konkani. That translation got published eventually (as have three others over the last decade), but the lack of information persists. So, before we look at *Yug Sanvaar* (*Age of Frenzy*, 2004), Mahabaleshwar Sail's historical novel, we need to look at Konkani, the language in which it was written.

Konkani is spoken in Goa and in parts of Maharashtra, Karnataka and Kerala that lie along the western coast. The oppressive linguistic policies of the Portuguese rulers in the sixteenth century ensured that Konkani disappeared from the public sphere in Goa and was spoken only in the privacy of one's home. The exodus of Konkani people from Goa and their subsequent relocation in these southern parts kept the language alive in these pockets. However, the influence of the majority language in each region resulted in the development of widely differing Konkani dialects and the use of the Devanagari, Kannada, Malayalam as well as Roman scripts.

A language thus marginalized by history's tide could hardly boast of any creative literature of note. It was only after Goa was liberated in 1961, after the Sahitya Akademi recognized Konkani as an independent Indian language and it was included in the eighth schedule of the Constitution, that creative writing received impetus with short story and poetry being the most favoured genres. It is against the backdrop of this nascent literary tradition that Mahabaleshwar Sail's *Yug Sanvaar*, perhaps the most ambitious of his five novels, should be viewed.

Yug Sanvaar deals with life in Adolshi village, home to a peaceful agricultural community that lives in accordance with age-old traditions, when the Portuguese arrive in Goa in 1510. The order passed in 1546 to exile Brahmins, ban Hindu religious practices and destroy idolatry in Goa forces entire communities to uproot themselves and move away in a bid to save their religion and their gods. Temples are razed and churches built on those sites. Those who remain behind are forced to convert to Christianity, but they often persist with their old traditions and culture. The Order of the Inquisition (1560–1812) unleashes ruthless, inhuman punishments on the new Christian converts in a bid to retain them within the folds of the Church. This causes a major upheaval in the socio-cultural history of Goa.

'I believe in God but not in any organized religion,' Sail claims in the foreword to the book. 'By confining God within the framework of organized religion we breed intolerance of other faiths. By interpreting the teachings of the prophets in a manner that suits our own ends, we create immense havoc . . .' It is this 'havoc' unleashed by a powerful conqueror with a crucifix in one hand and a naked sword in the other on an ignorant mass of people caught up in rituals and taboos, fragmented by issues of caste and social hierarchies that forms the theme of the novel.

A man's sense of identity is linked to his religion and the culture from which he springs. Faced with an ultimatum from a powerful State to give up his religion or face expulsion, arrest or death, each character in the book is forced to make this difficult choice. While Sukhdo Nayak, the first Christian convert in Adolshi, is tempted by the gold coins and portions of fertile community land being offered to new converts, henpecked Gaja becomes a Christian to spite his cruel, domineering wife.

For Ranu Kenkre, the wealthy Brahmin bhatkar (landlord), conversion is the only way he can retain his orchards and fields and continue to look after the families who work on his land. As for Duga Mhar and his son Ghungo, 'untouchables' who are condemned to haunt the fringes of Hindu society, it is the lure of an existence without barriers of caste or class, where everyone eats at the same table and worships in the same church.

The saga of choice plays out differently with other characters when they choose to safeguard their religious beliefs and move to unknown lands. Guna, the headstrong young man from the Nayak community, tries to instigate the villagers to attack the police camp set up in a local shrine. When no one responds to his call he destroys the large stone cross on the hill and cuts off the legs of two Portuguese soldiers before fleeing from the village in search of a new life. Nilu Nayak and his neighbours, however, choose to abandon their homes and their land so that they can carry their *kuldevata* (family deity) Ramnath to safer regions and consecrate the idol at a new site.

For Timanna Bhat, the sensitive younger brother of the temple priest, the desecration and destruction of the temple, which has been the centre of his existence, is too much to bear. His lifeless body hanging from a ravaged beam amidst the silent temple bells is an expression of his rebellion, and displays yet another aspect of this choice.

Sail received the Sahitya Akademi Award for his short story collection *Tarangam* in 1993, but his broad, sweeping style eddying into numerous subplots and cul-de-sacs and drawing deeply from dialect and folklore and indigenous religious practices is better suited to the novel as a literary form. *Yug Sanvaar*, with its vast historical canvas, gives Sail the latitude to tackle life in Goan villages revolving around the temple, the orchards and the fields and the upheaval created in this peaceful fabric by 'the white devils from across the seven seas'.

We accompany Sail to distant Spain and Portugal to see what makes the crusader's spirits tick. We are carried into the labyrinthine depths of the 'Big House', the seat of the dreaded Inquisition, 'where Death did not come easily'; where 'solitude and the huge weight of sorrow often killed the inmate long before he was sentenced to death'. We wonder what the future holds for those straggling hordes, forced to uproot their umbilical ties and head into unknown zones. And, like Sail, we hope that though today 'there is darkness without end on all four sides, who knows, the bright light of morning may reveal a new shore where their tiny footprints may eventually leave mighty impressions on the land'.

Much of this breadth of focus is possible because Sail does not follow a linear plot, nor does he confine himself to the fortunes of merely a handful of families during these turbulent times. The novel develops as a series of episodes peopled by a mosaic of characters, many of whom remain mere cameos caught up in the swirl of the narrative for only a couple of pages. But there are notable exceptions like Durga, the spunky Brahmin woman who decides to work in the family's fields challenging the Portuguese order that Brahmin landowners may no longer hire help. Or Camil

Ribeir, the local neo-convert who is now a Shef (chief official) in the Portuguese police, torn between the need to forcibly convert the villagers and a deep sympathy for the predicament they are in.

It is Padre Simao Peres, the genial Spanish priest who wanders about the village talking of love and compassion and forgiveness, who plays the central role in this novel. 'Some of our people are following the wrong path. They are followers of Jesus, too, but someone has led them astray. The path to Jesus goes through men's hearts. Nothing can be achieved through force,' he laments. He is an effective foil to Padre Paolo Colaso and the other Jesuit priests who clamour for greater use of force and more stringent laws to make Goa a Christian stronghold ruled by the Portuguese king. This Padre bappa's arrest and subsequent trial by the Tribunal of the Inquisition give Sail a chance to flesh out his character and explore the workings of his mind.

While religious conversion, the migration of communities and the excesses of the Inquisition form the three main planks on which the novel rests, Sail is also intrigued by the comparative ease with which a boatload of soldiers and religious practitioners could overrun an entire region. Hindu society, fragmented by divisions of caste and of class, and the Hindu religion, preoccupied with issues like untouchability, ritual purity and taboos of diet were unable to withstand these intruding forces.

The doors of Hinduism opened outwards – people were branded 'outcastes' and expelled from its folds. A hungry child from a Hindu family fed by a kind-hearted Christian woman or unsuspecting Hindus who cooked on a hearth that had been used by a Christian family were therefore tarred with the same brush. Once expelled from its folds they couldn't re-enter Hindu society; they could end their lives or accept the four gold coins offered to each new convert and get baptized, thus swelling the numbers of the Christian faith.

Sail claims that his imagination was fired by the unwritten stories, the drama, the conflict and pain that lurked in this period of Goan history, but he remained hesitant because this was an issue that concerned men's faiths. It called for much research into the historical and sociological accounts of the period. It had to be handled with sensitivity and restraint.

Yug Sanvaar testifies to Sail's mature handling of a turbulent period of Goan history, of interest to Konkani Hindus who flock to the resurrected temples of their kuldevatas even today, and to Konkani Christians in search of their roots.

Social and political upheaval and the resultant migration of communities have been spawning grounds for great literature all over the world. Creative writing born out of such ferment throws light on the collective consciousness of a community and the region it inhabits. *Yug Sanvaar*, if it transcends the boundaries imposed by language, has the potential to do just this.

MODERNISM AND ITS DOUBLES

U.R. Ananthamurthy's
Suryana Kudure

ASHWIN KUMAR A.P.

U.R. Ananthamurthy's *Suryana Kudure* (a collection of short stories first published in 1995 and translated as *Stallion of the Sun*) simultaneously operates in two registers: it is a modernist's elegy to a deeply ambiguous past (ambiguous because it is a monument to its own resilience as also a symptom of a degenerate society at the threshold of its own annihilation) and a moment of rupture in the very history of modernist discourse (rupture because here Indian literary modernism meets its own double: the aberrant, degenerate village simpleton transgressing both history and reason, not through an existential encounter with history but by simply falling through the cracks).

The title story itself is a staple of the Indian angst literature we are very familiar with. Returning to his village, the litterateur-author-narrator Ananthu discovers his old friend Hade Venkata (the nickname indicating the urchin that he was and continues to be) in a state of utter disrepair – unmarried daughters, a suffering, complaining and cursing wife, an errant and wayward son and Venkata himself in the midst of all this strife in his splendid, almost reckless, disregard for his lot. The subsequent narrative is a slow and painful unravelling of the minute details of Venkata's life and his moral failure as father, husband and above all provider of the family, occasionally interspersed with commentaries from the narrator, now on the abounding 'village idiocy' of Asiatic proportions and now about his own dread at the precarious distance that separates himself from Venkata.

The central drama binding the narrator and the narrated is an oil massage and a scalding hot-water bath given by Venkata to Ananthu, an art for which he is known far and wide, and the reason why Ananthu has come to Venkata's house this time. Venkata is supposed to have the ability to take his clients (who include not just local politicians and police officers but also the illustrious K. T. Basham) to the heights of bliss through his massages: 'showing the full moon', as he describes it himself.

At this point, the narrative shifts gear and we are no more in the familiar domain of the room-temperature social theory of Indian modernism with its well-worn antinomies: the alienated individual versus his rotting, self-amnesiac, non-modern counterpart, the dangers of urbane vacuity versus the ancient violence of ahistorical modes of life and formal knowledge versus native intuition. The massage slowly dulls the narrator's consciousness; standing behind him is the expert masseur Venkata chanting rhymes, mantras, Yakshagana lyrics and affected extempore poetry even as he is kneading, drumming, squeezing and twisting Ananthu's flesh, bending as it were the rigidities of both muscle and mind.

Both the narrative and the narrator from this point onwards acquire a suppleness and intimacy that dissolve the hitherto intellectual bravado and moral certainty of Ananthu and his puzzlement about the ways of Venkata. A process of healing has already begun for Ananthu where what requires healing now is not only the decadent human condition petrified in an antediluvian Asiatic mode, but also the rigid varicose of a historical rationality subsuming life to abstract and monstrous goals bypassing the dialectic of experience and reflection. Of course Ananthu experiences nothing of the 'full moon' after his massage, but by now the narrator has been so undermined that we cannot take this as proof only of Venkata's failure, but on the contrary also as a question about the capacity of the narrator to do full justice to his own experiences.

I strongly believe this narrative failure to be the real success of the story.

Readers of Ananthamurthy will know that this is no isolated work of his, but a central concern to which he returns repeatedly in his novellas and other short stories. Whereas works with this theme prior to *Suryana Kudure* suffer because he fails to sustain the essential ambivalence of this moral-historical situation, later works can squarely be seen as formulaic attempts to milk this theme to produce a world view (a gestalt that modern Indian literary history has shown us it is incapable of). In some senses, then, *Suryana Kudure* stands at the pinnacle of Ananthamurthy's achievement as a writer.

The story ends on an ambiguous note when the narrator, waking up early in the morning after a troubled sleep owing to a row between Venkata and his son, finds Venkata transfixed in the kitchen garden gazing at a grasshopper, the stallion of the sun of the title, which represents the lithe insect with the mythical capacity to bear the sun on its back as also the skill to be completely submerged in the colours of the background making itself innocuous. The stallion of the sun is only one small element in an entire matrix of mythologies shared by Venkata and Ananthu from their boyhood days. Seeing it as a metaphor or a symbol standing for some abstract idea is really beside the point. The stallion of the sun is only a point of entry into another completely different world of objects and relations, a world that is the common past of both Venkata and Ananthu, making them nothing more, but also nothing less, than two possibilities inherent within that world. The specific contours of that world will remain closed to the reader of this story but will reveal glimpses of itself throughout Ananthamurthy's work as so many human possibilities.

Ananthamurthy works with similar themes in some other stories in this collection: notable are the stories 'Akkayya' and 'Jaratkaaru'. In 'Akkayya' the two academics sharing over a glass of whiskey the story of Akkayya (a child widow and the matronly sister of one of them, similar to Venkata in the incongruity of her existence with the ways of the modern world) start drumming on the antique earthen pots decorating the interior of one of their American living rooms and mouthing absurd nonsensical rhymes in a bacchanalian moment. The story ends in their realization that it is probably in this moment that fuses their sentimental remembrances of Akkayya's life with the 'awkward and absurd' (in their own words) hankering after sensitivity and sensibility, that true authenticity is to be found.

Although this refreshing lightweight resolution to the story shows a full awareness of the traps of the authenticity-seeking modernist writer, in so far as it cannot shake the received antinomies of much of modernist writing, it remains an intellectual play of thin abstractions and does not push the narrative towards taking any real risks. In fact, both in 'Akkayya' and 'Jaratkaaru', the problem gets reduced to the great conflict of historical modes being played out in the battleground of the modernist artist-individual's consciousness. In all these stories the problem becomes one of seeking individual redemption from the gravity-free hell of modern alienation by finding an authentic mode of existence.

But what is the stuff of authenticity that modernist authors are so taken by it? The hankering after authenticity is in the final instance the desire to render one life-world completely in terms of the other. What then is the problem with it? Only that this necessarily intellectual task is converted into a problem of psychologies, of being able to *feel* or exist in a psychological state called authenticity. No doubt this is a critique of Ananthamurthy's work, but we owe a debt to Ananthamurthy for opening up the possibility for such a critique of Indian modernism and of the social function of writing in India. To slightly correct our previous evaluation then, both 'Jaratkaaru' and 'Akkayya' are in some senses the beginnings of a contrapuntal exploration of the artistic-intellectual problems inaugurated by *Suryana Kudure*.

SAVED BY TREES

O. V. Vijayan's *Khasakinte Ithihasam*

KALA KRISHNAN RAMESH

When I first read O.V.Vijayan's *Khasakinte Ithihasam*, I was fifteen, and the world it took me into was subtly bounded by the experiences of my parents — on whose feet I was comfortably standing at that time — thus everything in Khasak was mellowed by their innate simplicity and good nature. Twelve years later, when I reread it, I was on my own feet, staggering through adult worlds, a familiar negotiator with the chimeras that ruled Khasak and its inhabitants: self-knowledge, guilt and redemption. On this second reading, Khasak stretched out before me, unrefined and complex; *Khasakinte Ithihasam* (1969) was different from anything I'd read in Malayalam and also different from other books I'd read.

Khasak was a brave book: in it, O.V.Vijayan was taking on and rejecting the Malayali's unyielding materialism in its stubborn Marxist coat of arms and — perhaps more significantly — effectively writing himself out of reach of this world. Rejecting the Marxian envisioning of history and progress as a rational, outward-moving impulse, in *Khasak* he created a counter world, a world in which time was elastic and 'progress' often meant not just giving up goals, but also submitting to apparent chaos. In a single masterly stroke, Vijayan not only erased his own history of allegiance to Marxist philosophy and his commitment to realism and satire, but he turned against the Malayali grain of rejecting the spiritual-mystical as somehow less than, and outside of, 'real' literature (which was often a literature of social commentary).

The thing about *Khasak* is that it released the Malayali from a suffocating need to steer clear of the spiritual as a valid part of life and fiction. Thousands of young people – perhaps especially young men, because in some ways Vijayan is much more a young man's writer and much less a young woman's – took to *Khasak* as readers in the English-speaking world took to Salinger and his vision of a spiritual world. In *Khasak*, Vijayan re-enchants and spiritualizes the inner and outer worlds not only so that the book's hero Ravi can regain a sense of identity and belonging but also as some sort of ideal for himself, which he would then spend the rest of his life travelling and writing towards.

It's an oft-repeated truism that before *Khasak*, Vijayan was a confident communist, and in this book he had set out to write the great 'revolutionary' novel, but disillusioned by the Soviet Union's invasion of Hungary and the execution of Imre Nagy, he had, in an extended mood of self-inquiry, eventually turned his gaze inwards. During this time of disengagement, Vijayan refashioned the book's hero Ravi, melting him out of the 'mould of the urban revolutionary come to conscientize the village . . .' and recasting him as a 'spiritual wanderer'.

Khasak's protagonist Ravi, when we first meet him, has just struggled free of the straitjacketing and reductive grasp of the rational world, in which he is a sinner, frozen forever in time's irrevocable forward march. He has left his father's house – exiled also from the metaphorical security of the maternal embrace following a sexual liaison with his stepmother – and travelled to Khasak, which will eventually restore to him the timeless comfort of a kindly mother and relieve him of the overwhelming burden of guilt that he's carrying. This homecoming for Ravi is hinted at in *Khasak*'s opening paragraph: 'When the bus came to its final halt in Koomankavu, the place did not seem unfamiliar to Ravi. He had never been there before, but he had seen himself coming to this forlorn outpost beneath the immense canopy of trees, with its dozen shops and shacks raised on piles; he had seen it all in recurrent premonition – the benign age of the trees, their riven bark and roots arched above the earth.'

What an opening! Vijayan nicks away any readerly expectations that *Khasakinte Ithihasam* might be housed in a Marxist/materialist dwelling, by making it clear that Khasak is located in a spiritual place, a place that lives in and is governed by spiritual time.

As the reader goes further into Khasak, she will realize – as Vijayan himself said in an interview – that the basis for this spirituality is Hindu, in its broadest and most dynamic sense, reminding her that if Vijayan had been alive, he could have made valuable contributions to the discourse of liberal Hinduism, reminding us of the deep spirituality hidden within religion, which is almost inevitably connected to a vision of nature as intrinsic to human wholeness. The reader will also see how Vijayan has chosen 'time' to do battle with materialism and to spiritualize the world he has created in the novel. For *Khasak*'s time is enchanted; it curves into itself, so that past, future and present are coexistent in this enchantment. This timeless landscape re-enchants Ravi, cleansing him of sin and guilt: washed free of the stains of linear time, Ravi is absorbed into a kind of mythical time, into a mythicalized world.

Khasakinte Ithihasam begins with the hero Ravi arriving in Khasak and ends with him leaving it: his transformation through receiving the grace of Khasak occurs over a single school term at the Single Teacher School, where he has been contracted to teach. Ravi has just left Madras, where he, along with his lover Padma, has just finished an undergraduate degree in physics. Ravi apparently was so good at it that a visiting professor from Princeton, a friend of Padma's father, invites him to Princeton to study. In the months between Ravi's meeting with the professor and his decision to leave Madras and come to Khasak, much happens inside him. His guilt at having slept with his stepmother is deeply intertwined with the never-ending sorrow of losing his birth mother, who transformed his early days with stories that turned the clouds and everything in the natural world around into magical beings, imbuing the whole world with a preternatural magic.

Guilt and sorrow have also driven Ravi to the edge of his own interior landscape, which he now realizes he does not know anything of, always having looked out at the world around him, neglecting to travel across his own interiors. This combination of problems – that as readers we can see clearly – must be solved not just by looking inwards but also by reconciling the enchantment of his mother's world with the sense of sordidness that surrounds the place he is stranded in at the moment; he must reconcile the timelessness of the one with the cause-and-effect bounded chronology of the other. And by one of those momentous quirks of fate, Ravi senses that it is Khasak, which will enable him to do this, and so he gets on a bus and sets off. And our acquaintance with him begins there.

In Khasak, he meets people whose lives are almost mythical in their complete immersion in and surrender to nature and spirit, and where the landscape, filled with all those mythical trees, those deep, black wells that can drive a man to surrender himself to its depths, the half-boy-half-man Appukili, the mollaka, old and dithering, Nizam Ali, who is in a sense the carrier of the mystical seed, the irresistible Maimoona, the only substantial woman character that Vijayan ever created, are all a part of his cleansing and transformation. In Khasak, Ravi meets people who have such a keen feeling for the endlessness of time that they appear to be living in a place hollowed out of time's circularity; they have no will and are instead, it would seem, governed by a common will that extends from the natural world into their own natures.

In Khasak, Ravi also spends the days with the children who are his students and it is they, more than anything else, who return him to his mother's clasp, by asking awake his frozen perception of the enchantment of the natural world. Through his storytelling and his school activities, many of which involve going outdoors or looking at portrayals of nature, he is once again able to receive the signals that nature never stopped sending out.

Thus, in Khasak, Ravi is able to immerse himself in his search for inwardness and learn a willingness to participate in the swivel of nature without attempting to resist the gravitational force of its repetitive circular swing. He too learns to submit himself to nature and time, like the inhabitants of Khasak. Ravi is the student in Khasak, and everything: the people, the winds, the flowers, the sexual relationships, the toddy, the oracle, the deaths, the ideas, the children, the mullah, the khazi, are all teachers — Masters, in the old-fashioned sense — and he is their apprentice, giving himself up to their instruction. At the end, he is alchemized.

Ravi's search is agonizing and its conclusion is death, a death that appears at one level to say that the only logical end to such a search is death — whether literal or metaphorical — but the amazing thing is that the author, himself engaged in such an inward-looking endeavour, does not die or weaken. In real life, Vijayan himself was at the burning beginning of a spiritual quest no different from Ravi's and yet he never loses track of the fact that he is creating fiction: he tells a terrific story, the words continually embellishing

Khasak and its inhabitants, and not once does the veneer of fiction lose its shine, or the artifice become lifelike.

In *Khasakinte Ithihasam*, Vijayan makes innovations with language, theme and storytelling that are said to have left Malayalam literature so changed that Malayalis would ever afterwards refer to pre-Vijayan and post-Vijayan writing. But perhaps the greatest achievement of *Khasakinte Ithihasam* is how it asserts the possibility of re-enchantment, of returning to a natural world so spiritualized that it is clearly not just a container for human evolution and history – as the Marxists would have us believe – but something far more organic, extending into the human interior in a way that makes it impossible to separate the world into inner-outer, material-non-material.

I met O.V. Vijayan for the first time when he came to stay in Bangalore with his nephew, a few streets from where I lived, to work on the English translation of *Khasakinte Ithihasam*. I would walk down to the house twice or thrice during the week, after he had finished his work for the day. My daughter Gauri, who was then two – too young to go to Montessori – was always with me: she would sit looking at her picture books or drawing, sometimes Vijayan would engage her in talk. About five years later, we went to visit Vijayan in his sister O.V. Usha's house in Kottayam. Vijayan was by this time quite debilitated by Parkinson's and could just about make himself understood; he was frail, his white hair and beard wispy, but he was still animated with affection. My daughter stood as if she were seeing a vision, and then said, 'He's real. This is the man I've been dreaming of for so long. He sits in a grandfather's chair and nods at me, as if I'm telling him something.' And that, in many ways, is how I'd like to think of O.V. Vijayan (and *Khasakinte Ithihasam*): as an involved patriarch in a disenchanted world, insisting that we detail what we see so that we can look at what we aren't seeing.

THE MARVELS OF AN ICE-LIT DREAM-TIME

I. Allan Sealy's *The Trotter-Nama*

SAMPURNA CHATTARJI

The Trotter-Nama is a book built by icelight.

Icelight. It's that slippery spermy light that comes just before dawn . . . It freezes time, or rather, it traps it at that tremulous point just short of freezing, when time is neither solid nor liquid but simply a quality of light. It comes at the edge of sleep, when all those vivid fragments from the past float up to the surface hard and real but running away like lumps of ice. It allows you to get the past down, to copy it, after it's actually melted away. And the past alone is true. It's my livelihood anyway. Sans Souci, for instance — that's our ancestral home — I rebuilt it by icelight.

So says Eugene Aloysius Trotter, Chosen Trotter, herald of New Promise after six generations of Legend, Chivalry, Romance, Prose, History *(void)*, Decadence and Diaspora. Author of *The Trotter-Nama* (not to be confused with the *Tota-Nama*), '*The chronicle (not history) of the Trotters as set out by the Seventh Trotter*', writer of epic and ballad, forger of miniatures, paper-chaser of the past, lover of gulab jamuns, who only and always catches planes after the last and final call . . .

My exhilaration at the prospect of communicating just one small fraction of what Allan Sealy's magnificent debut novel meant for Indian fiction in English — what it encompassed, extolled, lampooned, what it revelled in, what it did for literature — is immediately followed by despair. It cannot be done. What *The Trotter-Nama* needs is the epic essay. A form as accommodating and inventive as the book itself. One that will allow for lists and interpolations, for interruptions, digressions, conversations, recipes, verses, inspired artistic passages, inbuilt disagreements, parodies. For hilarity and meditation. For detailed instructions on *How to critique an unclassifiable text* or *How a genuinely original book is made*. Instead, I must work within given strictures of format and word count.

And so I begin with (return to) the icelight.

Eugene Aloysius Trotter (E.A.T.), worthy stand-in for Irwin Allan Sealy (I.A.S.) as the author (one is tempted to use the word 'auteur') of this mock epic, proudly asserts that he rebuilt Sans Souci, ancestral home to seven generations of Trotters, by icelight. In truth, what his creator has done is far more ambitious — rebuilding the narrative of an entire community by icelight.

This book is that ancestral home. It is no accident that Sealy reiterates the fact that it is a Chronicle and not a History. As Walter Benjamin writes in his essay *The Storyteller* — 'among all forms of the epic there is not one whose incidence in the pure, colourless light of written history is more certain than the chronicle.' The writer of history is the historian; the teller of history is the chronicler. 'The historian is bound to explain,' but the chronicler has 'from the very start lifted the burden of demonstrable explanation from [his] own shoulders. Its place is taken by interpretation, which is not concerned with an accurate concatenation of definite events, but with the way these are embedded in the great inscrutable course of the world.' Within the generous enfoldments of *The Trotter-Nama*, the burgeoning, flourishing and subsequently fraying and frittering Anglo-Indian community finds its warmest, truest chronicler.

The book, in Sealy's own words, is dedicated to 'that protean people'. To my mind, the invisible presiding deity of this novel is Proteus himself, that oracular, all-knowing, hard-to-pin-down shape-shifter of Greek mythology, associated with the unconscious in Jungian psychology and in alchemy with the element of mercury. From the ice-lit dream-time of a mercurial imagination, vivid, fragmented, hard and real, yet elusive, melting away, full of a past that comes right into the present, *The Trotter-Nama* confounded, even annoyed Western readers when it first appeared in 1988. One critic, while rather grudgingly admitting that Sealy 'can often write prose supremely well', went on to say 'he's less good at that most fundamental task of the novelist', which he defined (rather limitedly) as 'making people live on the page'. All the riches that delighted me, and no doubt, other authors, reviewers and readers, he wrote off as cosmetic, whimsical, seemingly sophisticated, hopelessly redundant attempts at being a 'fancy modern novel'. What he, and many others, missed was the book's true originality.

As John Berger put it in *The Hour of Poetry* — 'original has two meanings: it means a return to the origin, the first which engendered everything that followed; and it means that which has never occurred before.' He goes on to say that only in poetry are these two senses united in a way that is 'no longer contradictory'.

But here is a modern novel that, far from being 'fancy' (i.e. decorative), is one that identifies and returns to its origin, only to come back from the journey with a wholly new rendition of an older form. In this case, Abu'l Fazl's *Akbar-Nama*, Firdausi's *Shah-Nama*, the *Babar-Nama*, the *Sikandar-Nama* . . . The energy it draws from these acknowledged sources proves, in Sealy's hands, to be extraordinarily enabling. There is a communicable charge that animates 575 pages of complex, allusive, sprawling, detailed, historical, metaphorical, literary prose. It is the presence of the writer who fears nothing, risks everything, and spins a jolly good yarn at the end of it.

Sealy's *Trotter-Nama* took giant steps in creating a genuinely Indian novel — namely an assimilative, multicultural, polyphonic place (following in the robust and rule-breaking footsteps of G.V. Desani's *All About H. Hatterr*, in which, as a learned friend put it, 'the mangling of language along with a manic energy are first expressed so fully'). Sealy places it within a tradition, and then shows (shews) how many traditions that really is. There is a hilarious section in which Sealy lists the ingredients for a Raj novel; another in which he introduces 'literary echoes' and does so, literally,* with panache. The word 'eclectic' has lost its edge through overuse. But Sealy's book is truly that noble thing. Through his eclecticism, Sealy achieves a universe of particulars, a particular universe. It is a place with a tenderness for forgotten pasts, forgotten people, forgotten objects. The doolie, so lovingly described, was what my grandmother called a meat safe. In the litany of humble everyday things, the invented histories of the invention of mango-fool and Trotter Curry, the many kinds of elbows (from those like tailor's chalk to those like beaten iron), the book is far from being a frippery of concoctions or a hot-air balloon, and is, rather, a capacious, compendious, exquisitely crafted magic box from which the marvels keep coming.

For all its humour and wise-cracking energy, there is a kernel of sadness at the heart of *The Trotter-Nama* — in the question of what home might mean to the 'country-born' Anglo-Indian, disowned

---

* DA! DA! DA! — *The Wasteland*, BOUM BOU-OUM OU-BOUM — *A Passage to India*, SUNYA! -NYA! -NYA! — *The Titar-Nama*

by both the foreign master and the native. Towards the end of the book, there is a beautiful passage where Eustace Trotter wonders, 'Could one have a home that one had never been to, that filled one's chest with a prickly longing, like the plainsman's longing for the mountains he has never known?' The memory of a glimpse of the snow-covered Himalayas comes back to him and with it the sensation that 'The white wall was not home . . . but it was a vital place to which his thoughts would go back again and again. It went deeper than the ordinary longing for a sense of quiet rootedness — it was the sense of a source or spring, maybe one that had to be invented.'

In his preface to the 1999 edition, Sealy writes, 'the novel is a product of the nineteen seventies. By the middle of that decade when I was carrying *The Tin Drum* everywhere, I had begun to feel that I could do a Grass on India. The question was: did I want simply to beat out an Indian march on a borrowed drum?' He didn't want to, and he didn't. And while Sealy names Laurence Sterne's *The Life and Opinions of Tristram Shandy, Gentleman*, Mervyn Peake (that idiosyncratic creator of works such as *The Adventures of Foot-fruit* and the *Gormenghast* trilogy) and Emperor Babar as some of his inspirations, there are umpteen other sources that animate this book. The references are rich rewards for the keen adept, the one who will rejoice in the allusion to Robert Frost in the note on ice; in Fonseca's son being named, significantly, Henry L(o)uis Vivian after the poet Derozio; the way in which the Great Trotter's last will and testament echoes the phrasing of Hiranyakashipu's boon; the nod to Coleridge's 'The Rime of the Ancient Mariner' in the Narrator's appeal to 'The Wedding Guest-and-gentle reader' . . .

Sealy takes wicked delight in jumping up and down on a verbal trampoline, punning, bringing together styles from Anglo-Saracen to 'Hindu-Gingerbread' (!), even taking the phrase 'a little bird told me' literally and turning it into a deft narratorial device. The

Narrator has invariably heard what he recounts to the Cup-Bearer (wonderful carping, cajoling, impatient, demanding stand-in for the reader) from a bird – the golden oriole, the Canada goose, the phoenix, the crow. These are never random, each is chosen with care and wit – the vulture after a battle, the dove after peace, the house sparrow on the proceedings in the British House of Lords, the adjutant bird on the events of the Sepoy Mutiny. And here's just one breathtaking example of the many risks Sealy takes in the course of the novel, when he interrupts the Chronicle (yet again) to reveal aspects of the 'World-Historical Water-Spirit (*Weltgeschichtlicher Wasser-geist*)'! Such fearlessness is radical. Not for Sealy the dread of putting off, annoying or simply losing the reader. He writes as he does, firm in the conviction that some will stay. And he is right. In the current climate, where being 'reader-friendly' (i.e., simple to the point of idiocy) seems to be key to a novelist's success, Sealy is a beacon. In a scenario of overnight sensations (that fade overnight), the time *The Trotter-Nama* took in the making (eleven years in all) is an object lesson in fortitude. And to any young Indian-English author, Sealy's oeuvre, reinventing itself with every new novel, is an inspiration.

In the Prologue, Eugene tells his fellow passenger that he keeps his life's work (*The Trotter-Nama*, of course) in a brown paper bag that travels with him everywhere. Instead of worrying about losing it, he tempts fate, taking the only precaution of making sure the bag bears his current address. And then he says, 'It's been left under bridges, on buses, in public toilets and telephone booths, on park benches, in Groppi's confiserie in Cairo, and it always comes back.'

Not feted as loudly and widely as it should have been, loved and maligned in unequal measure, more than two decades after its publication, *The Trotter-Nama* is that triumphant feat – modern, Indian, classic. A cult book with a following, alive and relevant as ever, disappearing occasionally, but in the end, always coming back.

THE BARD OF BORUNDA

Vijaydan Detha's *Rachna Sanchayan*

AKSHAY PATHAK

Words they are a-plenty. Numbers two or twenty. With the blessings of the lords of words there was once a man weaving them into worlds.

To begin talking about a writer like Vijaydan Detha it would be fitting to start with a *chougou* — a form of mostly nonsensical rhythm or rhyme he employed in most of his stories much in the oral tradition of storytelling that he finds himself most attracted to. That and the language.

Language flows in one's blood, believes the writer. The mind then plays tricks adulterating the language — a victim to the hegemonies and hierarchies languages face in the wake of power and its endless tyranny. The writer then resorts to counter that very power with a word and text so mighty it shakes things up.

Vijaydan Detha, popularly known as Bijji, is one such champion of language. Negotiating the promiscuous relationship of language and literature, he has managed to put together a body of literature to be read, told and cherished for generations, quite in the spirit of what he believes stories are meant for. A deliberate choice of writing in Rajasthani, a language yet to be constitutionally recognized and considered a poor cousin of the dominant Hindi, as well as compiling folklore, he has given the language new life by translating the oral to the written and transforming it richly in the process. His fourteen-volume *Batan ri Phulwari* (*A Garden of Stories*) is an unparalleled work compiling folklore from Rajasthan, which he adapts with his inimitable style and decorates with commentary, often citing the source of these stories.

Shying away from notions of ownership and copyright, he insists on his role as that of a storyteller as opposed to a story writer; a raconteur of sorts. Literature, like language, belongs to everyone. Stories are a collective wealth that the writer, according to Bijji, sifts through, adds to and mirrors to society. Well illustrated in the fact that he used to pay daily wages to women in the village who came and told him stories that they indulged in in *angan*s or behind closed doors in their veiled and secluded lives, while men were out either ploughing fields or amassing wealth in nearby towns. His stories have a sharp sensibility attributed mostly to the feminine, the music of a whirling sandstorm or, as he puts it, 'the stories of the desert are like its sand, fine and transparent'. And an imagination of the bonded. His freedom to create, he says, came from bondage: the bondage of society, the bondage of languages foreign, the bondage of a caste-ridden feudal existence.

A reaching-out, almost Freudian, to his early childhood, as pointed out by several people who know his work well, including his son Kailash Kabeer who has translated most of his works into Hindi, reveals a strong recognition of the power of the word as a force for social dissent. The leitmotif in his stories being a rebellion against the caste-based feudal system symbolized and perpetrated by powerful Brahmins and *thakur*s, the systemic hold of power and its inherent nature of exploitation. Anecdotal references bring one to the conclusion that his writing was a form of retribution, a pun instead of a gun. The genetic memory inherited as a prodigal son of a family of *charans* – courtly poets – excelling in their art of metric poetry informs and enriches Bijji's stories and the architecture of his sentence. More than the power of meaning attributed to words, he lays emphasis on the 'arrangement of words' (*shabdo ka niyojan* as he aptly puts it himself). The form then makes his storytelling unique in ways that leave the reader hooked to a story with its musical, lyrical, visual and sometimes very complex structures. This same richness of his story's texture has led to adaptations on stage as well as cinema.

The choice to write in his mother tongue Rajasthani came with its own set of challenges. Using idioms and phrases situated in the local gave a uniqueness to his stories and a chance to break free from the languages imposed on him by teachers in his childhood. However, he faced some resistance from his peers writing in the same language discrediting his colloquial use of the language, a polluting of the language for many. And then the rather shocking fact of the absence of a constitutional recognition for the language failed to bring his stories to a wider readership. But in the 1970s, Sahitya Akademi recognized his contribution by presenting him with an award, the first for a Rajasthani writer, which gave an impetus to the language which was largely and inaccurately considered a dialect of Hindi. Thereafter he got national recognition through some of the most prestigious awards – the Padma Shri, the Sahitya Akademi fellowship and the Katha Chudamani award among many others. A book brought out by Sahitya Akademi titled *Vijaydan Detha: Rachna Sanchayan* (2009) contains a comprehensive range of his brilliant short stories, some essays and other writings. It has been edited by his son Kailash Kabeer.

A storyteller mastering the short story form, he often mentions that his thoughts were hugely inspired by Chekov, Tagore and his beloved Sarat Chandra Chattopadhyay, but his style, he claims emphatically, belongs to his surroundings, his rural environment, to the inherited lyric of his forefathers. Of the dust-laden bookshelves and thirsty throats on a summer afternoon in the small quaint village called Borunda, where he has been living for half a century, collecting stories, retelling them and inhabiting a cosmos both fantastic and rustic, and almost always with a socio-political undercurrent.

A political writer, he insists on not wearing his politics on his sleeve but enjoys layering it in the folds of his stark stories, which take on the spectrum of social ills ranging from the oppressed state of women, *satipratha*, to the feudal hierarchies still prevalent in a post-Independence post-liberalization India. The subtlety at times betrays his pen and he renders stories with a force that hits the reader irrespective of the contextual reading that might colour it even more radical. That he deals with them in an unconventional manner would be a dangerous allegation that the urban reader often inflicts on a presumed 'simple' rustic – of a conservative convention.

Take his rather famous story 'Alekhun Hitler' ('Untold Hitlers') – a story of a day in the life of post-Independence India sampling the reader with a taste of the modern: farmers and their new-found affluence, the urban-rural contrast and the backdrop painted with the Hindu karmic ethos (in rather critical light) informing a collective understanding of the universe for his immediate and national environment. Visual imagery so powerful it recreates landscapes of a still painting interspersed with visuals of cinematic grandeur; the story with its poetic idiom builds up to a crescendo as the cyclist races alongside the newly acquired tractor of the rich farmer family, symbolism ripe with a critique of the politics and society without sparing individual responsibility.

Or his more popular 'Duvidha' ('The Dilemma'), also adapted to the screen twice, once by the late Mani Kaul and more recently by Amol Palekar (*Paheli*) – a story that deals with love, adulterous and pure at the same time, of giving voice to a woman's desire in the physical absence of an indifferent husband, of the prejudices rampant in a society that decides and dictates codes for pre- and post-marital existence. He weaves here an intricate story about a woman falling in love with a ghost who takes on the guise of her husband. She knowingly furthers the masquerade revelling in a clandestine love of an absurd manner where the truth is veiled except for the two lovers, till one day when the husband comes back. Painfully aware of the inevitable, the story paints a loss of love, of how one buries desire and hope. That this dealt with adultery is made digestible for a conservative society by making the protagonist a ghost, a non-human. In Bijji's hands the story takes on a humane role, almost feminine in its handling of love, a bold statement on the woman choosing her fate, her love, and daring to fulfil her desires.

Of the more radical of his stories, though one uses that word with some amount of urban prejudice as I mentioned earlier on in the essay, is his story titled 'Dohri Joon' ('Two Lives' / 'New Life'). The story of two women choosing to spend their lives together given the turn of events that brought them together speaks of nothing short of a rebellion against patriarchy, challenges notions of gender and openly celebrates same-sex relationships. One wonders, though, if Bijji was talking more about the freedom a woman needs from an oppressive marriage. There are strong undercurrents of greed for dowry among the parents and the twist in the tale leaves one sure about the underlining assertion of a desire to be loved and treated equally. Many feminists have expressed wonder at the rendition of the feminine psyche in this story. Bijji was told by many that only a woman could have written so lucidly about feelings that inhabit a suppressed sex. The story, one of my favourites, is rich also in language where you see the expression of love and accompanying lust handled delicately with a veiled (at times explicit) sublime eroticism. It was also adapted for the stage in the 1980s.

A more satirical story 'Putia Chacha' ('Uncle Putia'), ripe with very local humour, has at its centre a man always found in 'the company of women', a neo-Krishna revelling in female attention. The undercurrent of sexual tension and a certain control Putia Chacha exercises on the teachers in the school he manages are comical and at times hilarious. The patriarch is the object of everyone's humour. The pandering of his desire, to be at the centre of everyone's attention, by all the women in the school is sure to remind an Indian reader of that one uncle or neighbour in childhood who was the butt of every joke. His position of this dubious power when threatened by a young woman asserting her desire for an arch-rival presents the reader with an emotional story both funny and sad. The story is dotted with conversations written in a flow escaping simple dialogue. It has gems of retorts and repartees that Bijji employs famously in a lot of other stories.

Translating his works is as much a challenge as a delight for any translator who knows Rajasthani. A language with mostly oral existence, the script being a borrowed Devanagari, poses a challenge as does his style, which is deliberately colloquial and situated strongly in the local environment with its own smells and sounds. Universal themes relevant to the human condition and of power and powerlessness also manifest in ways very fantastical and other-worldly – talking animals or ghosts, for example. This has been negotiated brilliantly by Christi A. Merrill and Bijji's son Kailash Kabeer, who have brought out a two-volume collection titled *Chouboli and Other Stories* (published jointly by Fordham University Press in New York and Katha in India). The choice of stories offers a good range of Bijji's works from the essential folklore to the more topical stories that he has written prolifically for the last half century.

Bijji, having compiled the idioms of Rajasthani, has generously used them and even created newer ones in his stories. This finds its way very loyally and suitably in the translations in these two volumes. Particularly fascinating is the story of 'Chouboli' — a labyrinth of stories within stories true to a storyteller's magic of knitting a quilt of tales, as Bijji himself describes his craft. Other stories in the collection are equally engaging. 'The Crafty Thief', for example, is the lively, gripping and exciting tale of a thief who vows never to lie, landing him in situations bizarre as well as complex. Other stories include translations of the stories I mentioned earlier as well as some fantastical tales like 'The Dove and the Snake' and some very political ones like 'Weigh your Options' and 'A Hound's Pride'.

A writer for writers and artists, he claims his writing offers one the surprise he himself likes to have when he reads his own creations. At ninety he still sits in his study rereading and correcting his books, revisiting stories and still being surprised by what his pen magically poured out over decades of untiring and sincere writing.

Shy of narrating his person, his work reveals an unearthing of a huge treasure of stories in the folk traditions to be shared, cherished, retold and celebrated. I was most touched and thrilled to hear about Bijji's wonderful stories from an autorickshaw driver in Jodhpur, the town closest to his village, who has known of his stories for over forty years and was proud of having once driven Bijji somewhere. This detail is particularly relevant in the light of the fact that the other upper-class (mostly upper-caste) educated Jodhpuris I met pretended that they had heard of him and some not even that. A reminder also of the reach of Bijji's works beyond the educated elite.

Bijji was in the running for the Nobel Prize in 2011. He is now unable to write due to an accident a few years ago that left his limbs affected. He attributes this to mathematical justice: 'the need to stop writing as his input and output according to him seem to have matched well.'

Hailed commonly as the Shakespeare of Rajasthan, a crown that sits uncomfortably on his head as he deserves more than being a parallel, Bijji never offers you a stale word.

INVENTING A DALIT AESTHETIC

G. Kalyan Rao's *Antarani Vasantham*

N. MANOHAR REDDY

G. Kalyan Rao's novel *Antarani Vasantham* (*Untouchable Spring*, 2000) is a complex mapping of the life struggles, the artistic repertoire and the political economy of a people belonging to two major castes – the Malas and the Madigas – in the state of Andhra Pradesh in India. Written after two decades of a resurgent movement, it is the first Dalit historical novel in Telugu. It draws its insights from the author's grasp of local history and his own experience as a Dalit-revolutionary. The narrative captures the memories of Rubenu and his wife Rutu, memories riddled with the relentlessness of struggles against untouchability and upper-caste violence. The author captures the memories of a community of six generations of untouchables – Rubenu's ancestors as well as the couple's children and grandchildren – and turns it into an extraordinary novel.

Malas and Madigas of the Enneladinni village in the novel were neither allowed to draw water from the village tanks nor build a house of their own on public land. Upper-caste Brahmin-Karanams and Reddys had not only grabbed their land but also forced them to work in the same land as bonded labourers. Caste is the foundation on which such exploitation thrived. This episode is set in pre-colonial times. However, the strength of the novel lies in establishing the truth that caste has managed to sustain and reinvent itself through the age of colonialism and is a presence in independent modern India. Thus caste is represented here not as a pre-modern sociocultural phenomenon, but as an everyday contemporary reality, pointing to the hard fact that, in modern India, caste is pervasive and operates as a powerful form of social control and oppressive power. As the author puts it:

> In India, the air you breathe, the water you drink, the irrigation canal, the agricultural land, the school, the temple . . . the food you eat, the house you live in, the clothes you wear, the words you speak . . . literature, culture, the state, its law, its justice, its court . . . the dead body, the burial ground, god, devil — all have caste.

Malas and Madigas of *Antarani Vasantham* do not perceive themselves as helpless victims of caste oppression, like Mulk Raj Anand's untouchables or the 'Harijans' in the celebrated Telugu novel *Malapalli* which follows the Gandhian reformist approach to the caste question. Nor do they clamour for the cultural status of upper-caste Hindus, a notion termed Sanskritization by sociologists. Far from wanting to be 'uplifted', the Dalits of *Antarani Vasantham* fight for land, water and self-respect with determination, and rebel against upper-caste oppression and violence. They struggle not for an ideal, but for survival. Ellanna's wife Subhadra confronts Achhi Reddy in the fields when there is a dispute regarding water between him and the Malas and Madigas. When Narigadu, a Mala, is murdered by the Karanam for playing a key role in occupying public land for cultivation, in retaliation, Mataiah, a Madiga, kills the Karanam.

These struggles are revisited from the present and signify the arrival of the Dalit subject into the public sphere in India. The Dalit movement had consolidated itself as a significant political force by the 1990s, fighting against a series of atrocities committed against Dalits all over India by the upper-caste Hindus, which include the Karamchedu (1985) and Chunduru massacres (1991) that occurred in coastal Andhra, the region where the novel is set. After Karamchedu, two streams of Dalit consciousness emerged among the Dalit intellectuals and activists: one represents those who believed that their liberation was possible only through the armed struggle led by the communists, and focused more on the question of economic exploitation regarded simply as 'struggle against hunger'. The other stream, represented by the Dalit Mahasabha, is inspired by Jyotirao Phule's thoughts and Dr Ambedkar's ideas of 'annihilation of caste'. It focused more comprehensively, in addition to economic rights, on sociocultural inequality and self-respect.

In *Antarani Vasantham,* both hunger and self-respect are complexly intertwined with one another. Kalyan Rao, himself a Dalit, was also the secretary of Virasam (Revolutionary Writers Organization), an ideological arm of the Naxalite movement, which subsumes the caste question in armed class struggle and Marxist-Maoist revolution. Thus Kalyan Rao's writing *Antarani Vasantham* as a member of Virasam itself must be treated as a remarkable political act in the sense that it was a transgression of the laws and protocols of that organization. Such acts eventually forced not only Virasam but also most of the Left organizations to alter their ideological stand on caste.

Unlike Brahmanical literature in which Dalits appear as culturally impoverished people, in *Antarani Vasantham* they figure as bearers of a great culture. Chandrappa was a celebrated Urumula dancer. Naganna and Ellanna were great artists. Rubenu is proud of them. Dalit performative traditions include forms such as the Urumula dance of the Malas, Chindu Bhagotam and Vidhi Bhagotam of the Madigas and the puppet shows of Yanadis, Yerra Gollas, Malas and Madigas – all of which, for Kalyan Rao, constitute the untouchable 'Spring'. However, none of these art forms figures in Telugu literary and cultural histories, the norms of which are set by the concerns of contemporary literary culture in Telugu, largely defined by the left-of-centre standpoint influenced by Marxism. *Antarani Vasantham* engages with such discourses and alters the terms of the debate. Another aspect of the 'Spring' is the deep-spirited human relations among the untouchables, especially among women. Dispossessed of any property, all that they have is love and affection for one another.

As we read on, we realize that the novel is not simply a documentation of Dalit cultural life, but challenges the legitimacy of knowledge systems taken for granted as authentic. For instance, it poses several new questions to the literary authorities: How did Nannaya, an orthodox Brahmin who was supposed to have translated the Hindu Sanskrit text Mahabharata into Telugu, become the first Telugu poet, and not the Dalits who had produced great oral literature even before Telugu had a script? How does the history of Telugu drama begin in the colonial period when Dalits had a rich tradition of performing Vidhi Bhagotam in pre-colonial times? Why do we need Gidugu and Gurajada – the modern icons of Telugu language and literature – to start a movement to rescue 'people's language' when Dalits have always preserved the everyday richness of their language?

An equally or perhaps more significant aspect of the novel is its radical approach to the contentious issue of conversion to Christianity in India. Drawing from historical evidence and the experience of Dalits recorded in missionary accounts, the novel is able to construct a well-researched account of why Dalits converted en masse to Christianity in Andhra in the nineteenth century.

Chinnodu becomes Martin to escape the oppression of the upper-caste Chaudharys. During the worst famine, at the site where the Buckingham Canal was being dug, Rubenu's father Sivaiah discovers that hunger and labour too had caste. When he discloses his Mala identity, he is badly beaten up and chased away by the upper-caste workers. Eventually he becomes Simonu. Both Chinnodu/Martin and Sivaiah/Simonu, and thousands of others like them who converted to Christianity during the early nineteenth century and also during the height of the nationalist movement, believed in Christ to get rid of untouchability, to fight against hunger and to escape from being slaughtered by the upper castes. Within the missionary church for the first time in their life, Martin and Simonu were treated with the importance of human beings. Martin says it was a great experience.

However, conversion did not mean complete liberation from upper-caste oppression. Martin tells Simonu that only the Clough couple and Cotton were determined to stand by the untouchables while the other missionaries opened the church gates to upper castes, who became 'John Paul Reddys, Emmanuel Shastrys and Jehovah Chaudharys' and soon occupied positions of power in the colonial state machinery. Thus the novel exposes the vicious campaigns of the Indian social reformers and nationalists like Gandhi, who accused the missionaries of enticing Dalits with allurements. In fact, while Gandhi wanted to 'ban conversions' as part of the nationalist efforts to claim Dalits into the fold of the Hindu religion, Ambedkar declared in the same year that 'though I have been born a Hindu, I shall not die as Hindu'. This novel suggests that neither the Marxist historiography of India with its modern 'secular' nationalist perspective, nor the post-colonial scholarship which treats missionary efforts as part of British colonialism, seem to have paid enough attention to the politics of conversion.

Within the local public sphere of Andhra, *Antarani Vasantham* attracted some criticism, mainly from the Ambedkarite Dalits and a few Madiga intellectuals. Ambedkarites consider the concluding part of the novel – Rubenu's son Immanyuelu and the grandson Jessy joining the Naxalite movement – the weakest part and regard the conclusion to be uncalled for. They also point out that Jessy gets completely alienated from his community by the time he goes underground. Such alienation, it is said, is unwelcome since no anti-caste struggle has been possible so far without the participation of Dalit communities. Another important critique came from Dalit feminists, who insist that the protagonists or, perhaps, the true inheritors of the 'Spring' that the novel imagines are men – from Ellanna to Jessy – and thus the underlying assumption is that Dalit women are capable of performing only secondary roles. As far as the Madigas are concerned, they agree that the novel does make an attempt to bring Malas and Madigas together to fight against their common enemy. However, they point out that it does not address the crucial issue of internal hierarchy among Dalits, raised by the Madiga Dandora movement in 1994. Some have even argued that the novel primarily focuses on Malas and doesn't really represent the Madigas, their history and culture in a significant way. These are legitimate critiques and, if addressed seriously, will complement the debate that the novel sets up.

WITHOUT MISSING A BEAT

Gopinath Mohanty's *Paraja*

UTKAL MOHANTY

Even before receiving the Jnanpith Award in 1974, Gopinath Mohanty was a towering figure in Oriya literature, counted among its most prominent novelists with works like *Amrutara Santana*, *Paraja*, *Mati Matala*, *Rahura Chhaya* and *Laya Bilaya*. His distinctive voice can be found in his true-to-life, compassionate depiction of tribal life, which he had observed at close quarters, and in a sense pretty much lived, during his stints as a government official in the various backward districts of Orissa. Among his tribal novels, it is *Paraja* that stands out for its epic achievement. It is to our good fortune that the novel is available in an excellent translation by Bikram Das, published by Oxford University Press in 1987.

Paraja (1945) tells the story of Sukru Jani, a patriarch of the Paraja tribe in the Koraput region of Orissa, and his family – his two sons Mandia and Tikra and daughters Jili and Bili. It is a world where a tribal looks up to anyone who so much as wears a dhoti, as a symbol of unlimited power and complicated world view, which

92

he cannot begin to fathom. Their own world is remarkably simple, aligned totally to the rhythm of nature. They go out to work or in search of food in the jungle as the day begins. At dusk they come back to their modest homes to prepare food and retire, as the young boys and girls congregate at the bachelors' dormitories. The boys play their dungudunga and sing love ditties. The girls with flowers in their hair braided with castor oil, dressed in colourful but minimal attire, join them in dance. They drink locally made liquor to forget the hard labour of the day and their hundred mundane worries. 'Boys and girls in love had the inalienable right to elope, which they often did, and after that the only thing necessary to get their relationship legalized was a payment of about forty rupees by the boy to the girl's father, as the customary bride price.'

At the beginning of our tale, Sukru Jani is happy with his life. 'It has been as they wanted it to be, and some kind and benevolent spirit has made everything happy and beautiful for him.' The first blight of misery appears in his life when Jili, the elder of his two daughters, catches the eye of the lecherous forest guard, making Sukru Jani livid. Sukru Jani is charged with illegal clearing of the forest, even though the forest guard himself had given him verbal permission to go ahead. He is forced to cough up a fine of eighty rupees, a sum clearly out of reach for someone like Sukru Jani, or be sent to prison, a world totally beyond comprehension for a Paraja used only to the natural world. The only way out is to borrow money from the local landlord, offering himself and one of his sons as gotis, or serfs.

The sturdier of the two sons, Mandia, stays back, dreaming of setting up home with the girl of his choice, Kajodi. To put together the bride price, he begins to brew liquor, hoping to make a killing before the spring festival. But the excise officer discovers his makeshift vat, and a fine of fifty rupees or fifteen days in prison is announced. Following the arc of inevitability, Mandia too becomes a goti of the landlord, leaving the two girls to fend for themselves. The happy picture that Sukru Jani had imagined for his family recedes further and further away. Jili's admirer Bagala marries Kajodi, who was actually betrothed to her brother Mandia, shattering the romantic dreams of both brother and sister in a single humiliating blow. Sukru Jani makes a last attempt at putting his house in order, mortgaging his prized land to the landlord in return for his freedom. The younger son Tikra too looks at the future with optimism, stealing time from his duties as a goti to brew illicit liquor, putting together the money to get their land back.

But Sukru Jani's household keeps falling apart without the sturdy presence of Mandia and Tikra. The two girls yearn for new clothes, little trinkets and occasional admiring glances from young boys. But their world remains unchangeably grim. Then one day, Jili gives in to the overtures of the landlord, who has been visiting their village bachelors' dormitory, trying to lure the local girls. He sets up home for Jili in another village and Jili begins to enjoy her affluence and the respect she is shown as the landlord's mistress.

When Tikra earns the money that he thinks is enough to get their land back, the landlord laughs in their faces. The father and son decide to file a case in the town court as a last resort. This time the truth is on their side, they reason. They have witnesses. They have the money. But the cruel and complicated world of civil society foxes Sukru Jani and his sons once again.

With no fight left in them, they come to the landlord, pleading with him to return their 'rice bowl' to them. Sukru Jani sees his daughter Jili and calls out to her. The landlord twists his lips into a crooked smile and delivers the lines that sum up the power that landlords like him exercise over a poor Paraja like Sukru Jani: 'Yes Jili! And isn't there another called Bili at home still? Bring her to me, I have taken the land; I've taken the sister; and I shall take the other too. I shall take your wives; I shall drive you from court through the lengths of the country. I shall make you sweat out your lives as gotis, and I shall rub your nose in the dust.' Something inside the heads of the Parajas snaps at this and the story comes to its denouement.

The plot in itself is not too different from other such tales of exploitation, but what brings the narrative alive is the remarkable accuracy with which Mohanty captures the process of exploitation, not missing a single twist in the psychological game that the landlords and government officials play with the Parajas of the world. Remarkable too is the way the author desists from painting the Parajas as angels without blemishes. In this he is akin to Premchand, who understands all the weaknesses of the poor, whom he sees as no more or no less human than the rich. When the forest guard slaps a fine on Sukru Jani in clear breach of his oral approval, no one comes to testify in his support. 'Just because you were in the tiger's grip, are we to go and put our heads in its mouth? . . . You are angry with us, but there is nothing we can do. We too have our families and our children,' they proffer as an excuse. And the 'simple' Parajas are not above pocketing a few rupees for themselves from the fine money that Sukru Jani hands over to the village leaders for paying off the forest guard.

But what makes the novel a work of luminous beauty and power is the way it takes us into the very soul of the Paraja, allowing us to feel his every joy, every despair, every wonder, every rage. Unlike writers like Mahasweta Devi, who seem to write from a higher pedestal, offering an analysis of the socio-economic reality, Mohanty's is an insider's view, rich in empathy rather than analysis. It is a deeply pessimistic novel, but more than the pathos what is likely to stay in the minds of the reader are the joyous scenes of wild singing and dancing in the bachelors' dormitory, the lovers' tiffs and exchange of banter, and the sheer life force of the creatures of nature, their animal magnetism which contrasts with the wily city folks devoid of any physical grace. The language that Mohanty uses in the novel is half tribal lingo, half the author's own lyrical Odia laden with metaphor. Be it a tiger hunt or a visit to the weekly market, Mohanty's observant eye and robust prose bring the scene alive with colourful details.

The novel's contemporary relevance is to be marvelled at. For a novel written more than fifty years ago, it still engages us with its uncanny insights into the quintessential human, both as an individual and a social being. It could be Sukru Jani in the tight grip of a moneylender or a tribesman losing his cherished land, or it could be a city-dweller losing his home or a modern-day businessman caught in the web of speculative trading, losing his business and being forced to work for someone else. What remains unchanged is the hope in the human heart for a better tomorrow, the sheer will to live and the throbbing force in our souls that makes us fall in love, dance to music and battle on bravely. The novel happens to be set in a tribal setting, but the situations relate to the universal human condition, captured in vivid prose, and lit by a personal vision that is Mohanty's own.

THE GREAT GAME

Raja Rao's
The Chessmaster and His Moves

HARTOSH SINGH BAL

Even to say a flower, let alone Rama, you must be able to say it in such a way that the force of the vocable has the potency to create a flower. Unless the word becomes mantra no writer is a writer, and no reader a reader. For the right reader-to-be, the writer has therefore to become an upasaka of the word.

The term *upasaka* itself was used for lay attendants who had been initiated into Buddhism, men who served the right path much as Raja Rao served the word. Of all the Indian writers, no one was more of an upasaka of the word than Raja Rao: 'The writer or the poet is he who seeks back the common word to its origin of silence, that the manifested word becomes light. There was a great poet of the West, the Austrian poet, Rainer Maria Rilke. He said objects come to you to be named.'

This, beyond everything, was Raja Rao's quest, seeking the

common word back to its origin of silence, to the silence from where all things are named into existence.

Unfortunately, such a quest, of concern to all those who engage with the written or the spoken word, is hardly the stuff of literature as we have come to understand it in the cosseted world of Indian writing in English. Derived as our idea of literature is from the Anglo-American world, we are afraid of ideas. We have decided literature follows norms that have been dictated to us, embodied in that perfect example of middlebrow taste – the Booker. Afraid to tell our own stories in our own way, we have even refused to look at the larger history of literature in Europe.

Only in this sense was Raja Rao lucky that he found his way to France, for it has also meant that today, a few years after his death, he has been all but forgotten in India. Yet he was the most Indian of writers. The word and its origins are central to the Vedas, and long before modern linguistics dwelt on the origins of meaning in language, the poet and grammarian Bhartruhari had devoted a book to this very question. Raja Rao's quest, as he has said, was the most Indian of quests.

There is no shortage of those who claim such exoteric ideas of India are only another form of catering to the expectations of the West, ignoring as they do the reality of this country. But Raja Rao was well aware of such a charge: 'This exaltation for India, which we Indians ourselves share with others objectively, historically, spiritually, is not an indication by any means of the truth of India, but of the need for *an* India. If there were no India, with the Seven Seas to the south and the white-swan Himalaya to the north, if India did not have the holy Ganga and the Cape of the Virgin Goddess (Kanya Kumari), if India were not the land of the elephant and the monkey-world, of parakeets and peacocks, and of the saintly cobra – if India did not have the diamonds of Golconda and the pearls of Coromandel, if India did not possess muslin fine "as a cloud" or spice, holy, rich as sandal, with cardamom, cinnamon, aloes and musk – if India were not the land of sadhus and of the suttee, of Thugs, pariahs, devdasis and unbloody famines – if India were not the country of Asoka or Bhoja Raja, of Vikramaditya or of Akbar Padishah – India would still be. India is not a country (*desa*), it is a perspective (*darsana*); it is not a climate but a mood (*rasa*) in the play of the Absolute – it is not the Indian who makes India but "India" makes the Indian, and this India is in all: it is the centre of awareness wherein one's self dips again and again into the hearth of Agni, as the sacrifice is made. All acts are rites when "the perfect performance of our tasks, whatever they may be, is itself the celebration of the rite" – so says Ananda Coomaraswamy.'

In the perfect performance of his task, Raja Rao was perhaps our most successful writer in English. By success of course I do not mean the judgement of the market, where he barely registers, but in the use of English to represent our reality, whatever our reality may be. From the very first paragraph of the foreword of *Kanthapura*:

> There is no village in India, however mean, that has not a rich
> *sthala-purana,* or legendary history, of its own. Some god or
> godlike hero has passed by the village – Rama might have
> rested under this papal-tree, Sita may have dried her clothes,
> after her bath, on this yellow stone, or the Mahatma himself,
> on one of his many pilgrimages through the country, might
> have slept in this hut, the low one, by the village gate. In this
> way the past mingles with the present, and the gods mingle
> with men to make the repertory of your grand-mother always
> bright. One such story from the contemporary annals of my
> village I have tried to tell.

It is clear that this is a writer unlike any other in India in terms of his relationship to his land and to his craft.

Kanthapura remains his best known novel, perhaps because it is his most accessible work. But in the corpus of his work – a corpus that examines India as a *darsana* – *Kanthapura* is to *The Chessmaster and His Moves* (1988) as the Puranas are to the Vedas. Far less accessible, far more abstruse, it rewards those who are willing to struggle with it. Not for those weaned on Booker shortlists, it is the culmination of all that Raja Rao has written. In 1996, speaking of himself, he had said, 'I am no scholar. I am a "creative" writer. I love to play with ideas. It is like a chess game with horses, elephants, chamberlains, and the Kings which might fight with one another. The game is not for winning. It is for *rasa* – delight.'

This approach makes for what at first glance seems to be a frustrating and exasperating book. The plot seems to go nowhere, conversations seem set pieces, characters speak as no one ever has in life, and at the end of over 700 pages dotted with quotations in Sanskrit, Tamil and French, you find out that this is but the first part of a trilogy of which the other two have yet to be published, caught as they are in a dispute between the author's estate and the publisher. It should come as no surprise that almost all the publishers in the West wanted it to be cut down by a third.

Yet they would have been idiots if they had succeeded, indeed they are idiots for even having asked, and the existence of the book (published in full but badly produced) is another argument for us not to trust judgements passed elsewhere. The book that survives revolves around Sivarama Sastri, an Indian in Paris, playing the game beyond all games, that of mathematics. 'Indeed, I have a very private theory that mathematics was invented by Siva not to amuse Parvati, as he did many other things, but that one day as she sat for a game of chess, she was winning so quickly that he had to defeat her – if not, imagine the Absolute being defeated by its own expression, its companion, and if the Absolute is defeated, then what remains . . . so Siva invented puzzles much like Bhaskara, except Parvati could never solve them . . . and thus mankind was saved because the Absolute was not defeated.'

The victory of the Absolute can then only tempt a man to aim high: 'For me, the self-evident alone was the final, and most western positions appeared to me to be intellectually exciting but arbitrary. You establish a God or the First law of Newton, from which you build any castle you wish (or any paradise). But both God and Newton (and Newton, as is well known, believed in his God), both assumptions that work. I was not interested in what worked (and this was ultimately what utilitarianism is about, I imagine, but you know Socrates would have laughed at the Truth being what is useful), but in what *is*.'

In Paris, to separate what *is* from what *is mere appearance* is not easy. The young women who surround Sivarama in the city each enchant him in their own way: Jayalakshmi who is married and can never be his, yet is truly his consort; Suzanne the French actress who needs more from him than he can give, afraid as he is of reproducing himself in this world; his sister Uma whose central desire to conceive remains barren; and Mireille who is married to Sivarama's friend but participates in the play of desire without fear of the consequences that arise from tradition or biology.

But let us not wander among the complexities of plot, those are for the reader to explore, a reader who will eventually find a book that has no parallel in Indian writing in English. I certainly know nothing like it, even Desani's *All About H. Hatterr* seems a mere game of draughts in comparison. If it can be compared to anything at all, it is to Robert Musil's *The Man Without Qualities*: another unfinished trilogy centred around a mathematician, whose true quest is the only quest that matters, what Musil terms the 'other condition'.

The book, despite the publishers' naysaying, won the Neustadt Prize in 1988, placing Raja Rao in the company where he actually belongs – Czeslaw Milosz, Josef Skvorecky, Octavio Paz, Max Frisch and Nuruddin Farah. But even that is incidental, for a reader what should count is the quest at the heart of *The Chessmaster and His Moves*, born out of play and delight.

'I marvelled then, as always, of the connection of things, all equations instead of working themselves down, worked themselves up, and then with one final leap, we had, like Schrödinger's equation, one total answer . . . And that is how life should be. But how far away was I, with my dividedness, one part unequal to the other, yet the whole more than its parts, indeed twice or thrice its parts, fear and courage going sidelong, one pulling toward the normal, the settled, the nameable, the other wild, solitary, incommunicable, the ascetic and the sensuous pulling each their own way . . .'

IN THE WATER'S LIGHT

Ashokamitran's *Thanneer*

N . KALYAN RAMAN

Ashokamitran's *Thanneer* is considered a landmark novel in the annals of contemporary Tamil literature. The events narrated in *Thanneer*, a short work of no more than 100 pages, are woven around the first severe water crisis to afflict the city of Madras in the late 1960s. When it was first published in 1973, *Thanneer* (*Water*) took the Tamil literary world by storm. Connected intimately with life in a central locality of Madras, the narrative seemed to resonate strongly with its audience. The book was discussed extensively within the Tamil literary milieu, as much for its unflinching description of a crisis as for its path-breaking narrative technique. Many years later, when *Thanneer* was translated into English, making Ashokamitran's work accessible to a wider audience within India and overseas, it garnered substantial critical acclaim from non-Tamil readers and critics. Even today, *Thanneer* enjoys the status of a classic, along with *Pathinettavathu Atchakkodu* (*The Eighteenth Parallel*), a novel loosely based on Ashokamitran's teenage years in the erstwhile princely state of Hyderabad and the occurrences that followed India's Independence from British rule in 1947. Other important novels include *Karaindha Nizhalgal* and *Manasarovar*, both set in the south Indian film industry of the 1950s and 1960s; and *Otran,* with an international writers' programme in an American university as the backdrop

Given the author's wide-ranging and rich oeuvre, what makes *Thanneer*, a pitiless urban chronicle, an undisputed classic in the canon of contemporary Indian literature?

Thanneer is a multilayered narrative. Ostensibly about a set of main characters and others who are related to them peripherally, the novel is also a portrait of the many categories of people and social arrangements that enable life in a city. In that sense, it is also about the nature of the city and the world. The novel's main protagonist, Jamuna, is a young woman of twenty-eight, whose hopes of making it big in the tinsel world of films are fast fading. Following several twists of fate, she finds herself living alone in Madras – without hope or succour, her dignity compromised inexorably by the middle-class world that surrounds her. Overlaid on Jamuna's crisis is the unprecedented water crisis that beset Madras in the late 1960s and early 1970s.

How do ordinary people in an urban setting manage when their access to a basic requirement of life – water – becomes precarious? *Thanneer* offers a chilling existential portrait of a city under siege, overtaken by a pestilential lack. Despair, rage, trickery and monstrous selfishness, as also generosity and strength of character, are in evidence here, as individuals and families struggle to procure and store water under extreme conditions of scarcity. Indian novels have dealt with transformation of societies wrought by cataclysmic incidents and episodes (Partition and the anti-Sikh riots of 1984 come to mind) but the details and nuances springing from a protracted crisis — the subtle shifts in speech, disposition and character of common citizens in the face of a faceless strife — are captured for the first time in *Thanneer*. In this respect, it is somewhat reminiscent of the celebrated French classic *La Peste* by Albert Camus.

Ashokamitran has said that a young woman he often saw in the streets during that period, always alone and looking for water, was the inspiration behind Jamuna. Along with her failed aspirations for a place of distinction in the film industry, Jamuna's existence is entirely determined by the world around her. A young woman without the protection of family or spouse, Jamuna leads a life that is indeed precarious in every respect. She has no steady income and her stay in rented houses is hostage to the mercy of people who hold her in contempt for her lack of middle-class respectability. She is also marked by that special vulnerability of an unprotected woman. With her fast receding aspirations as the only pivot that will give her any purchase on life, Jamuna proves an easy prey to Bhaskar Rao, a married man from the film industry, who exploits her in many ways; but forsaken more or less completely by everyone else, Jamuna cannot find it in herself to get rid of him. For companionship and empathy, she must depend on her younger sister, Chaaya.

Chaaya is married to an army man who is away on a posting and whose return to the city is uncertain. Chaaya opts to live in a working women's hostel, which provides an easy solution to the problem of finding water. However, she is forced to leave her young child in the care of her maternal uncle, who also bears the additional burden of tending to her mother. Jamuna and Chaaya's mother is old and ailing, haunted in her senile dementia by copious memories of past cruelty. When the story opens, even as she longs for the protective company of her elder sister, Chaaya is at once terrified and repulsed by Jamuna's lifestyle, which she sees as foolish, reckless and degrading. She stays away, leaving Jamuna to her own devices.

Chennai's water crisis makes its fearsome appearance in this vale of horrors. Forced onto the streets and into the compounds of unfriendly strangers during the course of her daily struggle for water, Jamuna is even more susceptible now to the moral and economic 'superiority' of her neighbours, to their wounding behaviour, full of scorn and contempt for her irregular ways and circumstances. Contrite and full of self-loathing after indulging in a weekend of debauchery with two film producers from Andhra at the behest of Bhaskar Rao, Jamuna prepares to hang herself, but she is discovered and rescued at the last minute, ironically due to her lack of privacy.

A middle-aged woman who lives down the street from Jamuna, a primary schoolteacher who is known only as 'Teacher-amma', befriends her at an early morning fray near the communal water pump. Emerging from her own private hell, made up of an invalid husband and an ancient mother-in-law who is both spiteful and infirm, Teacher-amma seems to have achieved a kind of inner truce with the perils of the quotidian world. Her chance encounters with Jamuna are marked by an attitude that is part-solidarity, part-protectiveness. Humiliated and utterly desolate after her botched suicide attempt, it is to Teacher-amma that Jamuna turns for solace. In a seemingly inspired fashion, Teacher-amma delivers a catechism of sorts in plain, simple language – based on a vision of life as inexorable, endless suffering, not just for oneself but for every living person, a vision that can potentially help an individual to stop being a victim and recover her sense of agency in this world.

At some point, weeks or months later, it starts to rain – as it must, inevitably. The rain muddies the city's streets and makes the drains overflow, but still does not guarantee easy availability of water. At the end of the novel, in spite of being pregnant, Jamuna breaks away from Bhaskar Rao, asking him to leave. She and Chaaya, both sisters still stranded without luck, will live together — for now.

To the common run of people, lack of water might mean disruption and another source of misery. To Jamuna, almost without her realizing it, the quest for water brings many lessons. Jamuna sees quite clearly the ignominy and humiliation that will surely come her way before she can overcome the drought. When she goes hunting for water in public places and inside people's compounds, she comes face-to-face with what society thinks about her. Her neighbours end up denying her the water she needs. She also comes to discover Chaaya's exceptionally unfeeling nature.

Although Jamuna has acquired a keen sense of body, she has never gone looking for love as she hunts now for water. Even if she finds the water she needs for survival, her life will still remain arid.

When her false turn with Bhaskar Rao collapses and the false trust she has reposed in him is blown to bits, Jamuna seeks a counterfeit end to her troubles: her own demise. This death too fails to come off. Jamuna recovers from the illusory nature of the drought in which she is stranded. Water invades her consciousness and her actions, giving her intensity and a sense of purpose that she has never experienced before. It is precisely her alienated condition that liberates her from suffering and grants her an honest perspective: water is essential for living. Through water, Jamuna comes to nurture an essential confidence in life, undiminished by alienation of any kind.

The water crisis hasn't ended yet. She must still go in search of water, and be humiliated in the process. But this will only stabilize her, instead of sapping her strength. She will no longer seek false consolation. This is even truer of her relationship with Chaaya than with Bhaskar Rao.

Chaaya lives in a private world of her own filled only with her aspirations and values. Her values are not based on individuals and their contingencies, but related to an abstract 'society' and its norms. The anonymous puppeteer's string operates most ruthlessly here. Chaaya attacks Jamuna and also torments herself with all the violence of her compulsions. In the end, her fears for Jamuna originate from the same source. She has not yet reached a position where society, which she holds in high esteem (which has also imprisoned her), is ready to accept her – this is the sum of her conflict and her yearning. She tries to flee the water crisis, making her child stay in a place she herself can't bear for long. It is not struggle that blocks her awareness, but her own selfishness.

By the end, the sisters' relationship is liberated from dependency but it is Teacher-amma who faces the most severe drought: an utter lack of love and water. Looking for water does not change her in any way because she is already present in the world, alive in and through her awareness. She serves as an instrument for delivering Jamuna from her faux suicide. But not everything that Jamuna comes to learn is taught by Teacher-amma. In a sense, the latter's life is without any hope of deliverance. In her distraught condition, Teacher-amma perceives the inherent conflict between individuals but not that such conflicts are settled unjustly, always, by social arrangements. Her trait of living harmoniously with her environment makes her less than faithful to her own conflicts. Teacher-amma, who can vividly sense the prison that she is trapped in, continues to live inside that prison with compassion towards others.

How the water crisis plays out in the public space, comprising neighbourhood residents, government officials, workmen from the corporation, taxi drivers, ordinary people, forms another layer in the narrative. Through Ashokamitran's spare, nuanced prose, we understand that the crisis in society at large predates the present scarcity of water. The traits brought to the fore in individuals by the struggle for water – stinginess, greed, selfishness, despair, distrust – are not fresh consequences of the water famine. They are traits of habit, brought on by extant material arrangements.

To their lives, already arid and bereft of love, is added the actual famine of a water crisis. With lack of water acting as the catalyst, this aridity becomes even more intense. When water becomes scarce in a society founded on property rights, those rights also extend to water. Even ordinary life and its needs are brought under the ambit of property rights. This aridity will continue even after water begins to flow. There is nothing new that they have learnt from the crisis. Not wishing to accept and grant even the body's intimate need for water, they continue to hold the right to property as the fount of all life.

But the main characters in *Thanneer* are all intensely physical. For the first time, they become conscious of their bodies in public. This unusual circumstance frightens them. Their sense of shame conflicts with life's remorseless necessity. In the end, it is need that emerges the winner; the famine intensifies.

Ashokamitran's narrative technique in this novel, and indeed in most of his work, can be described as a kind of 'documentary realism'. He describes the surface of events, apparently choosing details with great care, but never spelling out what they mean. In this quiet and unobtrusive way, he brings startling epiphanies and blinding insights to the reader. In his foreword to *Sand and Other Stories*, Paul Zachariah, the eminent Malayalam writer, describes it thus: 'Ashokamitran leads his characters through a maze of life's ordinary, casual and dull details, guiding the reader into the lovely belief that . . . every little thing is part of life's grand plan . . . Then, like the final straw, he would add one more detail. And BOOM! The world explodes with a blinding flash. You are no more the reader you started out as. The illumination has consumed you.' (Orient Blackswan, 2002)

The forty years since the publication of the novel have brought irreversible changes to both Chennai and India. With unseasonal rains on their way to becoming a regular feature, Chennai is no longer thirsting for water as it once did. Our liberalized economy and its unabashedly commercial ways make efficient water supply possible, at least for those who can afford to pay. But *Thanneer* is less about water than about the framework and dynamics of a crisis, both individual and societal. Surely the prospect of a crisis and the need for an honest, redemptive awareness are not about to forsake us.

How are we to cope with this existential burden? '. . . in the last analysis, each of us is always responsible for what has been made of him – even if he can do *no more than assume* that *responsibility*.' (Jean-Paul Sartre, *The Necessity of Freedom*). In *Thanneer*, Ashokamitran arrives at and illuminates this truth not through the labyrinths of philosophy but through a narrative of contemporary experience, under specific conditions of history, society and gender, involving people we can recognize within the frame of a mirror and without. It is an illumination that we need direly in these dark times, marked by collective despair about the future of our world.

CAN THE MAD WOMAN SPEAK?

Triveni's *Sharapanjara*

P. RADHIKA

The Kannada novel *Sharapanjara* (*Cage of Arrows*, 1965) by Triveni can be seen as a wildcard entry to a list of the best Indian writing. But let us not forget that wildcard entries have the uncanny ability to justify their presence among the best and Triveni's *Sharapanjara* does not betray this trust. This claim can be made only with the recognition that the novel belongs to the genre of popular novels that are structured very differently from literary texts that possess formal and rhetorical complexity.

Sharapanjara, Triveni's last novel, can be read as a psychological novel because of its focus on the characters' interiority, the workings of their minds, their inner worlds (rather than the exterior world of reality). However, the twist that Triveni brings to the form is by introducing a woman protagonist who is not mentally 'normal'. Thus we have a perspective that is different from that of the conventional protagonist – the reasonable man.

The story of *Sharapanjara* revolves around Kaveri, who becomes afflicted with what is variously called 'hysteria', '*hucchu*' (madness), '*unmada*' (intoxicated, mad) in the novel. She is subsequently admitted to a hospital but returns home once she has been declared 'cured'. The novel, set in the post-cure phase, but revisiting her past through flashback, plays out in a stark manner: how a woman who was loved and respected by her family and society before she was labelled 'mad' is suddenly scorned by all after. By the end of the novel, Kaveri's hysteria returns due to this rejection and she is taken to the hospital once again. We could interpret the novel as an appeal against the stereotyping of the 'mad'. Triveni's painstaking descriptions of Kaveri's social ostracism by those shown to be steeped in superstition (Kaveri's servant, her cook) as well as the modern and educated (Kaveri's husband, her children's schoolteacher) is directed towards a scientific understanding that mental illness is like any other physical illness and is curable.

Let me, however, provide another interpretation that takes into account that *Sharapanjara* is a novel that needs to be read vis-à-vis portrayals of the 'mad woman' in earlier novels. Then, *Sharapanjara* is more than merely telling a new story or presenting a new theme around the 'mad woman' but confronting the very problem of her representability. That is, it seems as though when Triveni asks: 'How do I portray the "mad woman"?' she means 'What are the existing vocabularies and images that I can draw upon?' The writer is confronted with a problem that has no precedent; she has to begin at the beginning. Is this a tall claim? Surely earlier representations existed, but they drew on images and vocabularies that were fashioned from the vantage point of the norm – the normal, the normative. As the protagonist Kaveri thinks in the novel,

'People show excessive pity – "poor thing she is mad" they say.
Or excessive contempt – "after all she is mad" they say. Like

the marks of small-pox that remain on the body till death, will
the label stick to me till I die? Will people not allow me to live
like any other?' Wherever Kaveri turned arrows pierced and
left a deep wound in her heart – the arrow of pity, the arrow of
disdain, the arrow of whispers, the arrow of scorn, the arrow
of laughter – Kaveri was bound by these. Was there no freedom
from the cage of arrows?

The novel, as it were, embarks upon the task of re-presenting the
'mad woman', to present her anew in a way that accounts for her
experience. It seeks to un-stick the mark, the label 'mad woman' and
provide a re-description. No doubt, Triveni's writing that spanned
the decade between 1955 and 1965 was made possible by a historical
conjuncture: cheap publishing of paperbacks that allowed for a
proliferation of new writers to emerge, translations of Freud that
led to literary explorations into human psyche and sexuality, and a
new Indian nation that held the promise of rights and equality for
different sections of society – minorities, women, tribals. But what
Triveni does with those possibilities is something extraordinary.
For *Sharapanjara* exemplifies that move: of what it means to ask
questions of the psyche of 'woman', 'mad woman', of her identity
and that too in ways more than that of rights and equality. Let
me elaborate.

The characters in the novel are concerned about why Kaveri
turns mad. Her husband Satish is perplexed: 'What did Kaveri
lack? Love? Affection? Trust? Money? *What did she after all lack?*' The
servants say she is 'possessed'; the psychiatric opinion is that hysteria
is caused by 'blood deficiency leading to a depletion of bodily
strength'. The hysterical moment reveals to us readers that the
trauma is caused by the protagonist being raped by a male friend
with whom she had gone on vacation. The hysteria then can be read
as the surfacing of a repressed trauma, caused by the violation and a

societal morality that made it unspeakable. However, I ask if there is something more.

Is Kaveri's trauma a consequence of her experience-knowledge of *being the lack* in a cultural system that privileges the rational and the male, the 'reasonable man' who is the ideal in law, science and philosophy? Is the novel about the very erasure and absence of 'woman' and 'mad' in such a cultural system? The erasure of the 'mad woman' implies more than merely the incapacity of the norm (rational, male) to understand the 'other' (non-rational, female), something that can be remedied with effort; it signifies how the very foundations of the rational, male world is predicated on the exclusion of the non-rational, the female. It is as though the figure of the 'reasonable man' as the ideal comes into being through the erasure of another being, another way of being. If this indeed is the case, which is a signalling of a much more profound kind of othering than merely an attitude, stigmatization, what does it mean for the mad woman to speak? Is it at all possible? If so, how?

Psychoanalysis that inaugurated a new writing like Triveni's also tells us that the non-rational (and why not woman) speaks during unguarded moments such as slips of tongue, dreams despite the conscious rational ordering of selves. *Sharapanjara*'s uniqueness is in allowing us a glimpse of the non-rational and female through the excesses of the protagonist's speech and behaviour. Kaveri is no longer the sober, demure wife that her husband desires: she laughs and cries unnecessarily, she insistently questions her husband's changed manner towards her. The shift in Kaveri's behaviour from *miti* (moderation/limit), a much valued quality in Indian culture, to excess seems not only to be a symptom of the hysteric, but increasingly takes over Triveni's writing itself. Towards the end of the novel when Kaveri finally breaks down, Triveni creates a spectacle of Kaveri's hysteria:

Kaveri felt a volcano erupt in her head. Kaveri tossed from one side to another feeling the oncoming of a deluge that would destroy the world. There was an impossible sound in her ears, her head. Arrows coming from all directions formed a cage around Kaveri and bound her within. Outside the cage, thousands of people stood and laughed loudly: 'Kaveri is mad, mad Kaveri . . . See she is mad, poor thing! Her husband has kept a prostitute, poor thing!' Kaveri tightly covered both her ears. But the sound of people's laughter pierced her head till the nerves within burst. Like a deer that is caught in a net, Kaveri struggled. The people standing outside the cage started to throw stones at the imprisoned Kaveri. Leading the crowd was Satish who was throwing large boulders at her. A volcano that was coughing out lava and spitting balls of fire was forcing itself on Kaveri.

This excess is not to be read merely as the excess of a hysterical Kaveri. True, it is at one level Triveni's own attempt to work out the mechanics — words, images, metaphors — by which she can portray the hysteric woman. And it almost seems like Triveni's portrayal is like any other melodramatic depiction of hysteria. However, in the repetition of the spectacles of hysteria that surpass the narrative requirement, the novel makes you wonder what the portrayal is actually about. Madness when it attaches itself to woman harks back to the history of associations of woman with irrationality, madness, emotion (as opposed to reason) but in the novel also makes the reader reflect on and question that history. What the representation in its excess shows is the point at which the grand claims of the rational fails. The non-rational overrides, is present despite the rational logic of the plot, which condemns superstitious beliefs and sees mental illness from a scientific perspective. It is as though we fleetingly get to hear the mad woman speak. And what does she say? Nothing in terms of content but the very act is an enumeration of the non-rational woman speaking, showing up the limits of the rational, male norm, showing up a sphere that is not entirely graspable within the rational, male logic. If anything further can be gleaned from that speech, it is the plea to acknowledge and respect different ways of being. This emphasis on respecting 'difference' is more important in arriving at an egalitarian, ethical world than 'rights' and 'equality', values that have driven, among other things, much of feminist search in women's writing.

If *Sharapanjara* then is fundamentally about the question of the representability of the mad woman, both as a 'writing about' and as a 'speaking for' her, the novel exemplifies, within a popular mode, the struggle of such representability – the possibility but also its difficulty in the given culture. Written in 1965, before any signs in India of a disability discourse or even a feminist one, *Sharapanjara* offers not only a nuanced insight into the world of the 'other' but how that insight requires us to reframe our ideas of the norm and those who do not belong to it, something we have far from achieved almost half a century later.

RIVER OF TIME

Qurratulain Hyder's *River of Fire*

AAMER HUSSEIN

Qurratulain Hyder was born in Aligarh in 1927. Her parents were writers: Sajjad Hyder Yildirim, who wrote short stories influenced by Turkish and French fiction, and Nazar Sajad Hyder, a popular and prolific novelist who proved that women could be successful professional writers.

Hyder migrated with her family to Pakistan in 1947, living in Karachi with stints in London, and working in a variety of careers in the media throughout the 1950s. She wrote two novels and two collections of stories supposedly influenced by Western modernism. She transcended her influences and broke new ground in 1955 with *The Exiles*, an exquisite novella about Indian expatriates in London in the aftermath of Independence and the Partition of India.

Nothing, however, had prepared readers for the structural boldness and technical virtuosity of *Aag ka Darya* (*River of Fire*), first published in Pakistan in 1959, which was the sum of all her previous

work and the source of the brilliance to come. It was instantly
acclaimed as the finest novel ever to appear in Urdu, and fifty years
after its publication it retains that reputation. It also provoked
some controversy: Hyder's view of Pakistan and Pakistani identity,
it has been rumoured, was not in keeping with the nationalist
sentiments of Ayub Khan's regime. Literary rivalries possibly played
a part in such controversies. Whatever the reason, Hyder left
Pakistan for London, from where she moved to Bombay in the
early 1960s. She worked as a journalist in English-language media
and continued to write exquisite fiction, concentrating on short
stories and novellas. Some held that *Aag ka Darya* was a fluke until
her next major novel, *Aakhir-e-Shab Ke Hamsafar*, appeared in the
late 1970s and proved the contrary.

Many of the techniques Hyder introduced to Urdu fiction in the
1950s foreshadowed those of later writers, whose ambitious
reworking of history would bring Indian writing much international
acclaim towards the end of the twentieth century. Paradoxically,
however, her novels remained accessible only to Urdu readers (and
a couple, in transcript, to readers of Hindi) on both sides of the
border (the majority of them in Pakistan) and were praised by
those who could read them. Eclectic and iconoclastic, Hyder won
award after major national award, while most Indian readers had
read only a few of her short stories in English. Few regional or
vernacular writers break through the language barrier without a
dedicated and competent translator. But the bilingual Hyder began
at some point to translate her own fiction into English. In 1994,
Fireflies in the Mist, a translation of *Aakhir-e-Shab*, appeared and a
collection of her finest stories slightly later. But her uncompromising
stance would continue to limit her appeal to departments of Indology
in a period when new stars such as Vikram Seth, Vikram Chandra et
al. were leading Indo-Anglian fiction into new avenues of
cosmopolitan success.

Then in 1998 (in the sixth decade of her career, with the encouragement of enterprising editor-publisher Ritu Menon at Kali for Women) Hyder finally completed her long-awaited 'transcreation' (as she styled it) of *Aag ka Darya* into English, making available Urdu's most celebrated novel to an Anglophone audience, allowing them to see whether the fierce beauty of her imagination had traversed the borders of language and nation. Judging from the applause it has gained, it has had a significant impact on a new generation who set about discovering her work: Amit Chaudhuri anthologized Hyder in his anthology of the finest modern Indian writing; Amitav Ghosh saluted her as one of India's major writers and Pankaj Mishra praised her in the *New York Review of Books*; more recently, young critic Hirsh Sawhney acknowledged in the *Guardian,* her enormous talent and *River's* seminal place in Indian fiction; and Chandrahas Chaudhury anthologized a story in his anthology of Indian fiction. Beyond the South Asian realm, J.M.G. Le Clézio, in his acceptance speech, placed Hyder at the head of a brief list of great non-Western writers to whom he dedicated his Nobel Prize for literature.

River of Fire is set during four Indian epochs: the time of the Buddha, the time of the arrival of the first Muslims, the time of the British ascent and appropriation of power, and finally the novel's own modern post-national time. Each section is linked by characters that bear, in every period, the same names. Gautam, the troubled spirit of quest, begins and ends the novel. Champa, the enigmatic, embodies continuity, change and the experiences of Indian women. Kamal, a Muslim in each section, appears later in the proceedings just as the Muslim settlers did, and loses himself in the Indian landscape, just as Muslim culture took on local colours on Indian soil. Cyril, the Englishman, is the last arrival; never able to identify with the country his compatriots are attempting to subjugate, he remains, however, obsessed by the country and its women. The experiences of these figures, shaped by often confrontational relationships with their times, are disparate, but they reflect the similarity of experience across cultures and centuries. Instead of espousing nationalist or religious ideologies, Hyder argues for a syncretic reading of Indian culture, which she sees as multi-vocal and inclusive. Each age knows chaos and upheaval; mankind learns nothing, and continues to create greater and greater cataclysms of violence.

One of the novel's major preoccupations is the nature of time: the Urdu version begins with an extended translation from T.S. Eliot's *Four Quartets*, evoking the elusive significance of time as both preserver and destroyer and the inextricability of beginnings and endings. Hyder probably omitted it from the English edition because she wanted to introduce cultural and historical nuances to her new pan-Indian and probably international audience (an American edition did soon follow the Indian one) rather than to underline the novel's original modernist allusions. Hyder also deleted some of the metaphysical musings and lyrical flourishes of her youth, but the book's bold original architecture, the sheer scale of the endeavour and the range of imaginative resources remain unaltered.

Hyder's English prose is musical and witty, deploying a range of references, from the redoubtable nineteenth-century novelist Flora Annie Steel and the contemporary humanist E.M. Forster to classical Urdu verse and Faiz, the presiding genius of twentieth-century Urdu poetry. Hyder plays with genres, interweaving legends, dreams, diaries, pastiches and chronicles, extending the form of the novel in a way quite unprecedented in twentieth-century Urdu fiction, which had struggled to unburden itself from a heritage of literary fantasy and romance. The much discussed influence of Woolf is faintly discernable on the one hand: Hyder is credited with introducing the modernist technique of stream of consciousness into the Urdu novel and, according to critics, may have borrowed aspects of her handling of time from *Orlando*. On the other, Hyder herself slips in a sly reference or two to the traditional *dastan*, a form rejected as one of the most cumbersome legacies of Urdu fiction by her predecessors; in its epic and mock epic mode, its discursive technique and constantly shifting and decentred perspectives, Hyder's novel is occasionally reminiscent of that discarded traditional form, but not in a derivative fashion. It is possibly this debt that has led readers to compare Hyder to the Latin American magic realists, who hadn't yet appeared on the international stage when Hyder wrote her novel.

The longest and richest section of the novel is set in the mid-twentieth century, before and after Independence. It is recounted, in part, by Talat, who refers to herself as a dastango (narrator of a dastan) and might be an authorial alter ego, in a St John's Wood (London) flat. We follow the entangled destinies of a group of friends, both Hindu and Muslim, from Lucknow to London. Post-war, post-colonial Britain is vividly depicted with its artists, dreamers and revolutionaries. Tragicomedies of displacement, caused by conflicting nationalisms and Partition, are narrated; modern times mean unstable lives and, sometimes, a pervasive sense of not belonging for our heroes. Kamal is forced by circumstances to move from the anti-Muslim, anti-feudal tendencies of a traumatized India to Karachi, capital of a brash new homeland of Pakistan; a segment of the novel depicts life in both East and West Pakistan. Feckless, volatile Champa goes back to her homeland, becoming a fellow wayfarer of 'the veiled women and ragged urchins of her lane, the coolies with their push-carts'. The past, that foreign country, is not unredeemable.

Hyder herself moved from Bombay to live the last quarter-century of her life in Delhi. None of her work after her memoirs directly revisited the places of her own past, moving instead between historical settings and the harshness of present-day India. The reprinting of *Fireflies in the Mist* in 2008, a year after her death, raises the question, once again, of whether *River of Fire* is indeed her magnum opus in English. So, what qualifies this novel to be one of the best works of Indian fiction if it isn't even Hyder's best?

Its experimental structure, its range, preoccupation and sensibilities, its phenomenological view of ancient history, its lyrical imagination are undeniable. I've recently reread it in both languages. The original's mould-breaking place in Urdu literature is unassailable. But in my opinion, Hyder, by rewriting the book in her second language half-a-century after some of the events it chronicles, for a contemporary Indian and international audience, is asking readers difficult new questions: at the dawn of a globalized and postmodern new millennium, she demands their participation in a dialogue between past and present, between narration and the mind's divided nation. The two versions of *River,* framing Hyder's complex oeuvre, remain its cornerstones. And Hyder's evocations of Indians in mid-twentieth-century London — written from lived experience in one decade, rewritten from memory and the hindsight of maturity forty years later — is among the most beautiful and heartrending accounts of a community and a period I've read in any language.

THE MARGINAL AT THE CENTRE

Arundhati Roy's
The God of Small Things

ANITA ROY

When first reading *The God of Small Things* (1997), before the hype and hoopla that accompanied its winning the Booker Prize, it didn't seem likely that this slender, tender story of two children's lives in a small Kerala village would become one of the most political novels to have come out of India in the twentieth century, and its author the country's most famous political activist. The story opens quietly, vividly:

> May in Ayemenem is a hot, brooding month. The days are long and humid. The river shrinks and black crows gorge on bright mangoes in still, dustgreen trees. Red bananas ripen. Jackfruits burst. Dissolute bluebottles hum vacuously in the fruity air. Then they stun themselves against clear windowpanes and die, fatly baffled in the sun.

From the first page, the reader is plunged into the world of the
novel, surrounded by colour, sound, texture, smell, taste. It is a
hallucinatory, mood-altering experience.

David Godwin, Roy's agent, described it as 'a shot of heroin in
the arm' and as she describes their first meeting to me, it is clear
that it was this comment, rather than the promise of huge advances
or worldwide publicity, that convinced Roy to sign up with him.

Sanjeev Saith, the photographer and friend whom she chose to
take the cover picture, and who set up the publishing company
India Ink to bring out her book in India, was likewise overwhelmed.
'I read the first chapter, and then stopped. I rang her up and said,
look, it's so visually powerful that I can't read any more until after
I've done the shoot,' he recalls. Saith and Roy travelled to Ayemenem
and spent days drifting along the backwaters in search of the
perfect image. Yet, when the selection was sent to London, to Roy's
UK publishers, HarperCollins, they finally chose the first image
that he had taken – ironically, not in Kerala at all, but in the lotus
pool outside the India International Centre in New Delhi. Roy,
with characteristic single-mindedness, insisted that this image appear
on the cover of every single edition of the book worldwide. It has
become one of the most iconic covers of all time.

A few months after the book was released, the judges of the
Booker Prize announced their verdict. In a more or less time-
honoured tradition, Roy's novel, like Booker Prize winners before
and after it, provoked strong reactions. Gillian Beer, professor of
English literature at Cambridge and the chair of the jury, praised
the book's 'extraordinary linguistic inventiveness', while the
previous year's chairperson, publisher Carmen Callil, pronounced
it 'an execrable book', which did not deserve to be on the shortlist,
let alone win.

Reactions – both positive and negative – tended to revolve
around the novelist's literary style. What for some was overwritten,

self-indulgent whimsy, for others was lyrical, heart-rending, inventive and unique. My own feeling is that far from imposing her own literary flourishes on the tale, the voice in which it is told is entirely contiguous with the characters it revolves around. Estha and Rahel, the twins around whom the story unfurls, are linguistically adventurous. They speak and relate to each other and their world in secret tandem, almost like wolf children. Words are chopped up into their component parts: Ei. Der. Downs. Or gleefully strung together: Orangedrink Lemondrink. Misheard ('porketmunny') and deliciously onomatopoeic ('*Hslip Hslip Hsnooh-snah*'). Phrases, repeated, take on a nursery rhyme cadence and grammar submits to a child's understanding ('Margaret Kochamma told her to Stoppit. So she Stoppited.'). The result is a vertiginous ride through the English language, piloted by a trapeze artist of consummate skill and recklessness.

The God of Small Things is as structurally inventive as it is stylistically unorthodox. The entire plot of the novel is revealed in the first few pages. The reader quickly learns that when they were seven, the twins' nine-year-old half-English cousin Sophie Mol had died. That the guilt associated with her death has marked their entire lives. That their mother Ammu died soon after, tragically young. That Velutha, the low-caste 'untouchable', was killed in connection with Sophie Mol's death. And that Velutha and their mother were in love.

It is this love story, ironically, that is the most overtly political element in the book. The fictional transgression of unwritten laws – the 'Love Laws . . . that lay down who should be loved, and how. And how much.' – provoked a real legal case, in which the author was charged with obscenity. The case didn't amount to much, but I cannot help feel that the fact that it happened at all must have delighted the author: a resounding confirmation that she had hit a very raw nerve.

But the political import of *The God of Small Things* is by no means confined to an attack on horrors of the caste system, nor even to its stinging critique of Communist Party politics, the Syrian Christian Church or patriarchy (although it is simultaneously all of these things). The clue lies in the title: a phrase that, like the other big Indian Booker, *Midnight's Children*, has entered into common parlance. Roy's presiding deity is not the all-seeing, omnipotent God of organized religion.

> Who was he?
> Who could he have been?
> The God of Loss.
> The God of Small Things.
> The God of Goose Bumps and Sudden Smiles.

By placing the marginal at the centre, by giving the silenced a voice, by bringing the overlooked under the magnifying glass, she articulates a profoundly humanist politics in her novel, which all her subsequent non-fiction writing – against nuclear arms, against rapacious mining corporations, against a violent bureaucratic state – reconfirm.

This is profoundly linked to the question of style. Roy has faced considerable criticism for the literary style she deploys in her political writings: for bringing the personal into the political and resolutely refusing to divorce the two. In response to the most outspoken attack on her by historian Ramchandra Guha, Roy writes: 'My style, my language, is not something superficial like a coat that I wear when I go out. My style is me – even when I'm at home. It's the *way* I think. My style *is* my politics.'

Sitting with her, sipping coffee in her light-filled apartment in New Delhi as the short spring wheels into summer outside, glazing the new leaves lime-green, it is abundantly clear that for all her firebrand radicalism, the most potent weapon in Roy's considerable arsenal is humour. She smiles a lot, laughs easily. I get the impression that if you gave her a high horse she would give it a lump of sugar far sooner than clamber on top of it. She's someone who clearly takes her work extremely seriously, and herself not at all. 'I used to go to these meetings and stuff,' she recalls, 'and it was like bringing a Kalashnikov to a cocktail party, you know?'

One of the most delightful things about *The God of Small Things* is its lightness of touch – we are invited to enjoy the absurdity of those who are used to being taken Very Seriously Indeed.

When Roy says that there is 'really not much difference between my fiction and my non-fiction writing', what she means is not that the two are interchangeable, but that, on the contrary, the form and the content are similarly intertwined in both. But to me, there *is* a difference – one that calls to mind the words of another radical thinker and the progenitor of the modern environmental and social justice movements of which Roy herself is so closely allied: Henry David Thoreau. When he wrote, 'Electricity kills darkness, candlelight illuminates it,' he could well have been describing the different ways in which non-fiction and fiction work in order to shed light on a particular truth. What is sometimes lost in Roy's political writings is the journey that the reader makes *towards* a realization: her position is crystal clear from the outset, and the reader is swept along with the author's emotional conviction rather than the cool construction of an argument. The novel works very differently, telling the truth but 'telling it slant', in Emily Dickenson's phrase.

Whatever else it is (and it is many things), *The God of Small Things* is a book about truth and lies, the hypocrisies of polite society and the horrors that they elide. It is a book about how the big things in life are actually the small ones. The way an unthinking comment can leave an indelible scar on a child's mind. The fact that life is precarious and everything can change in a day. The fact that the love between a man and a woman can precipitate calamity.

Roy's novel has sold in excess of five million copies and has been translated into at least twenty-one languages worldwide. Each of her subsequent five collections of essays has been a massive commercial success. She is perhaps India's most widely read author writing in English and has been translated into many Indian languages. She has used her success as a novelist to bring into the mainstream the voices and stories of those who are routinely marginalized and silenced by the machinery of the state and the seemingly unstoppable march of globalized corporate capital. The fact that her writing (particularly her political writing) touches people living outside India's elite metropolitan centres is, she says, 'the greatest gift any writer can have. It's like . . .' she goes on, unconsciously echoing Godwin, 'straight into the bloodstream of the society that you live in, that you love. That you hate.'

Her agent was right: reading Arundhati Roy is like a shot in the arm: a powerful jolt, a kind of awakening. The emotional resonance that *The God of Small Things* found in readers across the world bears witness to the power of a story well told, of characters who live beyond the page, of imagery that seems to tap into our most intimate dreamscapes, reminding us of our common humanity — the frailty wherein lies our strength.

CHARISMATIC REBEL

Ismat Chughtai's *Terhi Lakir*

AMINA HUZFAR

Ismat Chughtai's *Terhi Lakir* (1947) is an exceptional novel in more than one way. Rich in characterization, incident and insight, it defies the cultural mores of the conservative Muslim society of the 1930s and early 1940s, as well as the often heard criticism levelled at women writers that they have a limited canvas. Chughtai's canvas is worked with a richness of theme and depth of perception rarely found in Urdu literature.

The novel is an illustration of her consummate talent for storytelling. Though the central theme concerns a girl from a Muslim middle-class background, there are several motifs in *Terhi Lakir* which, with slight modifications, could become compelling stories in their own right. It is rightly said that Chughtai is first and foremost a writer of short stories.

Shaman (short for Shamshad), the protagonist, is the tenth child in her family (Ismat was the ninth in hers). Left by a worn-out mother to be fed and cared for by a young wet nurse, Shaman becomes extremely attached to her. The girl has to be discharged for immodest behaviour and the responsibility for Shaman's care devolves on to Manjhu, one of her older sisters. But before long, Manjhu is married and this second surrogate mother too abandons her; and once again Shaman is the lonely, uncared for child in a teeming household of immediate and extended family.

Shaman could never brook pity or condescension, and she emerges from her loveless childhood with her dignity intact. There are few deprivations as tragic as indifference and lack of love in a child's life, and Shaman has suffered both; but Chughtai has no taste for tear-jerking descriptions, and in any case she is busy bringing the situation alive with a wealth of detail that tells its own story. The childhood of this neglected girl, drawn with lifelike vigour and a total rejection of sentimentality, is itself a motif that is a remarkable and rare achievement in Urdu literature.

Shaman is sent to a boarding school. This live coal of a girl, used only to rejection and suspicious of all overtures of kindness, finds herself in a totally unfamiliar environment. And now surfaces the most powerful underlying theme of the novel — sexuality. It is of course female sexuality that Chughtai deals with — she is a writer who never wanders very far from her own experience, and *Terhi Lakir* is quite candidly autobiographic.

Actually, sexuality is never absent from any part of the novel. In Shaman's childhood its presence is like that of a stream in the dark, visible only now and then, by an evanescent moonlight. There are hints of it, as when she stuffs her doll's waistcoat with two pellets of cotton wool — and is chastised for obscenity when discovered. It becomes more explicit in her school days, beginning with her infatuation with her teacher, Miss Charan; though it is still a long time before she can look into its eyes and recognize this powerful force in her life.

Shaman was sent to a local mission school when she failed in her first school. There she had to cope with the arrival of her menstrual period and observed with horror the accompanying bodily changes in herself. Chughtai achieves another first in Urdu, when she describes the advent of puberty and the girl's reaction to it. Shaman, the bold and precocious girl, who came from a home where bringing babies into the world was the chief occupation of the purdah-observing ladies, thought she had delivered a baby, which for some reason was being kept from her. She thought further, that she had been blessed with a virgin birth. And why not, had not God made that happen once before?

In contrast to the hypocrisy that she saw around her and detested, Shaman's own feelings were vivid and intense. Her rage was pure untarnished fury and her revulsion was, well, the prototype of revulsion. Rasool Fatima, her room-mate, adored Shaman with a lesbian intensity. And Shaman reacted to her love with equally strong loathing. But life sometimes turns the tables on us with its ironies. As soon as Shaman had got rid of Rasool Fatima, she herself fell in love with Najma, a friend of her friend Saadat, though here the game was played in subtle moves. This motif of homosexuality too could stand on its own – the chase is seen in two different situations, though in my opinion the rendering of revulsion in the first situation is worth turning the page back for.

Female sexuality is the theme of many of Chughtai's short stories, most famously in 'Lihaaf', for writing which she was charged with obscenity but later acquitted. In *Terhi Lakir* she has explored its manifestation in a variety of forms and themes. Male sexuality enters this domain only where it serves to draw out its female counterpart, and is not examined from within.

Yet, impressively, each of the male characters who engage Shaman in this way (whether to entice or to repel) is a credible individual, and their sexuality pours out in distinctly different moulds. There is the unctuous Ajju with his odious and covert advances; Rasheed, who pulls on Shaman's heart strings with tactics akin to those of a lowbrow Urdu novel's hero (the purloined handkerchief acting as a lever for the libido), Iftikhars the ailing but diehard Casanova; and finally, the Irishman, Ronnie, with whom Shaman's imagination did not embark on romantic flights. But perhaps the most captivatingly portrayed relationship is that between Shaman and the zestful Rai Saheb.

In college Shaman had a friend called Prema who took her to her home, where Shaman met Prema's father, Rai Saheb. Prema's household, the antithesis of Shaman's, comprised the motherless Prema and Narinder, and their only surviving parent. Rai Saheb was a much loved father who danced and painted, joked and played with his children and welcomed their friends warmly. Unused to such lively familiarity from a man who was not a close relative, Shaman was fascinated. He teased her, joked and was affectionate, all apparently without any sexual motivation; but Shaman, the greenhorn in both social and sexual matters, lost her heart to him.

The Shaman-Rai Saheb motif, which has to be read in Urdu to be properly appreciated (particularly in Chughtai's vibrant prose), is in the opinion of this writer one of the gems in this book.

Here is Rai Saheb, dancing to oblige an importunate audience of his children and their friends:

At first Rai Saheb was quiet. Then, he dropped his cigar in a saucer and stood silently with his back to the lamp. The music played on and he stood staring at the wall before him, his feet in place. Slowly, taking off his kurta, he flung it up in the air, and began to stroke his arms. And then, as Shaman gaped in astonishment, he turned around with the speed of lightening and his powerful body began to undulate to the rhythm of the music. It was as though a stone idol had stretched itself and awoken. The body that only a while ago gave a suggestion of age was responding like a pulled string in a sitar. Boundless movement of joints, powerful curve of ankles, the grandeur of a broad chest . . . the music seemed to be coming not from any musical device but from the flowing motion of those supple limbs . . .

There is more, gaining in beauty, until the music stops and the dance ends, leaving Shaman numbed and dazzled.

This narrative leaves one wondering if the widowed and aging Rai Saheb did not in his heart feel drawn to his daughter's friend, but was too wise to acknowledge it. The doubt adds depth and beauty to the vignette, as unexplained things often do.

In college Shaman grows up. Her intrepid and direct style, wit, and impatience with hypocrisy (all Chughtai's own qualities) win her many admirers. Meanwhile, unwilling to return to the stifling conservatism of her family, she finds a job as the headmistress of a school, lives alone and enjoys lots of male attention.

Notwithstanding her independent mind and rebellious spirit, Shaman does, unalterably, have her roots in the powerful UP culture. She is also a faithful daughter of the times, her mind, as that of other thinking people of the era, preoccupied by the trauma of the pre-Partition years, a mental state intensified by the impact of the World War.

In the end Shaman marries Ronnie Taylor, an Irishman introduced to her by her Christian friend Alma. One cannot but admire the dialogues between them before and after their marriage in which Chughtai's art manifests itself in the entirely plausible characterization. Her dialogues and characterization almost always ring true, but in this case Ronnie is a foreigner and one could have understood if she were a little less accurate. However, though Ronnie's uncomplicated and gentle temperament seems to augur well for the marriage, Shaman's passionately held and openly expressed views do not. Ronnie is the reasonable colonizer, but Shaman is the angry colonized, fiercely protective of her independence. Moreover, such equal, interracial marriages between the West and the East are not the order of the day, and Ronnie begins to feel the breath of societal disapproval wafting over him from his compatriots.

The marriage between a Western man and an Eastern woman, undertaken confidently by both, without sharing the decision with their families (especially in the case of the woman), is another first for Ismat Chughtai. She has described here a situation long before she could have studied it in real life, or perhaps she did, but whatever the case, she creates here yet another motif that is capable of standing on its own, thanks to the mental stimulation it offers and the skill and aplomb with which it is crafted.

The end of the story is a liberation or a subtle tragedy — depending on which way you look at it and on whose side you are.

A LITERARY HAND GRENADE

Nabarun Bhattacharya's *Harbart*

ABHIJIT GUPTA

Harbart was a Molotov cocktail hurled at the heart of the literary establishment at a time when the Bengali novel increasingly resembled a never-ending tele-serial. Nabarun's earlier novels (*Juddha Paristhiti, Khelnanagar*) had been equally unsparing of the status quo, but had languished unnoticed at the borderlands of little magazines and small presses. Then in 1993 came *Harbart*, winning a clutch of awards and suddenly making Nabarun a household name. More incendiary projects were to follow, such as the 'Fyataroo' stories and the rambunctious *Kangaal Malsaat*, but it was *Harbart* that marked the true moment of rupture.

Harbart is about the life and death of Harbart Sarkar, son of Shobharani and Lalitkumar, a failed film magnate. After the deaths of Lalitkumar in a car crash and Shobharani in an accident with an electric cable, Harbart is brought up in neglect in his uncle's family. The men in the extended family are either scoundrels or syphilitic or both, with the exception of his nephew, the revolutionary Binu, who is murdered by the police for being a Naxal. Binu's dying declaration to a grieving Harbart launches him into a most unlikely career, that of communicating with the dead. With the aid of two tattered volumes on occultism and a signboard, Harbart takes his first steps towards a career, earning the grudging respect of the family and the loyalty of the local youth. His modest success attracts the attention of an entrepreneur who proposes to set him up in a more sophisticated setting. But soon retribution arrives in the form of a society of rationalists bent on exposing godmen and charlatans, who arrive at Harbart's door carrying camcorders and dictaphones.

From the very first pages of the novel, Harbart's destiny is a foregone conclusion. Nabarun is not interested in narrating a consolatory tale that would soothe our collective bad consciences. What he seeks to recover are the epiphanies of Harbart Sarkar. On the rooftop of their north Calcutta house, Harbart fashions a kind of childhood from fragments: an aerial flotilla of kites, stolen glances at a girl on the neighbour's terrace, the refuge of a defunct water tank, reveries of an angel's statue in a shop window. In the family, the only person who regards him as remotely human is the aunt, *jethai-ma*, who herself is trapped in a nightmarish marriage with a husband who has gone mad from excessive whoring. In rare moments of communion, both aunt and nephew cry together, the aunt for herself, Harbart for everything, in a way that touches the heart of all sorrow and loss.

But such moments of tenderness are rare: for the most part, the novel veers between the grotesque and the carnivalesque. In the opening paragraphs, the Bakhtinian idea of the carnival is vividly enacted as Harbart's drunken companions piss and vomit in wild choreography. Other characters revel in a Rabelaisian excess of scatology and debauchery, with Harbart's ancestors appearing to him in his dreams in a grotesque danse macabre. As in the later

'Fyataroo' stories and novels, Nabarun writes with great affection and humour about the class designated 'lumpen' by middle-class sensibilities. Unemployed young men, petty criminals, prostitutes, lunatics, poetasters, hitmen, street dogs and cats – these are the data of Nabarun's fictional terrain. They are celebrated, reviled, laughed and wept over, but never patronized, or made the subject matter of a grim or sentimental realism. In celebrating their small triumphs and offences against polite taste, Nabarun decisively parts company with a generation of Bengali novelists who are chronically unable to write about anything outside their own comfort zone.

In an introduction to a collection of short stories in 1995, Nabarun wrote: 'Every day, I see . . . new kinds of exploitation imposed on new groups of people; the handcuffs and blinkers of new colonialisms and cultural imperialisms. These are more heinous and criminal than the explicit tyrannies of feudalism or capitalism in their fledgling states . . . But this status quo must change. It must. And literature must do its bit in creating a new consciousness which can make this change possible.' Nabarun's early stories are brutal in their assault on polite sensibilities and in the creation of a poetics of violence, which draws as much on Nabarun's politics as on the availability of the city of Calcutta as a locale. Almost the entire body of Nabarun's fiction is borne out of an acute apprehension of urban spaces and demographies, especially in the post-liberalization era. In both *Harbart* and the 'Fyataroo' stories, urban space becomes the site of an increasingly uneven contest between the forces of exclusion and inclusion, the licit and illicit, the civic and the intimate. It is as if there are two cities – one that tries to sanitize itself from the promiscuity of the street and another that legitimizes infringements on civic space.

In the rationalists' bearding of Harbart in his own den and his consequent unravelling, the inequalities of this contest are most vividly dramatized. But in the end, whose is the triumph? As

Harbart's body is taken in a procession to the crematorium, the grief turns into celebration as his companions erupt in a cacophony of slogans, claps and whistles. The shades of his dead parents watch this spectacle, and his father comforts his weeping wife with the words: 'Why do you cry, Shobha? Look, it is a carnival.' At the moment of bodily dissolution, Harbart turns the tables on his tormentors in an astonishing narrative coup, and the unfinished project of his dead nephew Binu returns to electrify the novel. This climactic moment is perhaps the most satisfying of all epiphanies, imparting a terrifying clarity to the life and death of Harbart Sarkar, but also inscribing him within the ongoing narrative of the history of our time.

SO MANY SITAS

Ambai's *In a Forest, a Deer*

NIRMALA LAKSHMAN

In his brilliant and engaging book *How Proust Can Change Your Life*, the writer Alain de Botton, drawing from the ideas of Marcel Proust, the great French philosopher and novelist, speaks of what he calls the 'finger-placing ability' of fiction. De Botton elaborates on a Proustian observation that the value of a novel is not just limited to its depiction of people and emotions which makes it recognizable in our own lives, but also 'stretches to an ability to describe these *far better* than we would have been able to, to put a finger on perceptions that we recognize *as our own*, and yet could not have formulated *on our own*'. This precisely is the effect and power of great fiction. In its depth we can discover what is truly close to us and yet the words and ideas are collated in ways that are also in many ways beyond us, creating that 'aha' moment that makes our own humanness instinctively recognizable to us as readers. This recognition of the familiar that simultaneously challenges notions of what life should be about, forms the substratum of the

powerful short story collection *In a Forest, a Deer* (2000) by Ambai
(C.S. Lakshmi), one of the finest Tamil writers of the day.

This particular collection spanning ten years was published in
various Tamil journals and has been translated by Lakshmi
Holmström. In the author's note to the book, Ambai says, 'It is a
strange feeling confronting a translation of one's stories.
The characters seem different; the images are sketched differently;
the colours are not what one imagined and the words sound
different. And then as one slowly gets into the mood one sees one's
stories . . . take wings, traversing the distance between the two
languages . . . After my stories come back to me . . . there is a
moment of non-recognition, but that is soon transformed into
the magical experience of the stories becoming my own.' This
ability speaks not just to the obvious talent of the translator but also
to the potency of the writer's craft, which builds on the underlying
truths of the human condition, so that the language in which the
stories are first written is really no bar to their wider appeal
and recognition.

Ambai's tales are wry, inventive, and full of wit. Her narratives
are marked by irony and a sensibility that blends the personal
experiences of her characters and their history with a wider
landscape. *In a Forest, a Deer* takes the reader from rural Tamil Nadu
to Bombay and also to the Indian diaspora in America, exploring
through each story the individual struggles and triumphs of women
(and men), the boundaries of gender, the need for freedom and the
oppression of identities while questioning received and perceived
notions of society, history and continuity.

There are many things that make these stories compelling. The
form of the short story itself, which imposes a strict discipline on
the writer, also transfers to the reader; a tacit understanding occurs,
and the reader looks beyond the stated and the obvious. Ambai's
stories are full of this: things said and not said. Beneath the

impressionistic delineation, layers are always present. There is a woman who wants to sit alone on the single seat at the front of the bus in 'Journey 1'; she knows that 'this seat is her only line of defence' against her fellow travellers who will 'expect her to lay her entire life out before them' by the time the journey ends. Of course there is resistance.

'Won't you move over to the Ladies side?' he asked, pointing to the corner of a seat which already held three people . . . he was attempting to pierce through her line of defence . . . 'No I will not,' she replied with determination . . . 'Ladies shouldn't sit here *amma.*'

'Why, is there some rule to that effect?' she asked.

'There isn't a rule as such. But I usually sit here and go on chatting with the driver-*annacchi.*'

'Well I too intend to sit here and go on talking to the driver-*annacchi,*' she told him. The driver looked at her in surprise.

We know more about this woman and less too; in the earlier part of her journey she displays her annoyance when a baby next to her wets her sari and chews on her handbag. Her fellow travellers assume that she is unmarried and has not experienced motherhood on account of her irritation with the baby, and also because of the lack of a *thali* around her neck, the typical symbol of marriage for south Indian women. She is in fact married. She is then splattered with tobacco juice from the mouth of an old woman and another woman drools on her as she dozes on the bus. Are these the only reasons that she needs to sit alone? And yet as she does so, on her journey back, her unexpected encounter with a young boy who happens to sit near her, and their quiet connection make this part of the journey redemptive. We don't get to hear a whole lot more and perhaps we really don't need to. This vignette says it all.

Ambai's women move beyond their prescribed structures. They

lead ordinary lives but with extraordinary insights and skills. They weave their strengths and courage into their humdrum routines and are often transfigured by them. Consider the title story, 'In a Forest, a Deer'. Thangam Athai with beautiful dark skin and white hair has never 'blossomed' as her young nieces have heard (they are never quite sure what it actually means), and yet she is the one they all turn to when things get rough. 'Through her touch . . . through the firm pressure with which she massaged us with oil, a life force sprang towards us from her body like a river breaking past its own banks. It was at the touch of her hands that cows would yield their milk. The seeds that she planted always sprouted. My mother always said she had an auspicious hand.' It is Thangam Athai's hands that soothe the agony of childbirth, hers are the words that lull, and she is the one who finds a second wife for her husband and yet proclaims that she is a queen and that her house is full of children who are hers. She does not accept that her body has any limitations. 'Why, what's wrong with my body? Don't I feel hungry at the right times? Don't I sleep well? The same properties that all bodies have, this one has too . . .'

At night, Thangam tells the children the story of a young deer that gets separated from the herd and strays from its familiar forest. Terrified and alone, it panics, but when the full moon rises it slowly grows familiar with its surroundings and begins to understand the secrets of the new place. As the children listen they too are at peace. The reader is left with the poignant image of Thangam Athai surrounded by her wisdom and her sleeping children, gazing (perhaps a little wistfully) into the dark night before her.

There are other such women. Strong and unafraid, but often pegged to a social construct that overtly or subtly constrains them. One of the finest stories in the book, 'Forest' is about a woman who has not been professionally accommodated by her husband's business partners and sets off alone to reflect and perhaps write in a forest guest house. Chenthiru's husband disapproves of her plan. 'It was most appropriate (only) for a woman to be a *rishi-pattini*, spouse of a sage, journeying along with her husband. If she did go there on her own, it would only be as the seductive Menaka . . . for a woman a forest is a place where she cannot find her way.' She only smiles and tells him that perhaps it is time 'to rewrite the epics'.

Interestingly, as Chenthiru explores her newly unstructured world, she crosses social boundaries and makes friends with three local women who call her 'Chendiyabai'. After they introduce her to their lives and share their food with her, it occurs to her that in their light banter and natural kindness is another way of looking at life.

The poignant parallel story of Sita also unfolds in 'Forest'. This is a different Sita (is it Chenthiru who writes her?) who tells the sage Valmiki that his Ramayana is not for her and *she* will write Sita's *ayanam*. For this Sita, the forest was both a sanctuary and a prison, and as she rewrites her life reflecting on her weariness, her pain and the final betrayal by Rama, she declares that 'her journey lay in a different direction'. Chenthiru too understands from the old ustad whom she meets in the forest that in life, the perfect musical pitch must constantly be sought after. And in the parallel story, the legendary Sita too moves beyond her traditional ending. She will not let an ageing Ravana pick up the *rudravinai* and hand it to her. She must pick it up herself. 'It is my life, isn't it?' she asks. 'A life that many hands have tossed about like a ball. Now, let me take hold of it; take it into my hands.' Sita's moment becomes ours.

Not all the stories, however, are women-centric. As the writer herself says, 'I do write with a feminist perspective, but all my stories are not about women's lives alone. They are about moments, experiences and memories of experiences . . .'* Images of food,

---

* C.S. Lakshmi's comment to Nirmala Lakshman, September 2011.

music and poetry are woven with effortless beauty into these experiences; they seem to be the epiphanies that make life bearable. Eight stories out of the eighteen in this collection, including 'Journey 2', 'Camel Ride', 'Direction' and 'A Saffron Coloured Ganesha' are multilayered explorations of the self, the community, the small exchanges, the everyday quandaries and also the boundaries that we must necessarily cross to find meaning in our own lives.

Among the powerful and evocative themes that Ambai keeps revisiting in these stories is the question of what constitutes identity for women and for men as well. (Most of them move beyond the stereotype; many of her male characters love cooking, for example.) A woman's identity and worth are not circumscribed by her way of life, whether old-fashioned or radical. For example, in the moving story 'Parasakti and Others in a Plastic Box', the traditionally inclined Amma with her suitcase full of little gods and home-made pickles goes to America to support her newly divorced daughter Bharathi. Amma makes *paal kova* for the neighbouring pregnant American women; but she also talks politics with local Indian grocers and with 'the speed of a whirlwind' creates numerous jobs for herself. Her presence is both irritating and healing for Bharathi. Her sister Dhanam, who is equally exasperated by Amma when she moves into her atheistic house with all her gods and numerous belongings, becomes aware of Amma's inner strength and broadness of vision. Dhanam finally declares to Bharathi, 'Amma isn't just an individual, she's an institution.'

In 'A Rose Coloured Sari' the narrator attends a Festival of India during a visit to America. She thinks of home, of the smells, the images and the fragments of experiences that make up her being. 'The smell of cooking when a properly-soured batter is just spreading on a . . . *dosa* griddle. The smell of sesame in the chilli powder. The smell of gingili oil, unrestrained, fresh from the oil press. The tenderness of Bhimsen Joshi's Lalit *raagam*. The voice of her Tamil teacher who loved and read Tirumular . . . The poet Ghalib pleading. "Lord they have not understood me . . . give them different hearts. Or at least give me a new language . . .'" She wonders which of these things her mind draws from, and will it seek these deeply embedded things always? She is moved by the sight of an adopted Indian baby who reaches out to her from her American mother's shoulders. The narrator covers the baby with a piece that she tears from her rose-coloured Benares silk sari, a sari that carries history and memories in its folds, a sari that had soaked up family lore and happenings, a sari that was worn on special occasions and travelled all over the country, echoing the beauty and poignancy of those who wore it. 'In its silken threads there was the touch of Ganga's waters. The winds from the mountains. The heat of the sun and the coolness of the moon.' As she leaves the fabric on the sleeping baby, the narrator wishes that the silk threads would fall softly on the little one's body. 'May the swans and birds and vines spread over her. And ground her.' This is an affirmation of a whole body of experience, of nostalgia, history and memory, and yet in the giving away of a bit of the sari lies an acceptance of mutability and transitions.

Perhaps the most powerful story, one that is most overtly political in this collection, is 'A Movement, a Folder, Some Tears'. From the heart-tugging narrative of a precious and steadfast friendship among three idealistic young women, it stretches to examining the seeping poison of identity politics after the anti-Muslim riots in Gujarat. When Sakina dies after falling from the seventeenth floor, Charu and Selvi, her beloved friends, are devastated. Selvi agonizes about Sakina's suicide. She who had endured the anguish of witnessing her mother's murder, she who had grown quiet when old friends and the young ones whom she had carried and cared for turned away from her and spurned her connection because of her religion, she who had caught 'the whiplash change' in people's eyes, and who nevertheless worked tirelessly to create awareness of a common humankind, why did she of all people suddenly give up hope, Selvi wonders. In the end, across the boundaries of pain and death is the hope of a song that will still continue and voices that will safeguard our humanity. And in that hope, it seems to Selvi, Sakina lives on.

These are stories that vigorously probe what humanness means today. They stride across a happy canvas of everyday lives filled with food, music and celebration. But they also remind us of the tears that lurk just beneath. They are stories about those who defy and dare and also those in whose outward surrender is an astonishing grace. The interwoven narrative voices, the almost lyrical expression of the blending of joy and pain, as well as the transcendence that is glimpsed make this brilliant collection of stories uplifting and memorable.

A HINDU SENSE OF IRONY

R.K. Narayan's *The Guide*

PANKAJ MISHRA

Many of R.K. Narayan's novels open promisingly and then end slightly unsatisfactorily: the characters emerge from the world of custom and ritual, briefly and futilely experiment with alternative selves, and then drift back to the passivity of pre-modern India. *The Guide* (1958), Narayan's most intriguing novel and the fullest realization of his art and vision, is no exception. It shows yet again that human connections are not achieved easily in Narayan's fictional world. Indeed, what often strikes you about that world — something well concealed by Narayan's instinct for humour — is its extraordinary lovelessness. A Brahmanical formality circumscribes the relationships within families, the father being especially aloof, often cold, and romantic love, when it occurs, is either a loss of self-control (as in *The Guide*), or so beset by anxiety and fear (*Waiting for the Mahatma*) that its failure comes, as in *A Painter of Signs*, almost as a relief to the protagonists.

Narayan never casts sufficient light on the larger social and historical setting of his fiction, the major historical events – British colonialism, Indian Independence, the Emergency – through which his characters drift. Even a real setting goes under the imaginary name of Malgudi; and only a few, easily missed domestic details hint at the fact that Swami and Chandran, along with many other of Narayan's main protagonists, are Brahmins, marginalized by a fast-changing world.

Nevertheless, the lack of direct political comment doesn't prevent one from seeing now in Narayan's novels all the anxieties and bewilderments and disappointments of a generation of Indians expelled from the past into a new world. This tortuous initiation into modernity, which Narayan himself underwent, is what gives his work, particularly the early novels – and despite the inevitable comedy of small-town ambition and drift – an unexpected depth of suffering, which is all the more greater for not being perceived or acknowledged by the characters in his novels.

Narayan, by writing from deep within his small shrinking world, came to acquire an instinctive understanding of it. He developed with it the special intimacy that is sometimes capable of taking the novelist, if not the essayist, to truths deeper and subtler than those yielded by an analytical intelligence. It is the unmediated fidelity his novels have to his constricted experience, that makes them seem so organic in both conception and execution, and that also makes him now, remarkably, a more accurate guide to the inner life of modern India than such later self-conscious makers of historical narratives as Salman Rushdie and Rohinton Mistry.

The early novels with their energetic young men (Swami, Chandran and Krishna), the middle novels with the restless drifters (Srinivas, Sriram) and the later novels with the men wounded and exiled by the modern world (Jagan, Raman) map out an emotional and intellectual journey that many middle-class people in formerly colonial societies have made: the faint consciousness of individuality and nationality through colonial education; confused anti-colonial assertion; a post-colonial sense of inadequacy and failure; unfulfilled private lives; distrust of modernity and individual assertion; and, finally, in middle or old age, the search for cultural authenticity and renewal in the neglected, once-great past.

'The silent spirit of collective masses is the source of all great things,' Renan wrote at Turgenev's death. That silent spirit is what Narayan, writing in his own untutored way about men and worlds condemned to ambivalence, renders eloquent in his best novels. His characters don't leave the pages of his books without having achieved a kind of nobility, as part of an all-encompassing vision in which everything is accepted and forgiven. The characters, for instance, in *The Financial Expert* – small-time con men, greedy landlords, ingrate children, embittered parents, unhappy wives, exploited villagers – are like people locked in a trance, in Maya: the immense illusion of existence. They busily deceive each other and themselves; and everyone seems lost in the end. No liberation of the spirit, you feel, is likely to happen to these characters. Yet Narayan considers them with sympathy, even affection. We see them as the creator of Maya himself, that great ironic illusionist, would see us. It is this religious-seeming acceptingness that gives Narayan's novels their peculiar irony – an irony rooted in not scepticism and disbelief, but faith; an irony that belongs less to the European tradition of the novel than to a Hindu view of the world, in which the conflicts and contradictions of individual men and societies, however acute and compelling, are in the end no more than minor disturbances in the life of an old and serene cosmic order.

The Guide exemplifies this philosophical vision most vividly. Its last pages find Raju, the chief protagonist, at the end of a lifetime of insincerity and pain. As a professional guide to Malgudi's environs, he invented whole new historical pasts for bored tourists; he seduced a married woman, drifted away from his old mother and friends, became a flashy cultural promoter, and then tried, absent-mindedly, to steal and was caught and spent years in jail, abandoned by everyone.

His last few months have been spent in relative comfort as a holy man on the banks of a river: a role imposed on him by reverential village folk. But the river dries up after a drought and his devotees start looking to him to intercede with the gods. Raju resentfully starts a fast, but furtively eats whatever little food he has saved. Then abruptly, out of a moment of self-disgust, comes his resolution: for the first time in his life he will do something with sincerity, and he will do it for others: if fasting can bring rain, he'll fast.

He stops eating, and quickly diminishes. News of his efforts goes around; devotees and sightseers, gathering at the riverside, create a religious occasion out of the fast. On the early morning of the eleventh day of fasting, a small crowd watches him quietly as he attempts to pray standing on the river bed and then staggers and dies, mumbling the enigmatic last words of the novel, 'It's raining in the hills. I can feel it coming up under my feet, up my legs . . .'

Characteristically, Narayan doesn't make it clear whether Raju's penance does actually lead to rain. He also doesn't make much of Raju's decision, the moment of his redemption, which a lesser writer would have attempted to turn into a resonant ending but is quickly passed over here in a few lines.

What we know, in a moment of great disturbing beauty, is something larger and more affecting than the working out of an individual destiny in an inhospitable world. It is — and the words are of the forgotten English writer William Gerhardie on Chekhov, but so appropriate for Narayan — 'that sense of the temporary nature of our existence on this earth at all events, that he seems never able to forget, through which human beings, scenery, and even the very shallowness of things, are transfigured with a sense of disquieting importance. It is a sense of temporary possession in a temporary existence that, in the face of the unknown, we dare not overvalue. It is as if his people hastened to express their worthless individualities, since that is all they have, and were aghast that they should have so little in them to express: since the expression of it is all there is.'

'ALAS, MY HOUSE IS EMPTY . . .'

Rabindranath Tagore's *Ghare Baire*

ANANYA VAJPEYI

I began teaching *The Home and the World*, the English translation of Rabindranath Tagore's Bengali novel *Ghare Baire* (1916), in the fall semester of 2008. In the next four years, I must have taught it to half a dozen different classes, and at some point I began screening Satyajit Ray's film of the same name (*Ghare Baire,* 1984) alongside teaching the novel. Unlike many other works that I included in my history syllabus for a survey of colonial India from 1857 to 1947, I never got bored of teaching this book, nor the movie that went with it. In fact, I enjoyed both more, each time I taught them. Whatever my other difficulties in teaching American undergraduates at a poorly funded state university about Indian history, I knew I could always count on the two weeks set aside for Tagore to go smoothly.

In 2009 and 2010, I spent most of my time, apart from teaching, in writing my first book. Here too, Rabindranath and his nephew Abanindranath Tagore figured prominently, and each one had a

chapter devoted to him. I don't read Bengali, although I can follow
it with some effort if people are speaking around me, but I found
myself returning to *The Home and the World* to understand many of
the lineaments of Rabindranath's political thought. Now some
time later, my book is complete, I am no longer teaching those
classes about colonial India in America, and I am back to living in
India. What I realize as I look back over the past four years is that a
great deal of Rabindranath's perspective on political ideologies as
well as human relationships has seeped into my consciousness and
become an intrinsic part of the way I look at the world. Without
realizing exactly when this happened, I internalized the novel,
began using it as a dictionary with which to decipher life.

In my book, *Righteous Republic: The Political Foundations of Modern
India*, I have written at length about Tagore's politics, and argued in
some detail why and how he cannot be called a nationalist, even
though he has been designated India's national poet. Without
reprising my arguments here, I do want to note that for me *Ghare
Baire* turned out not just to be useful as an aide to think about the
Swadeshi movement and its failure in Bengal in the first decade of
the twentieth century; that it did not just prove to be an excellent
companion piece to Tagore's three lectures, collectively titled
Nationalism (1917), which spell out his opposition to nationalist
ideology. Rather, it helped me recognize that there are ways and
ways of being politically cognizant and morally active; that even the
smallest gestures, the most private decisions we make can sometimes
be the indices of our real convictions and the giveaways of our most
secret compromises. The political life finds its truest staging ground
deep in the human heart, a region excluded from any ordinary
study of politics. Tagore makes this unusual claim and I think he
is right.

It is not so much a matter of what one might do for love, or
whether one values persons more than convictions (or indeed

convictions more than persons). If those had been the limits of Rabindranath's enquiry into the political, then Bankim had already written political novels in Bengali well before him. In my view, his questions are deeper: which actions, which beliefs and which attachments count as political, and which do not? Where does the home end and the world begin? Is there a threshold over which one must step in order to enter into the zone of the political, or is that threshold coincident with the very shape of one's being in the world? In our modern lives, is there a place to retreat into and hide in − a metaphorical equivalent of the kitchen, the bedroom, the women's quarters − when we find ourselves confronted with stark political choices? How do we negotiate contradictions between personal and political loyalties; how do we manage conflicts between personal and political betrayals? Put starkly, the question becomes: Is it possible to refuse politics altogether?

If Tagore's novel is radically modern it is because it seems to suggest that politics is inescapable, it is also modern in its view of intimate relationships between men and women. Tagore never really had a modern marriage in his own life and yet he seemed to get it right, with all of the intelligence, sensitivity and imagination that characterize the entirety of his oeuvre. The love between Nikhil and Bimala, the physical chemistry between Bimala and Sandip, and the love-hate relationship between Nikhil and Sandip make for an almost archetypal triangle. It turns out in fact that there is a perfect coincidence between Bimala's sexual infidelity and her ideological error. She fails to understand both the true nature of her husband's love and the actual implications of her lover's politics. In thematizing sexual love both within and outside the marital frame, placing the onus of choice upon the female character despite her apparent sequestration within the four walls of patriarchy, and tying the political and the personal into one inextricable knot, Tagore writes a novel that hits home even a hundred years later.

The plot is by now familiar even to those who may not be dedicated or enthusiastic readers of Tagore, partly because of Ray's film – starring Soumitra Chatterjee, Swatilekha Chatterjee and, in a memorable performance, Victor Banerjee – and partly because the novel is so widely taught in Indian university curricula. Nikhilesh is a landlord and lives with his wife Bimala and other female relatives in a big house on his estate. The couple is childless but happy. One day Nikhil's college friend Sandip, who is involved in Swadeshi politics, comes calling, and needs to stay the night. Sandip's arrival brings for the first time into their home and into Bimala's sheltered consciousness an intimation of the political turbulence that is engulfing all of Bengal. Nikhil encourages Bimala's curiosity about Swadeshi in hopes that Sandip will initiate her into a political education. Unfortunately, Bimala and Sandip are drawn to one another in ways that are not just about her exposure to politics but also about their charged and illicit dynamic. Nikhil senses trouble but is unable to stop whatever it is that is brewing between his wife and his friend. Bimala is too smitten by Sandip's rabble-rousing charisma – his nationalist songs and fiery speeches, his flattering and deceitful conflation of her with a glorious image of Mother India – she is too dazzled by the prospect of a revolution to keep her head straight.

Sandip takes base advantage of the gullible woman, and eventually attempts to cheat her and outright rob Nikhil. Nor is his role in local politics exemplary – he foments trouble among Nikhil's subjects and disturbs the peace of the estate just as severely as he disturbs the harmony of his host's home and marriage. A series of catastrophic revelations opens Bimala's eyes to the truth, and husband and wife are momentarily reconciled. But no sooner do they decide to renew their vows than the situation outside explodes. Nikhil must rush away from a contrite Bimala to rectify the damage done by Sandip – alas he is not fated to return. The novel leaves the ending slightly enigmatic, but the film clearly shows Bimala transformed from a happily married woman into a grieving widow. Apart from the havoc in Nikhil and Bimala's relationship, Sandip's wake of destruction includes theft, arson, drowning, communal violence and the death of one of his young acolytes whom Bimala treats like a younger brother. Sandip – who stands for Swadeshi – tears through Bengal like a tornado, whipping up political and personal passions. He represents a wild, surging energy that promises transformation but delivers only mayhem.

Using rubrics like 'social history', 'national movement', and 'gender studies', scholars have analysed every aspect of Tagore's novel as well as Ray's film over the past twenty-five or thirty years. But two properties of this book that make it especially precious have, I believe, been ignored or passed over without much comment. One I will call an element of quiet, which to me sets the tone of the entire story. What we read are the minds of the three protagonists; we enter the guarded precincts of their consciousness and follow along with recollection, reverie, regret, revenge and other absolutely private, unarticulated thoughts as they come to Nikhil, Bimala and Sandip, one after the other. It's as if Tagore is reminding us that the most terrible breaks in a relationship, the most awesome realizations, the truest knowledge of past or future to which we may have access, all these are events inside our heads: what lies within is what is important; what happens out there is but a pale shadow or a faint echo of the drama of our secret selves. The placid surface of the narrative form conceals a turbulence that affects not just these three individuals but an entire society at the time of the first iteration of Swadeshi nationalism in Bengal.

Things happen quietly but with an implacable relentlessness that is in fact rather frightening: Bimala is drawn to Sandip, Sandip seduces Bimala, Bimala and Nikhil's marriage falls apart, Bimala is let down by Sandip and realizes her mistake, Nikhil is called away on a mission that turns out to be fatal. The flip side of the quietness is the real and present danger: danger to this marriage, to this home, and in some sense to this larger social setting where Hindus and Muslims, landlords and peasants are about to be horribly – and in the long run, permanently – sundered from one another. Danger for me is the second underestimated quality of *Ghare Baire* as a literary work. A thunderous speech, a rousing song, a cup of tea, a passionate kiss, and the world is turned upside down for all those who are drawn into the vortex of nationalist politics. Bimala becomes unmoored from her domestic life and moral centre, never again to come home to safety. Nikhil is deeply and irreparably hurt, his journey abruptly truncated from horseback to hearse. Sandip falls from a golden and melodious heroism to a tawdry and mendacious cowardice. Beware the enemy disguised as a friend; the stranger at the door asking for shelter; the lover who loves only himself. How vulnerable a space the home is, how fleeting, how exposed at every moment to the depredations of an unbidden, unmarked and unexpected danger!

In Delhi in early 2012, I watched a rendering of the *Dastan-e-Ghare Baire*, the story of Tagore's novel, by Mahmood Farooqui and Danish Husain, in an Indo-Persian style of recitation and performance dating to the nineteenth century that these two artists have revived in India in recent years. Farooqui told the story in a mishmash of Urdu, Hindustani and Bengali, with Farsi words thrown in for good measure. He wrote the script himself, based on a Hindi translation of the novel by Prayag Shukla. With his usual brilliance, his polyglot sensibility as well as linguistic virtuosity, Farooqui managed to convey the rhetorical power of Sandip's grandstanding, the tenderness of Nikhil's love for his wife, Bimala's moral conundrums and political confusions, the era of Swadeshi nationalism with its slogans and chants, the quietness and the danger, the power and the pathos of the saga of these three persons joined in love and broken by doubt.

After years of developing a thorough familiarity with Tagore's novel, I was once again riveted as though at the first telling of this story. I considered my own life, and paused, discovering that Rabindranath had somehow guessed its secret dilemmas, entered my heart as he did Bimala's, and laid bare the chaos within.

A JAGGED EDGE

Bama Faustina Soosairaj's *Karukku*

S. THEODORE BASKARAN

Karukku is a short novel, barely a hundred pages. Devised as an autobiographical novel and narrated in the first person, it marked not one, but two new literary milestones in Tamil literature: for the first time a Dalit woman was writing of her experience of being a Dalit in her own voice, and also for the first time this was a voice that belonged to a Dalit Christian. This is the story of Bama, a Catholic Dalit woman who fled the nunnery, unable to withstand caste discrimination and related humiliations within Catholic institutions.

When *Karukku* was released in 1992, it became the focus of an intense debate on the nature of literature, on the kind of language it used and on Dalit life. The book rejected the prevailing literary conventions and forms and demonstrated that literary trends are born out of path-breaking works such as *Karukku* and not the other way around. Translated into a number of languages, it was prescribed as a textbook in universities and discussed as a hot topic in several academic seminars.

When I first read Bama's *Karukku* I was struck by the fact that the whole story is narrated in spoken Tamil. The people who inhabit the novel are Tamil Catholic Dalits. There is a specific jargon associated with this area and people – a rich, vibrant, spoken Dalit idiom that Bama employs with telling effect. Having grown up in a Tamil village and studied in a Catholic school, I could relate immediately to every sentence Bama wrote.

Dalit literature in Tamil blossomed late, compared to Marathi and Kannada. By the late 1970s, novels such as *Kaanal* (*Forest*) by Daniel and *Piragu* (*Later*) by Poomani had Dalit themes. A discourse slowly emerged on the need for such literature and what constituted it. Meanwhile, more Dalit writers appeared on the scene and articulated the purpose of Dalit writing as rediscovering their roots, recognizing their cultural identity and looking at society and history from a Dalit perspective. By the 1980s Dalit writing emerged strongly in Tamil Nadu and Bama's *Karukku* became an important high point of this literary wave.

Bama says that putting her life story on paper in the form of a novel was a therapeutic experience. 'In 1992 I looked upon myself as a bird with the wings clipped. Now I see myself as a falcon soaring high in the sky.' She also says, '*Karukku* gave me a new hope, brought in a new sense of responsibility and provided me with clear-sightedness. It made a big impact on those who read it. To those caught up in the tentacles of caste oppression and were being destroyed, to those who have been marginalized, the book gave confidence. The novel gave them optimism to continue their journey, to break the mindset and live with self-esteem and freedom, with their head held high.'

Born into a Roman Catholic Christian Dalit family (Parayan caste) Bama Faustina Soosairaj and her siblings were taken care of by their mother, who struggled as a farm hand, while the father was most of the time absent, serving in the army. The hierarchical inequality of life in a village, the day-to-day ordeals and the awakening she experiences in the nunnery about her life's calling form the crux of much of the story. She gives a detailed description of the places she has lived in, the schools she attended, and the places she worked at. The underlying theme in all these accounts is the degradation meted out to her on the basis of her caste.

The novel debunks the popular myth that there is no casteism in Christianity. In fact it is deep-rooted, and since the novel's publication, it has come out more into the open. Though Dalits outnumber other castes in the Church, upper-caste priests dominate every aspect of the order. Bama's *Karukku* is a courageous exposure of the caste-based injustice of untouchability in the nunnery, where upper-caste nuns keep a tight control over the convent.

Karukku refers to the jagged edges of the leaf of the palmyra palm, the state tree of Tamil Nadu. This is a story set in south Tamil Nadu, a village nestled in the slopes of the foothills of the Western Ghats. Here we deal with rural, Dalit, Roman Catholic Tamil society. Though there are some upper-caste characters, Bama plucks her characters mostly from the Dalit communities. The essence of Bama's writing is that it captures the suffering of Dalit women. The oppression, the life of torment, helplessness and thralldom are brought out by the phrases she chooses, the idioms she uses, the very earthy adjectives and the searing expressions she employs.

Words of abuse with sexual connotations occur in the novel not only as words uttered by different characters, but also by the author in the narrative. This aspect has been pointed out by scholars as being an essential characteristic of Dalit literature. For instance, the terms *kandaaroli* (one who fucks anyone) and *mayiru* (pubic hair) occur with ease. In an interview, Bama defended the use of such terms and says for a Dalit woman her only weapon is 'dirty' words. In villages you can hear these words crop up casually in everyday conversation. I think that these terms, expressions and related proverbs are part of the heritage of the language, albeit the spoken variety. Bama has retrieved those words from being lost to the literary world, since they were hitherto considered unfit for print.

Life in the Church and in school gets close attention. In India, indigenization of Christianity happened more naturally and in a deeper way in the Catholic Church than in the other denominations. The concept of female deity, so strong in India, has been neatly incorporated through the different forms of Mary. So you have Mary of Poondi, Mother of Velankanni and so on. The small icons (*soruoobam*) they use as pendants and the chariot festival (*sapara thiruvizha*) are part of this culture. There is even a story in the novel about a vision of Mary that appeared near her village to a travelling priest, a common legend in Tamil Nadu about the origin of some Catholic shrines.

The names of biblical characters have been Tamilized by early translators as part of the indigenization process, and they are still used, both in the Bible and in naming children. Ignatius becomes Innasi, Sebastian is Sevathaiyaru and Joseph is Soosaiyapparu. These names occur frequently in the novel, as Bama effectively captures the ethos of that society. Bama, with her keen ear for spoken Tamil, its imagery and speech pattern, is able to deftly capture the idiom of the language. The proverbs and the smutty swear words all form part of her vocabulary. When some attempts were made to offer oral poems and ballads in print, the editors brought out a sanitized version. But the Dalit writers are now recording their dialects. This is a literary phenomenon of the past decade, which characterizes Dalit literature. Just after reading a page or two, you can immediately identify it as a Dalit work. The text, through the earthy, pungent language employed, brings out the life experience of Dalits.

Ghosts move in and out of the story like any other character. Villager Pondhan steals some money from the shrine of a folk deity in the forest. Muniyandi, the resident ghost, is after the thief. Here is the account, in Bama's own words:

> Since then every night Muniyandi the ghost strode through our street with rage. 'Return my money and restore the bell in my shrine, otherwise I will scorch down this whole street,' he would rant. He appeared to many people. They could not understand what was going on. When they enquired, Pondhan's father, oldman Savarinayagam, narrated what had happened. The villagers gathered and persuaded Pondhan to go, tie the bell and put back the money he stole from the shrine. Pondhan then walked up towards the shrine, all the while making the sign of cross on his body, placed back the money he had pinched and tied the bell. After that was done, the motherfucker of a ghost never showed up in our street again.

I was happy to see that Dalit writings document this feature of spoken Tamil and through their writings this dimension of the language will be preserved. In a later autobiographical novel *Siluvairajin Charithiram* (*Story of Siluvairaj*) by Dalit ideologue and Tamil scholar Raj Gauthaman, Bama's older brother, one can observe similarities in the way both use language. She acknowledges that he was a strong influence.

A very important dimension of *Karukku* is as a social document. Bama writes about the ways in which Dalit children were subjected to humiliation in schools. If anything in the class or in school had to be cleaned, the teacher would ask a Dalit child to do the work. In one instance, the headmaster accuses Bama of stealing a coconut and when she denies it he says, 'You have displayed your paraya character.'

She records a fight among the Dalits, between Parayan and Pallan castes, though both are oppressed by the landowning castes. We read about the nature of landholding in the village and how the

Dalits are only the tillers of land, not owners. The traditions of
Tamil Dalits are described: on a festival day, a bull is slaughtered
and the meat is shared. A brief beef recipe also finds a place.
Electricity comes to their village and Bama records the experience.
The thrill of seeing the light come on like magic as a switch is
pressed: there is no kerosene oil in this system! Similarly, cinema
arrives in the village in the form of videotapes and a deck during
festivals.

By meticulously recording the geography of the village, the
trees, plants, birds and animals, this short novel morphs into an
ecological document. This is bound to be so as Dalits live close to
the earth. Her description of the external world is evocative and
accurate. Bama talks about the different kinds of fish caught in the
lake and the varieties that are eaten by the poor and the ones that
are eaten by the well-to-do. She describes the hunting expeditions,
assisted by hounds, which the villagers periodically indulge in,
defying the Wildlife Protection Act that came into force in 1972.
Animals such as chital and even the elusive Nilgiri tahr are killed
and shared. But the prize catch is a boar, and when one is brought
down, the carcass is decorated and taken in a celebratory procession
before it is cut into pieces and shared.

Bama's subsequent writings, the novels *Sangati* and *Vanmam* have
shown that success as a writer has not diminished her obsession
with her past or the bitterness, which is evident in her works. But
in the rich details of their lives is the celebration of their closeness
to nature, which has sustained them through centuries of oppression.
'My ambition,' Bama once said, 'is to communicate the dreams and
aspirations of my people, who have remained on the fringes for
centuries in Indian history.'

THE LOST WORLD OF CARVALHO

Poornachandra Tejaswi's *Carvalho*

BAGESHREE SUBBANNA

Back in 1997, the ever-opinionated Salman Rushdie declared that Indian writing in English was proving to be a stronger and more important body of work than those in the 'so-called vernacular languages'. Some Indian language writers responded to this with justifiable outrage, while others laughed off the comic ignorance.

I don't recall Poornachandra Tejaswi – one of the most loved and critically acclaimed Kannada writers – reacting to this debate. Had he done so, it surely would not have been in a tone of high seriousness. I happened to be rereading *Carvalho*, a slim novel he wrote in 1980 and arguably his best, as yet another Rushdie saga unfolded in the 2012 edition of the Jaipur Literature Festival. I couldn't help thinking that Rushdie, capable of being at the centre of ever so many sticky situations, is just the kind of character Tejaswi would have loved to put in his novels!

In one of the many hilarious episodes in *Carvalho*, a grand Independence Day celebration organized with a minister as the chief guest plunges into utter chaos as the din of bugles, cymbals and drum results in a swarm of bees going berserk. The police swing into immediate action, suspecting a conspiracy, and arrest a bunch of schoolboys.

Writing a review of *The Vintage Book of Indian Writing* edited by Rushdie, which carried the infamous dismissal of 'vernacular' writers, Tarun Tejpal said that *Carvalho* was among the 'odd gems one encounters every now and then in unhyped translations'. He described the novel (translated into English by Dr D.A. Shankar) as 'a stunning revelation of the class and sophistication of ostensibly mofussil writers'. *Carvalho* in theme, resonance and narration 'could knock quite a few of Rushdie's charmed 32 clear out of the ring'.

Not that Tejaswi has ever required endorsements of literary critics. Most of his books – which includes an impressive body of writings on science, ecology and agriculture, besides fictional works and translations – are what booksellers call the 'fast-moving' variety read not just by a small elite schooled in literary criticism. In 2012, *Carvalho* entered into its twenty-seventh edition. Tejaswi consciously shunned the dominant Navya (modernist) style of the 1960s and 1970s, which he felt was a 'bad imitation' of European modern writers with Brahmin writers at its helm. He chose to write in what is called, not without a hint of derision, the 'popular' mode. *Carvalho*, like much of his other writings, is lively, fast-paced and reads like a thriller peppered with comic interludes.

While his first two novels do not escape a somewhat self-indulgent Navya style – though one of the characters declares in his first novel *Swaroopa* that he is no longer willing to write 'university stories and university poems', reflecting the writer's own stand – it is in *Carvalho* that Tejaswi seems to really come to his own.

Carvalho is the story of a motley bunch of people's search for the flying lizard in the dense evergreen forests of the Malnad region of Karnataka. The reptile is believed to hold the secret of a crucial missing link in the chain of evolution.

The central character of the novel is Carvalho, who is as much a philosopher as he is a scientist of international repute, intent on unlocking the mystery of evolution preserved for '3 with 7 zeroes in front of it' years in the flying lizard. For most in the village, Carvalho is a madcap, 'chasing after a worm as if it is god'. Some even wonder if he is a foreign agent or a timber smuggler in the guise of a hawk-nosed scientist. At the other end of the spectrum of this assorted team that sets out to find the lizard is Mandanna, a 'natural naturalist', completely unaware of his own abilities. He has no aspirations beyond landing a permanent government job as a bee-keeper so that he is deemed fit enough to marry the big-breasted Raami. Carvalho, who recognizes Mandanna's brilliant indigenous talent, is intolerant of the latter's 'petty' ambitions.

In between are several characters with amazing idiosyncrasies – bow-legged Biryani Kariappa with a special talent for climbing trees, pickpocket-turned-helper Pyara who speaks a peculiar language that appears to the narrator like he is 'holding language by the scruff of its neck to extract meaning', Yenkta of a traditional hunting tribe whose sexual mores are beyond the comprehension of the middle class, Carvalho's helper Prabhakara who possesses an admirable equanimity, the dog Kiwi and temperamental swarms of bees among others. The dense forest is also a character in its own right, like in many of Tejaswi's works.

Tejaswi, as a farmer and a writer, is himself a character in *Carvalho*. He is the narrator of the story who lives within the village community. And yet he is an outsider who is by turns baffled, intrigued and impatient with the people around him. A failed farmer on the verge of abandoning farming to return to the city, he joins Carvalho's flying lizard expedition, as the scientist rekindles his innate curiosity for the mysteries of nature and a desire to unravel them. The narrator's fascination for the characters of Mandanna and Carvalho too, who seem to be opposite poles on many counts, seems to be added attractions in joining the team.

At the heart of this novel is an exploration of the human being's awe and curiosity for the endless riddles and mysteries that nature challenges him/her with. However hopeless the quest to crack the mystery may be, the irrepressible human spirit that seeks to do it is worthy of celebration. Interestingly, Tejaswi's father Kuvempu, an iconic writer who brought the first Jnanpith Award to Kannada, also wrote extensively about nature. But unlike Kuvempu, who portrays nature as benign and all-giving, Tejaswi sees nature as an awe-inspiring, mysterious entity that also has a malevolent face. He is also acutely aware that nature is threatened by human greed and ignorance.

The search for the elusive reptile is a methodological scientific quest, but a humanist like Carvalho also lends it a philosophical orientation. (Incidentally, Tejaswi was impatient with efforts to read too much symbolism into his realistic novels.) Carvalho tells Prabhakara at one point in the novel that an entire lifetime will be spent without a 'glimpse of the truth' if one can't transcend the illusion ('maya') of him being a great professor and Mandanna a village bumpkin. There is also a hint that a system that lacks imagination and is caught in such binaries, insisting on hammering round pegs in square holes, has little hope of redemption. While Carvalho sees Mandanna as inevitable to this ambitious expedition, the local police are busy framing him in a spurious liquor case.

The quest to unravel the mystery of nature in *Carvalho* also turns out to be an attempt to grapple with the enigma of human nature, which can suddenly soar from the most mundane to the sublime and plunge right back. Every character in this novel opens a fascinating world, each representing a different caste, class and cultural milieu. The characters — viewed with sympathetic, non-judgemental eyes — provide a counterfoil to each other, sometimes creating completely comic situations. For example, Kariappa's obsessive search for a wild goat for the next biryani meal often interrupts the narrator's reveries on their impossible attempt to defy the forward movement of time or his absorption with the fascinating wild world unfolding before him for the first time. Prabhakara, meanwhile, is desperately trying to keep intact his telescope and other apparatus – which Mandanna looks upon with disdain as completely unnecessary impediments – in the rattling bullock cart moving on a hilly terrain. At one point the narrator is disconcerted by the absence of any thread of commonality in the group, and yet it holds together, which is an enigma in itself.

The diversity of characters and the cultures they represent in this small world is a reflection of the close sociological understanding of Tejaswi and his diverse 'non-academic' interests. Tejaswi shunned the world of academics and chose to be a coffee planter in the hilly Malnad region and experimented with all the things that life presented him with. Talking about what his interest in photography (one of the his many pursuits alongside music, fishing, painting, bird watching and tinkering with motor vehicles) lent to his writing, he once wrote: 'The first discipline is that photographer cannot be the hero of his statement . . . Whereas in writing you can be a hero, in photography, you can exist only as a perspective, as an interpreter, not as a hero . . .' This statement is also an extension of his disdain for the modernist school of Kannada, which he was scathingly critical of, among other things, for being individual-centric. *Carvalho*'s narrator never becomes self-indulgent or overbearing to the point of overshadowing all other people and things.

More importantly, what shaped his perspective was his long, if somewhat volatile association with the important social movements of the 1970s and 1980s in Karnataka. A staunch follower of socialist political leader Ram Manohar Lohia, Tejaswi was involved with organizations such as Samajwadi Yuvajana Sabha (a socialist youth forum inspired by Lohiate thought), Karnataka Rajya Raitha Sangha (a farmers' organization) and Pragatipara Okkuta (a forum of progressive writers). Anti-Brahminism and anti-casteism shaped his consciousness as a writer and social observer. These values were also at the root of his disenchantment with the established literary canons, which he found too entrenched in Brahmanical values.

One could even argue that the zeitgeist of the 1970s and early 1980s, marked by a social and political fervour, had a strong role in making *Carvalho* very unique within Tejaswi's own oeuvre. We see a gradual shift in his subsequent three novels (published between 1985 and 2006) towards a more cynical view of social movements and all shades of ideological stances, as his caricatural representation of activists and activism suggests. He shocked his old associates by arguing that economic liberalization holds the potential to throw new challenges and shake up a stagnant system. Some of his close associates say that he had begun to realize, towards the end of his life that the opening up of the markets was not so benign after all.

The world of Carvalho that Tejaswi constructs, however, is still not the Brave New World of the big markets, but one governed by the principles of Nehruvian socialism. Carvalho's scholarship here comes coupled with a humanist and inclusive world view. He believes that the pursuit of knowledge is also the pursuit of the larger human good. Despite his international fame, Carvalho is an employee in a government department and can advise a farmer in distress on pest control based as much on common sense as it is on the knowledge of science. The simple village people around him can hardly relate to his achievements as a scientist, and yet he is an organic individual who can relate to a character like Mandanna and identify his special talents.

Reading the novel thirty-two years after its publication, one wonders where Carvalho would be in the 'knowledge society' in the era following economic liberalization. Could a man like him have been in a government job in a remote village? Would the 'native' knowledge of someone like Mandanna have been a tool for bio-mining in the hands of a patent-grabbing multinational corporation? In this sense, looking back at Carvalho and the world around him is also like looking for our missing links with the world around our own selves.

BETWEEN FACT AND FAIRYTALE

Amitav Ghosh's *The Shadow Lines*

ANJUM HASAN

The first pact a person hoping to write fiction makes is with an admired novel. I am quite certain that I would never have worked up the courage to write novels myself unless I had read other works of Indian fiction not just with pleasure, but also with that other emotion that reveals fiction's possibilities to us — a sense of recognition. I'm talking about novels written not just in English, but in a kind of English that echoed familiarly in my ear, that had the shape and sound of an instrument I might use to create narratives out of *my* way of experiencing the world. The work of I. Allan Sealy, Arundhati Roy, Upamanyu Chatterjee, Rohinton Mistry, Amit Chaudhuri and Kiran Desai all spoke directly to me, but the one novel that buoyed me most intensely and continues to do so is Amitav Ghosh's *The Shadow Lines*.

This is because *The Shadow Lines* (1988) is not just a tremendous work *in* fiction but also an argument for the power and potential *of* fiction. It is an answer to the question: what can the novel do? Or, since this is a novel about acts, events and memories that genres other than the novel also speak about: what can the novel do that the political speech, the newspaper report, the history book cannot?

The novel can, first of all, illuminate. *The Shadow Lines* is a tapestry of connections, overlaps and attachments. Every single moment in the novel touches off another. Each of its specific details is significant in itself as well as crucial for how it acts as a mirror to other details. I know of no other Indian novel that so fully exploits the potential of storytelling as a mirroring device, as a form of *reflection*. What emerges is a picture so angled and textured that one cannot but keep returning to it, a picture whose meaning is never exhausted.

This is not just technical virtuosity but also an argument against closure. Tridib, the novel's hero, tells us that one can never know anything except through desire, 'a pure, painful and primitive desire . . . that carried one beyond the limits of one's mind to other times and other places . . .' *The Shadow Lines* is itself an expression of this desire – the wish to not abandon to the quotidian what we habitually consign there, and yet not yield to the abstractions of politics that in fact have meaning only when located in the minutiae of everyday life.

A second thing that fiction does is show us how to defend ourselves against what J.M. Coetzee calls 'the brute facts'. When the unnamed narrator of *The Shadow Lines* is living in London in the 1980s, he often, despite himself, starts walking towards Ila's house in Stockwell. These expeditions are futile; they are driven by desire for a woman who is already lost to him. As a measure of his love for Ila, he calculates to the last foot the distances he walks. Why does he do this? Why do we try to express love in ineffective ways?

I could think of no answer, except that it is because that state, love, is so utterly alien to that other idea without which we cannot live as human beings – the idea of justice. It is only because love is so profoundly the enemy of justice that our minds, shrinking in horror from its true nature, try to tame it by uniting it with its opposite: it is as though we say to ourselves – he bought her a diamond worth exactly so much, or she gave up a career that would have earned her precisely so much – in the hope that if we apply all the metaphors of normality . . . we shall, in the end, be able to approximate that state metaphorically.

The contrast between love, which is the most extraordinary subjectivity possible, and justice, which is based on the dream of complete objectivity, mirrors, as I see it, the contrast between the possibilities of fiction and the limitations of 'brute fact'.

The brute facts in the world of *The Shadow Lines* concern riot-related statistics and war-driven allegiances, the stamp in a passport, and the 'science and factories' through which national borders are maintained. *The Shadow Lines* shows us that just as the idea of justice can never approximate to the idea of love, the brute facts, much as we rely on them, can be chimerical in relation to human experience. Just as love cannot be measured, however much we try, the facts do not add up to what we have experienced in their name. Only fiction can express this ineluctable subjectivity of human experience and *The Shadow Lines* illustrates as well as argues for the value of this subjectivity by being, in multiple ways, a novel about love.

The novel's first sentence tells us that Tridib, the narrator's beloved uncle, went as a child to England during the war years. Tridib and his parents stay with the Prices in London – the two families are bound by a friendship that stretches a generation back. At the time of the visit, Tridib is eight years old and May, the Prices' daughter, an infant. When they are older, Tridib and May will, even before they have met as adults, fall in love with each other. This is not only on the basis of the letters they exchange but also because they are aware of a shared history – the time that Tridib spent with the Prices as a child, as well as the even older history of friendship between their respective grandfathers.

But despite this common past, when Tridib writes to May, he says he wants to meet her as a stranger, '. . . the completest of strangers – strangers-across-the-seas . . . in a place without a past, without history, free, really free . . .' What would it take for them to meet in this way? Tridib believes that we live in invented worlds and that each one of us must create these for ourselves or we will never be free of other people's inventions. But this is one story that he cannot invent for himself and May: this Tristan-like story of a love-across-the-seas.

He cannot invent it because, genuine though his yearning is, he has another, equally strong yearning. This is to experience things not outside history but squarely within it – to use, as he tells his nephew, one's imagination with precision. Where might such precision lead us?

Tridib remembers a great deal about his childhood trip to England, and these images sometimes have a clarity that could not be born out of memory but is simply the result of that imaginative hunger for 'other times and other places'. He remembers standing by the window at twilight one day at the beginning of the War and watching three young leftists – Dan, Tresawsen and Francesca – walking down the road, going home together. 'But he knew that the clarity of that image in his mind was merely the seductive clarity of ignorance; an illusion of knowledge created by a deceptive weight of remembered detail.'

Later in the novel, Ila and the narrator are talking about the very past that Tridib remembers as captured in that image of three friends walking down a twilit street. For the narrator, the image represents a time when politics was more serious. Ila says that he is naïve, that he has idealized England and actually knows nothing about the country. To which he says, 'I gave up then, for of course she was right: I knew nothing at all about England except as an invention.'

So even though we cannot but invent the worlds we live in, even though we *must*, there is also that other thing contained within the fictiveness of the novel – the pull of ignorance, self-deception, illusion, play. We encounter all these elements in *The Shadow Lines*, and we also encounter – as when Ila reminds the narrator that he has dreamed up England – critical responses to them. It is as if the novel were having a conversation with itself about itself – emphasizing the necessity of the imagination and at the same time asking when the imagination should yield to another kind of knowledge, which lies outside the boundaries of the novel. This internal dialogue is a third thing the novel offers us.

Twenty years after Tridib and May's story is over, the narrator seeks out May in London because of his stake in that story. They meet because of the bonds between their families and because they have grieved over a common loss. It is not possible to imagine May and the narrator meeting without this context. In their entangled friendship, there could never be room for a Tristan-like story of a love-across-the-seas.

This then is the axis on which the novel places the idea of love – a state that will free one from the bonds of history as well as, seen from another point of view, a state that secures one within those bonds. At one extreme is a fairytale and at the other extreme are brute facts. The novel itself is written on the shadow line that separates them.

'KEEP IT IN WRITING'

Tarashankar Bandyopadhyay's
Hansuli Banker Upakatha

BENJAMIN CONISBEE BAER

I first became interested in Tarashankar Bandyopadhyay, because as a writer he seemed in many ways to brush against the grain of his times. His elegies for a certain rural Bengal are gothic, macabre, often comical, and yet filled with intimate details of the multilayered textures of the structures and patterns of rustic and small-town life. His language is strange: sinewy and additive, stark and hypnotic, simple and garrulous at the same time. Rabindranath Tagore praised these differences, both the language and intimacy that at best made Tarashankar's writing stand apart from the Santiniketan scene's tendency to a romanticized bucolic. Tarashankar also maintains a distance from the genre of the moral parable or socially reformist novel (Premchand's brilliant novels of the 1930s, for example).

Hansuli Banker Upakatha (or *The Tale of Hansuli Turn* in my translation) engages the specificity, the singular weirdness and texture of Bengal's Rarh region (the red-earth western fringes adjoining the Chhotanagpur plateau). In doing so it reflects upon the task of making a rustic underclass tale (an *upakatha*) survive within the form of a novel (an *upanyas*). *Hansuli Turn* represents an attempt to imagine itself as a response to a call from below; a response to an imperative to preserve a tale that itself has been kept in the heart and voice of an old woman. For this novel is perhaps above all about how, in what form or forms, the rural imagination (and especially the imaginations, stories and imperatives of India's most marginalized peoples) can live on as their existing patterns of life are, for better or worse, broken up and dispersed.

At a moment when, as Ashis Nandy and others have pointed out, the 'rural imagination' of India is being forgotten in a rush for the metro-centric celebration of the nation's economic 'rise', it seemed important to me to bring out a translation that might remind us of the paradoxes and dilemmas of such processes of social and economic development. Of course, 1940s' colonial India during wartime in *Hansuli Turn* is by no means identical to today's independent India enmeshing itself in globalization. Yet war as depicted in *Hansuli Turn* is a powerful mechanism of 'development' that translates into environmental pillage, uprooting and internal migration or diaspora; the sub-proletarianization of the rural peripheries. To give a different example, the ration cards introduced during the Second World War are still a part of everyday reality for the poorest inhabitants of rural India; and they appear here as an alien innovation, an object of contention in the community depicted in *Hansuli Turn*.

The first version of Tarashankar's *Hansuli Banker Upakatha* appeared in the Durga Puja special edition of the Bengali daily *Ananda Bazar Patrika* in 1946. That year, publication of the *Ananda Bazar* Puja number was delayed by over two months because of pre-Partition rioting in Calcutta. Tarashankar worked *Hansuli Turn* up from a novella-type sketch into a novel of more than 300 pages over the next several months, and the first book version was published in June–July 1947 by Bengal Publishers of Calcutta. Between 1947 and 1951 further re-edited versions appeared, changed by Tarashankar to reflect what he saw as the prevailing mood of the newly independent country. Various editions thus emerged across the tumultuous cusp of Independence and Partition, a period combining intense celebration of new nationhood with unprecedentedly violent dispute about the felicitous inhabitants of India. One could hardly call *Hansuli Turn* a 'Partition novel', though, as it depicts rather a different set of Indians whose status would be contested by Ambedkar and Gandhi, Verrier Elwin and G.S. Ghurye.

The collective protagonist of *Hansuli Turn* is a group of 'untouchable' sharecroppers tenuously holding onto a residual caste-based occupation of palanquin-bearers (hence their name, Kahars). Categorized as a 'Criminal Tribe' by the colonial state in the nineteenth century, the community in the novel has struggled slowly to extricate itself from this appellation and to establish itself in the quasi-feudal milieu between rising businessman-farmers, fading zamindars and now the wartime industries of the *mofussil* rail junction and aerodrome. Signalling prior sediments of movement and settlement, and perhaps the imminent decolonization of the country, the novel depicts the Kahars as inhabiting the ruins of an English indigo plantation. It stages historical transformation through an intergenerational conflict between headman Bonwari and young rebel Karali. A dispute over the meaning of a mysterious sound emerging from surrounding woodland engenders a crisis and an irreparable fissure within the group. Attacking all the signs of the village elders' dharma, Karali fights them in the name of undoing caste oppression, allying himself with the wartime industries and transportation networks of the local town. In this manner, *Hansuli Turn* approaches a deeply uncomfortable double bind: a suggestion that a certain allegiance with the violence of colonialism and war can also translate into a limited emancipation from the violent strictures of indigenous caste-based oppression.

An especially innovative aspect of *Hansuli Turn* is that it asks the reader to imagine a world of peasant farmer-businessmen, landlords, landowners and rural gentry from the vantage point of the landless sharecropper eking out subsistence in a remote place that is yet untouched by global crisis. The novel is the most sustained experiment of this type of focalizing gesture in its time. Moreover, it seems to me to be a modernist experiment in dramatizing the possibility of an interface between an emergent public sphere and those whose position does not give them access to that sphere. I emphasize that *Hansuli Turn* is a literary experiment: it does not provide any kind of blueprint for actual practices of 'inclusion' in post-Independence India. Its formal organization – especially the innovative mechanism of a special glossary that is woven into the fabric of the text – makes *Hansuli Turn* the most significant effort of its times by a literary author from the upper classes and castes to imagine and portray changes in mindset and social space in a space drastically different from his own. We have had to wait for Mahasweta Devi until anything else quite like this to have emerged. From such a novel we might learn the value of continuing to work on that interface in the drastically different circumstances of the present, experiencing our reading of Tarashankar as a singular site at which aesthetic pleasures and ethico-political imperatives coexist in productive unease.

A note on my translation of the title *Hansuli Banker Upakatha*: I chose to translate the Bengali word '*baank*' as 'turn' rather than the more obvious 'bend' for several reasons. First, it was an aesthetic or poetic decision: 'turn' has a less clumsy and more alliterative relation to the other words in the translated title. This alliteration is an attempt to mime a translation of the 'a' assonances in the Bengali name of the novel. Second, and perhaps more controversially, the word 'turn' begins to suggest for the reader not only the sinuosity of the river that defines the novel's geography, but also the twists and turns of the narrative itself and its final Moebius-strip-like turn into a gift from the Kahar tale-teller. Finally, 'turn' in English hints at the work of tropes and figures that comprises the textuality of the novel itself.

A BOOK I COULD NOT
STOP READING

K.M. Munshi's *Gujarat No Nath*

MEGHNAD DESAI

I began to read at the age of three or maybe earlier, since I don't have any memory of a time when I could not read. I read whatever came to hand and in my family no one restricted my reading activity – till I came across Kanaiyalal Munshi's great novel *Gujarat No Nath* (*The Master of Gujarat*). It was published in 1920 and by the time I must have come across it at the age of six or so, it was already in its tenth reprint. I was fascinated. I needed to read it again and again. I would finish it and then go back to the beginning and start all over again. My father finally had to forbid me from reading it any more. I had read the novel about thirty times by then.

It is not a children's story though it is full of adventure. Munshi was often accused of copying Alexandre Dumas. After a while, he said he did admire Dumas and found him a good model but had not plagiarized his work. He was more like Walter Scott, in that he invented an entire history and tradition from a few scraps of information. For Gujaratis who are not known to be militaristic and have few soldiers in their pantheon of heroes, Munshi provided swashbuckling heroes and made the small-time kings of medieval Gujarat larger than life. At last we had heroes to emulate, heroes who fought battles and rode horses and camels through long stretches of Gujarat now relabelled in a Sanskritic manner — Broach/ Bharuch became Bhrigukatcch, Ahmedabad is Karnavati and Khambhat (Cambay) was Stambhatirth.

Gujarat No Nath is the second novel of a trilogy, the first of which was *Patan Ni Prabhuta (The Dominance over Patan)* and the last was *Rajadhiraj (King of Kings)*. But the other two pale beside the middle one. They all related to the career of Siddharaj Jaisingh, the king of Patan, in the late eleventh–early twelfth century. Patan is besieged by crises. The child king, who succeeds his father Karnadeva, is challenged by his cousins and other lords who had pledged allegiance to his father. His mother Minal* takes him away and after some adventures in which his minister Munjal, who is hinted to be a secret but platonic lover of Minal, plays a pivotal part, restores him to the throne. That is the plot of the first novel of the trilogy.

Gujarat No Nath starts at a time when Patan is again about to be attacked by the king of Malwa. The young king and Munjal (his Richelieu), are away on a trip to Kashi. Patan shuts its gates at sunset in fear of the likely attack. Then on a cold night, with refugees waiting on the wrong bank of River Saraswati, a soldier

---

* Mrinalla, a Karnatak princess, but in this one instance her name was de-Sanskritized. She was a fascinating figure, a subject of many Gujarati novels, one of which, *Rajkanya* by Dhumketu, was made into a film (without attribution to the author) by Vijay Bhatt. *Patrani*, starring Vyjayanthimala and Pradeep Kumar, was a flop despite the brilliant music of Shankar Jaikishan.

arrives post-haste on his camel. He brings good news of urgent military help. His master Tribhuvan, the king's cousin, is marching to Patan with an army. He needs to give this news urgently to the king. Kak, as the soldier is called, is our hero. He is a poor young Brahmin with little or no education, but brave and valiant in battle. He meets another young man who is at ease with being left on the wrong side and who is sceptical of the power of the king Kak has come to help. Krishnadev and Kak become friends. As they talk and as Krishnadev deplores the state of Patan, they (and we readers) don't know that overhearing them are Siddharaj and Munjal, who hasten back and wait incognito along with the others to cross the river when the gates open the next morning.

What follows is a fascinating romantic story. Krishnadev is in disguise. He is the prince of Junagadh, a nearby Saurashtra kingdom. He is well known in popular legend as Khengar (Kshemraj), who steals Siddharaj's beloved Ranakdevi. She marries Khengar, and when he dies fighting Siddharaj (in the final novel) she commits sati rather than marry her old lover Siddharaj. This well-known folk story is woven into the trilogy. In *Gujarat No Nath*, we are told the story of how Khengar/Krishnadev stole the king's beloved. It is later in the novel, when Kak has to take a secret billet-doux to Ranak on behalf of the king. He has to seek Krishnadev's help as he is under some vigilante threat. It is thus that Krishnadev finds out that the woman whom he is giving a message to is not Kak's beloved but the king's. This then will be his mode of attack on Siddharaj.

But that is not the main story. With Siddharaj back and Tribhuvan at his side, the threat of attack disappears. There is truce between Malwa and Patan. Tribhuvan and his wife Kashmira are a dazzling, glamorous pair almost like Lancelot and Guinevere in Camelot. Kak is now part of the king's retinue. Kak is tasked to check out rumours that Udayan (Uda) Mehta, the local chief of Khambhat, has been unjust and unfair to his people, especially the local Muslims. It is when he is there that he meets and rescues Manjari, the beautiful but fiery daughter of a Brahmin priest, well versed in Sanskrit. She is grateful for her rescue but cannot respect Kak when she finds out that he cannot appreciate or even understand Sanskrit poetry, which she joyfully recites when she sees a river flowing. Kak is duly humbled, but captivated by her.

But there are complications. Uda Mehta is also after Manjari whose poor family had been pressed into offering Manjari to Uda Mehta. Back in Patan, Manjari knows this and so does Kak. Kashmira, his master's wife, arranges a quick marriage between Kak and Manjari though Manjari is not sure Kak deserves her. But then Uda abducts Manjari and imprisons her in an intricate system of underground rooms hidden around a deep well. There is yet another young man who catches Munjal's eye. He is Kirtidev, the deputy of Ubak, the Malwa general. Kirtidev is also imprisoned by Munjal as he suspects his motives. Manjari and Kirtidev find themselves in different rooms. They communicate in Sanskrit, composing suitable shlokas, which tell each other who they are. It is when Manjari hesitatingly tells Kirtidev that she is married to Kak that she is astonished. Kirtidev thinks the world of Kak, his bravery, his sagacity, etc. Manjari's heart is penetrated for the first time.

When rescuers come in the shape of Kak and Tribhuvan, they find Munjal in their path. But by then Kak can reveal the real dark secret of Munjal's life. Kirtidev is his long-lost son whose mother suffered neglect at Munjal's hands. Manjari is happy to be reunited with Kak in what is as yet an unconsummated marriage. Uda Mehta's atrocities are exposed and he is punished at the great durbar Siddharaj holds. Kak is rewarded and promoted.

Yet Manjari is not happy. Kak is still too fearful of approaching her to assert his conjugal rights. On her marriage, she had extracted from Kak a promise that he will take her to her grandfather's home

in Junagadh. To her disappointment, he means to fulfil his promise.
Off they go. Along the way they also witness Krishnadev's real self
as Khengar. He has to visit his dying father King Navghan. The king
had been humiliated by Siddharaj in a battle in which Kak had
helped. Now, as he lies dying, Navghan asks his sons to avenge his
defeat and humiliation. Khengar agrees to do it. It is as part of this
that he steals Ranak. But it is along the journey that Kak finally
fathoms that the beautiful, haughty Manjari is now in love with
him. She is pining while he is cool. She finally has to practically kick
him into responding to her eager heart. On a lonely mountain trail
on a moonlit night, the couple have their honeymoon. The novel
ends with a lovely chapter: 'What did the dawn (Usha) see?' It is
about the couple Kak and Manjari entwined around each other,
now openly and madly in love.

Munshi captured the reading public in Gujarati for three to four
generations. *Gujarat No Nath* has an intricately constructed plot
with many surprises, such as the relationship between Kirtidev and
Munjal, the complex course of the love of Manjari for Kak, the
heart-rending love of Munjal for Minal which must remain chaste
as conventions demand, the adroit way in which the romance of
Ranak and Khengar is constructed as a side show in Kak's story. For
us Gujaratis, this was high adventure romanticized and it gave us
pride while entertaining us.

I had the time of my life reading and rereading *Gujarat No Nath*.

SULTAN OF THE BLUE LIGHT

Vaikkom Muhammad Basheer's
Poovan Banana and Other Stories

KALA KRISHNAN RAMESH

Basheer is one of the most fascinating, eccentric and charming characters in Malayalam literature and without doubt one of its best storytellers. His biography is a gripping tale of the unpredictability and instability as well as the rewards of the writerly life. In this tale, Basheer is always the quintessential author: perpetually engaged in making up stories, dressing up characters and always – as we've seen from his life – with one foot in fiction.

It's difficult to pick out one or two pieces of fiction as Basheer's best; indeed, it is even difficult to actually be able to say that his stories are his best fiction, because his letters and non-fiction writing (and his life) are also great stories! For the purposes of this collection, however, I'm looking at *Poovan Banana and Other Stories* (1994 translation) which has some of his most remarkable stories: 'The Blue Light', 'The World-Renowned Nose', 'Walls', 'Elephant Wool', 'The Love Letter', etc.

'The Blue Light' is one of my favourites; it is a wonderful little story that Basheer later turned into a screenplay, for what is regarded as the first Malayalam horror film – *Bhargavi Nilayam*. When the story opens, a writer has just moved into a charming old house, which he is surprised to find lying vacant, till he discovers that it is haunted by the ghost of a woman who jumped in a well and died after being cheated in love. The story's movement comes from the writer's relationship with the ghost; he begins by looking into the well and requesting her to leave him alone as he means no harm, but this soon becomes a daily ritual with him regarding her as a co-occupant of the house and talking to her about whatever's happening to him: the music he's listening to, his writing, his life, what he's thinking, feeling, where he's going, what he's going to do, and he also talks to her about the few details that he has of her life and death. This sets up a double movement between the real writer, Basheer and his engagement with the characters in 'The Blue Light' and the fictional writer in 'The Blue Light' and his engagement with the character of the dead woman, now a ghost. At the story's close, the writer has gone out to get kerosene to refill the dying lantern and continue writing, and when he returns, he is filled with an unaccountable sadness, and opens the door to the room he had left in darkness and finds it filled by a blue light: 'The entire room and its white walls were illuminated with a blue light. The light came from the lamp . . . two inches of blue flame . . . I stood there struck with amazement. Who had lit the lamp which had gone out for want of kerosene? Where did this blue light come from?'

Where indeed did this blue light come from, if not from the ghost's affirmation of the writer's presence and his writerly occupation, of the power of the word to bridge the apparent chasm between the human condition of the this-worldly writer and the condition of the other-worldly ghost?

Friends of Basheer tell of how he often spoke about his characters as if they came alive to him while he was creating their stories. It was one such account that made me want to reread Basheer. In a Basheer Memorial issue of a Malayalam magazine, a friend of the writer describes how he went to visit Basheer one evening and found him in a thrum of excitement because 'she' had just visited. He was unusually animated as he proceeded to describe her betel-stained lips, her demeanour, her words, etc., and it took a while for the listener to realize that the 'she' in question was a character in the story Basheer was writing!

This is one of the many things that make Vaikkom Muhammad Basheer so fascinating: here is a writer so affected by the fiction that he gave himself up to it, and fed on the life-giving potency of the stories, lived in there as much as outside, where he was the active life-giving creator. Basheer's genius is organic to the fact that he let himself be carried away by and into the fiction, rendering the boundaries between reality and fiction so fluid that at times he was made incapable of distinguishing between the two. There came a time when this condition had to be institutionalized under the containing rubric of mental 'illness'. Twice, Basheer was in mental asylums, though he recovered both times; and one of his most acclaimed and accomplished works – *Paathummayude Aadu* – was written during one such internment. Basheer, popularly referred to as the 'sultan of Beypore', was, as they say, 'quite a character' and stories about his eccentricities are as popular as are the ones he authored.

Whatever one writes about Basheer's fiction, one writes with the awareness that he turns the world into a story and inhabits his stories as if they were the world and that making sense of a Basheer story accommodates this constant shift of location between the two.

Basheer often appears to write himself into the stories, making the fiction seem to be an account of a 'personal' experience restructured for the page. It seems as if the world of the fiction corresponds to the world in which the facts of his life exist. Stories like 'The Birthday' and 'The Mother' are filled with details that match known facts about the author's life. In 'The Birthday', which begins with the line 'Inne ente janmadinamaane' (Today is my birthday), the character, a struggling writer who wakes up on his impoverished birthday and spends the day trying to round up money for tea, is also trying to sit down and write the story before it loses its heat, much as we can imagine Basheer doing. 'The Mother' too has details that appear to be identical to Basheer's life's circumstances. This tension between apparent correspondence to the real, lived life of the author and the function of these events/details in the story – as something that serves the semantic and stylistic needs of the story – is a distinct characteristic of Basheer's writing.

As much has been said about the importance of Basheer's stories in the Malayalam literary canon as about the difficulties of translating Basheer and, curiously, similar characteristics appear to be determinants of both positions: language, theme and the implicit complexities of meaning-making in stories in which author identity plays an active and apparently deliberately confusing role.

With Basheer, you can't tell what's coming, his methods are varying; he is unpredictable when it comes to treatment and manner and he cannot be expected to uphold any conventional hierarchies, such as of language and subject matter. With Basheer, even binaries lose their tension and one thing colludes into its opposite: the lofty becomes the base; realism is also a sort of fantasy, or vice versa, as in the story 'The World Famous Nose'. This is the story of a man who has just lost his job as a cook in a household, when his nose, which has grown all the way down to his navel, becomes an object of people's curiosity, preventing the cook from doing his job. After days of hunger and poverty, the cook and his mother accidentally find a means of livelihood when people start offering to pay to view the 'world-famous nose'. 'The income of the long-nosed one grew day by day. Need one say more? In six years the poor cook became a millionaire. He acted in films thrice. What vast audiences were attracted by the technicolour feature film, "The Human Submarine"! Six poets wrote epic poems about the noble qualities of the long-nosed one. Nine well-known writers wrote biographies of the long-nosed one and won wealth and acclaim.' And he goes on in this tone, which is realistically absurd and absurdly realist.

Basheer's ability to be absurd, to talk in lofty terms about what seems to be a ridiculous topic – such as a nose – but to bring into it a certain grandeur, makes it seem as if Basheer is not talking about the nose, or whatever he appears to be describing, but is really talking about the writer's ability to construct an artifice of words, a world in which the words create meaning through the manner itself, in which the meaning is dressed.

In his non-fiction writing as well, in letters and reminiscences, these elements appear in good measure, entertaining but also disorienting the reader enough to blur the lines between fact and fiction. This must be why it was not difficult to turn a couple of his letters into short stories, like 'Ente Nylon Kuda' ('My Nylon Umbrella').

The best of Basheer's fiction seems to affirm the legitimacy of writing and fiction and to underline the impossibility of being able to separate in his stories 'real' from 'fictional', 'realistic' from 'fantastic'. It also reiterates the difficulty, if not impossibility, of the writer being able to extricate himself to a safe distance from the fiction he is creating. For Basheer, life was fiction and fiction was life: his stories used his life, his life was used by his stories; his letters were never realistic, his reminiscences were not factual.

A reading of Basheer can be as frightening as it can be elevating, for reading Basheer is to be intimate with an author who found it unnecessary and beyond him to distinguish between real and make-believe.

It is evidence of the versatility and inventiveness of Basheer's genius that while he gave us stories that are also not stories, he crafted into these very stories a way to read. And this reading sweeps the reader into a topsy-turvy, funny-sad, serious-ludicrous world in which it is difficult to retain a sense of life and of reading and writing as an orderly activity.

THE BOOKER OF BOOKERS AND
A PAIR OF PAJAMAS

Salman Rushdie's *Midnight's Children*

ANIA LOOMBA

It took me a long time to appreciate Salman Rushdie's *Midnight's Children*. Although it was first published in 1980, it was not until nearly fifteen years later that I read it in its entirety. I always felt there was something lacking in me that I could not appreciate a book that is undoubtedly the most celebrated and influential piece of Indian writing in English. It won the Booker Prize and the James Tait Black Prize in 1981, and was judged the best Booker of the last twenty-five years in 1993, and the best Booker of the last forty years in 2008. Marking a dramatic break with the form and content of its predecessors, *Midnight's Children* has become *the* iconic 'post-colonial novel', drawing critical admiration as well as ire for its commentary on post-Independence Indian history, as well as upon the writing and nature of history itself (the 577,000 hits on a Google search go some way towards indicating how widely it is taught and read).

But every time *I* embarked on it, I lost interest midway – my response always reminded me of an anecdote I had read in British critic Graham Hough's book about William Wordsworth. When he was in prison during the Second World War, Hough writes, he tore a copy of Wordsworth's poems in half, and exchanged it for the bottom half of a pair of pajamas; he thought the deal was well worth it. Whereas Hough was making the point that Wordsworth's later poems just didn't have the sparkle of his earlier ones, I wished Rushdie's novels were shorter, crisper; I often felt his brilliance with wordplay ran out of steam after a point. I still think this is the case with many of Rushdie's works, but I changed my mind about *Midnight's Children* when, many years later, I did manage to read it all, and began to appreciate the organic connection between form and content in this sprawling saga of modern India.

The book has been enormously influential in terms of its method of storytelling (often referred to as 'magic realism'), and its innovative language. Rushdie cheekily imports Hindustani words or phrases, or creates new terms by translating them into English, but never glossing them as earlier novels had done, so we have 'funtoosh' (the name of a 1956 movie starring Dev Anand), 'whatsitsname' or 'nakoo'. Rushdie also draws upon geographically, temporally and formally diverse writings – Gunter Grass's *The Tin Drum*, Gabriel Garcia Marquez's *One Hundred Years of Solitude*, Laurence Sterne's eighteenth-century blockbuster *Tristram Shandy*, epic and religious tomes such as the Mahabharata, Ramayana and the Koran, *The Arabian Nights*, as well as earlier experiments in 'Indian English' such as G.V. Desani's *All About H. Hatterr*. But Rushdie also turns to the form and style of newspaper accounts, detective stories and above all Bombay cinema to craft an ambitious, potentially unwieldy, yet tightly constructed narrative.

Midnight's Children tells the story of India's transition from the British Raj and the first thirty-one years of its Independence, ending with the clamping down of Emergency rule by Indira Gandhi. At the same time it questions the assumption that any history can be reliably or objectively captured or narrated. The lineage, birth and life of its central protagonist, Saleem Sinai, become an allegory for political and social developments of the nation. Saleem's birth at midnight on 15 August 1947 (Rushdie himself was born on 19 June that year), plays upon Jawaharlal Nehru's famous declaration on that date that India had finally awakened 'to life' at 'the stroke of the midnight hour'. Saleem is 'mysteriously handcuffed to history, my destinies indissolubly chained to those of my country'. Thus *Midnight's Children* promises to be a *bildungsroman*, a novel that tells the tale of a young hero's growth to maturity and integration into the social or national fabric. But it departs radically from the genre, almost inverting it, for Saleem's growth is a process of emotional and intellectual alienation, as well as a disintegration, both metaphoric and literal. By the end of the novel, on his thirty-first birthday, Saleem is cracking and dying, just as by that time India has become fragmented by partitions – political, linguistic, religious – and regional differences, and distorted by various types of intolerance and bigotry. Saleem's body is a metaphor for India, but somewhat contradictorily: the nation is also represented by a thousand and one children who were born in the same hour as Saleem. By 1957, the book tells us, only 581 (the number of seats in the Indian Parliament) have survived. Their shared hour of birth does not mark them as a unified collectivity, however, and by the end, it is the enmity between Saleem and Shiva, the two children born closest to the exact stroke of midnight, that is the most bitter and devastating.

Thus, *Midnight's Children* grafts *bildungsroman*, family saga and national history upon one another. The story of Saleem's family is also that of the nation, but which nation? India, Pakistan or

Bangladesh? The Aziz/Sinai family spans all three, and thus is, in one sense, larger than the nation. National partitions carve up families, but families also straddle many nations. Bloodlines are not what they seem – Saleem, it turns out, is not the real son of Ameena Sinai, daughter of Aadam Aziz, a Kashmiri doctor with an aristocratic nose and ice-blue eyes, whose early life the book's memorable opening chapters narrate. Nor is Ahmed Sinai, Ameena's husband, Saleem's real father. Saleem's nose and eyes are inherited from William Methwold, a departing British colonial, and his mother is Vanita, the wife of a poor street performer, Wee Willie Winkie. Saleem has been switched at birth with Ameena's real child Shiva, who is brought up by Winkie. This common literary device is turned on its head by Rushdie to show how class and religious identities, which shape the bitter rivalry and political choices of Shiva and Saleem, are a matter of upbringing rather than lineage. Familial, national or racial ideologies are fiction, but are nevertheless enormously powerful: as the narrator puts it, 'Reality can have metaphoric content; that does not make it less real'. When Saleem later falls in love with the Brass Monkey, the Sinais' daughter with whom he has been raised, he explains to her that there is no real incest involved. But he finds that 'although what he was saying was the literal truth, there were other truths which had become more important because they had been sanctified by time, and although there was no need for shame or sorrow, he saw both emotions on her forehead, he smelt them on her skin, and what was worse, he could feel and smell them in and upon himself'.

When the Sinais move to Pakistan, 'the land of the pure', official doctrines of devotion and patriotism ensure that 'purity became our ideal'. The Brass Monkey is transformed from an irreverent Bombay tomboy into Jamila, a decorous burqa-clad singing sensation. Saleem, however, 'was forever tainted with Bombayness, his head was full of all sorts of religions apart from Allah's', but eventually, no individual can resist the power of history. Following a series of catastrophes, Saleem Sinai finally 'learned the arts of submission and did only what was required of him. To sum up, I became a citizen of Pakistan'. Saleem becomes a 'man-dog', a sniffer, who works for an elite unit of the Pakistani army (dubbed CUTIA, Hindi for bitch) to hunt rebels in Bangladesh. Although the novel repeatedly contrasts the richness and diversity of life in Bombay with the claustrophobia of Karachi ('I never forgave Karachi for not being Bombay'), it does not posit such a contrast as emblematic of the two nation states, for 'nobody, no country, has a monopoly for untruth'. If the Pakistani army hunts out Bangladeshi rebels, the Indian forces ensure that the radicals among them are eliminated. If Saleem enables Pakistani repression, Shiva eventually becomes the right-hand man for the repressive Indian state during the Emergency.

The last section of the book bitterly charts the brutality and megalomania of Indira Gandhi's regime; set in the slums of Delhi where Saleem lives in a magicians' ghetto, it moves away from middle- and upper-class lives to reflect on the miseries of the poor, and the utter callousness and indifference of the regime to their well-being. The magicians are all 'Communists, almost to a man' and Saleem begins to lionize their leader Picture Singh and his vision of 'a socialism which owed nothing to foreign influences', but finds that the Reds are racked by internal divisions and dissensions. He marries Parvati, also a street performer, and adopts a child birthed by her but fathered by his arch-enemy Shiva; thus lineages continue to be broken and fractured. Parvati is killed in the levelling of slums led by Shiva, and Saleem ends his days contemplating his distance from Kashmir, the land of his forefathers who are really not his forefathers, as well as musing upon the 'privilege and the curse of midnight's children to be both masters and victims in their times'.

No plot outline can convey the novel's political and philosophical vision, which is embedded in its language and method of narration. Famously, it delights in a mixture of the everyday and the improbable that is often described as 'magic realism' and credited to writers like Marquez and Rushdie himself. So, for example, a character called the Rani of Cooch Naheen, involved in the Indian nationalist movement, begins to 'go white in blotches, a disease which leaked into history and erupted on an enormous scale shortly after Independence'. The Rani diagnoses her illness precisely: 'my skin is the outward expression of the internationalism of my spirit'. Or when the financial assets of Ahmed Sinai are frozen by the government, he says, 'the bastards have shoved my balls in an ice-bucket'. In bed, his wife discovers that this is literally true: 'Oh my goodness, janum, I thought you were just talking dirty but it's true! So cold, Allah, so coooold, like little round cubes of ice.' Rushdie continuously draws the attention of his readers to his method. The allegorical relationship between the Sinai family and history, or Saleem and India, the novel often reminds us, is constructed by Saleem himself, who, like any other individual, often misremembers or is only able to view reality from a particular vantage point. Saleem is often interrupted by Padma, a pickle maker, to whom he is telling his life story at the end of his life. Padma is impatient with Saleem's flights of fancy, digressions, ruminations and self-criticisms; she demands a more linear, conventional narrative that would safely adopt a single vision. Thus readers are constantly asked to think about the differences between various methods of narration, and their implications.

Many critics have interpreted this novel as emblematic of a 'postmodern' philosophy that suggests the impossibility of comprehending reality, and a 'cosmopolitanism' that critiques the post-colonial nation-state from an alien perch in the West and addresses itself to Western readers. In an important essay called

'Imaginary Homelands', Rushdie himself anticipates such critiques, explaining that it was the frustration of trying to recall the Bombay of his childhood from his home in north London that impelled him to confront the necessarily partial nature of memory, to abandon his previously 'Proustian ambition to unlock the gates of lost time', and to acknowledge that 'my India was just that: "my" India, a version and no more than one version of all the hundreds of millions of possible versions'. But he also realized that 'the broken mirror may actually be as valuable as the one which is supposedly unflawed'. As Saleem says to Padma, 'If you're a little uncertain of my reliability, well a little uncertainty is no bad thing. Cocksure men do terrible deeds. Women too.' Saleem's worry about his own possible megalomania, about 'his desperate need to distort everything – to re-write the whole history of my times purely in order to place himself in a central role' is a comment on authoritarian regimes that actually do precisely that. Indeed, Saleem's ultimate act of megalomania may be to imagine that *his* self-identification with the nation has leaked 'through the osmotic tissues of history' into the mind of Indira Gandhi, under whose rule it was declared that 'India is Indira and Indira is India'.

But the novel does not simply celebrate unreliability or partial vision. Aadam Aziz falls in love with Naseem because he has only viewed different parts of her through holes in a sheet; both more than a little disappointed upon coming to know each other as whole beings. Somewhat later, Saleem discovers 'an error' in his earlier narrative: 'The assassination of Mahatma Gandhi occurs, in these pages, on the wrong date. But I cannot say, now, what the actual sequence of events might have been; in my India, Gandhi will continue to die at the wrong time.' In other words, there can never be a 'right' time for Gandhi to have died. The novel's critique of historiography's truth-claims can be seen as giving 'the lie to official facts', which Rushdie has described as necessary function of literature. In this way, *Midnight's Children* actually underscores a commitment to narrating the past: 'for we are a nation of forgetters'. On the question of whether 'those of us who write from outside India' have 'any right to speak at all', Rushdie writes: 'Literature is self-validating. That is to say, a book is not justified by its author's worthiness to write it, but the quality of what has been written.'

Looking back from today's vantage point, it is especially significant that *Midnight's Children* begins in Kashmir, now routinely characterized as the most dangerous place on earth. In Amritsar, caught up in the throes of anti-colonial nationalism, Aadam Aziz tells his wife to 'Forget being a good Kashmiri girl. Start thinking about being a modern Indian woman'. The relationship between these terms – 'Kashmiri' (and indeed others such as 'Naga', 'Mizo', 'tribal', 'Dalit' and so on) on the one hand, and 'Indian' on the other – has become increasingly fraught, scrutinized, debated and in crisis. The failure of the modern Indian state to include large sections of the people in its vision of the future has become increasingly apparent. From this perspective, *Midnight's Children* does not seem a postmodern celebration of hybridity and uncertainty so much as a timely comment on the passing of nationalist certainties, and a warning against the erosion of democratic freedoms in the subcontinent.

While Rushdie did return to some of these themes in later novels such as *Satanic Verses* and especially *The Moor's Last Sigh*, in the last decade he has also become an apologist for the war on terror and the US invasion of Iraq. The scepticism of *Midnight's Children* towards Islamic, Hindu and nationalist pieties, and Rushdie's accompanying remarks on the politics of literature thus mark a moment in his career to which it seems all the more important to return. Today, when India's Muslim population is increasingly targeted by Hindu fundamentalists, I turn to the passages in *Midnight's Children* that deal with the shooting of Mahatma Gandhi. The Muslim Sinai family breathe a sigh of relief as it is discovered that Gandhi's murderer was a Hindu fanatic, for their own lives would have been in danger had the killer turned out to be Muslim. This scene has a different power in post 9/11 United States, where I have, since the bombings of the Twin Towers, regularly taught this novel.

I don't always like Rushdie's writings or agree with his public statements, but the novels I do admire are concerned not only with religious bigotry but with a closing down of debate and discussion that are also possible in societies that like to think of themselves as secular. Today, I would not exchange the last half of *Midnight's Children* for even the top half of a pair of pajamas!

WHEN MARATHI FICTION WAS
CAUGHT NAPPING

Bhalchandra Nemade's *Kosala*

ABHIJEET RANADIVÉ

Kosala's publication in 1963 caused a sensation in Marathi literary circles. Critics were split into two camps, with one side refusing even to call it a novel and the other claiming that it was the greatest event in contemporary Marathi literature. The famous writer P. L. Deshpande was to declare later (in 1974) that by writing it, the young Bhalchandra Nemade 'caught us (the older generation of writers) napping'. Examining how justifiable this claim seems today and how the passage of time has treated *Kosala* will hopefully serve as an appraisal of its claim to greatness.

Kosala's plot can be outlined in a single sentence: Pandurang Sangvikar, an adolescent from a small town, arrives in Pune to enrol as an undergraduate student there; eventually, he goes back home defeated, depressed and disillusioned, to shut himself up from the world, as if in a cocoon. (*Kosala* means cocoon in Marathi.)

The novel uses a first-person narrative. Pandurang's story starts by summarizing his childhood experiences concerning his family and small-town life. The largest part of the novel describes his student life in Pune. This is dominated by descriptions of his college mates, teachers and others. The narrative is peppered by his wry observations about life and human civilization, which turn sombre and even philosophical as the novel's mood changes. The last part of the novel describes Pandurang's life after he is back in his hometown as a dejected good-for-nothing.

Kosala defied many conventions of Marathi novels at the time of its publication. The opening sentences read thus:

I'm Pandurang Sangvikar. Now, for example, I'm twenty-five years old.

Actually, that's all, et cetera, that's worth telling you.

Ill-placed words like 'for example' and 'et cetera' are repeated throughout the initial part of the novel. Taken in the context of the standard Marathi used in literature at that time, this and other aspects of *Kosala*'s language, such as the use of profanities, jarred some readers to the point of seeming shockingly inappropriate. The chatty, fragmented nature of the text and the circumvention of standard punctuation also confounded some critics. Nemade refused to use quotation marks. The fact that rules for standard writing represented the establishment and breaking them was apt in a first-person narrative of someone enraged by the establishment seemed to escape people.

Speech in *Kosala* was revolutionary for another reason: it was realistic to the point of being shocking, since until then, Marathi novels used rather artificial, formal speech. *Kosala*'s imagery also proved powerful. For example: 'yawn-sized paper', 'peanut-sized pleasure', 'metaphor-like Pune' – such usages were unheard of in Marathi literature but aptly depicted Pandurang's sensibility. His narration has an unusual but poignant lyricism:

I decided, I'd tell you everything. Oh yes, I would . . . but I won't just tell you everything. Because even my shirts know it.

Throughout the novel, Nemade defines new and expressive idioms (such as the one with shirts above). *Kosala*'s rejection of conventional narrative created further problems when it was published. At that time, Marathi fiction required a strong plot with a central problem and its denouement. A certain post-Independence idealism further demanded that protagonists be heroes; that is, they should have positive characteristics so that readers could identify with and hopefully look up to them; a good-for-nothing protagonist who resigns himself to a nondescript life was discordant with this. *Kosala*'s dedication — 'To 99 (people) out of 100' — speaks for ordinary people, but the fact that Pandurang hails from a well-to-do farmer family, thus facing no socio-economic inequities or a struggle against social injustice, does not help.

This, however, does not mean that Pandurang faces no struggle; in fact, the nature of his struggle and his futile attempts to get a grip on life elevate the novel above just another rebellious work breaking conventions for the sake of breaking them.

Pandurang is intelligent enough to sense the absurdity of life and sensitive enough to be hurt by it. The initial section shows him describing his father as a harsh, hard-nosed, selfish man oblivious to Pandurang's sensitive character. One paragraph describes a big, prize-winning bull owned by Pandurang's family that other townsfolk find useful (presumably for mating with their cows) and the next describes Pandurang's disgust for his father's big, powerful body (Pandurang finds it 'obscene'). A childhood incident follows, in which Pandurang tries growing some flowers, but his father destroys the flower bed, saying that if bananas were planted instead, they would yield more money. The father is said to be well respected in the town, but is depicted as an insincere person, lying and deceiving others for petty gains. These incidents are used to justify

Pandurang's hatred for his father but they also depict his rage against phoniness, crudeness and insensitivity. Many variations of this theme appear later in the novel, depicting corrupt and cruel people. There is an iconoclasm evident in depicting grown-ups as selfish bullies. Conventionally, respectable father figures were either revered in Marathi literature or they had to have much greater faults to evoke the reader's disgust; adjectives like 'obscene' were sacrilegious for a character like Pandurang's father.

In contrast to this, it is his own sensitive, incorruptible nature that drives Pandurang's rage and makes him cynical but ultimately impotent. A key incident in the initial section of the novel shows Pandurang hunting and killing rats in his attic after some rats kill a baby rabbit that he had brought home as a pet. Pandurang hunts like a madman, in a frenzy driven by the brutal death of his cuddly pet; but it is also obvious that the rats (like the prize bull) are not unlike his father.

Throughout the novel, Nemade shows Pandurang's tenderness in many forms. Weak people, such as Ramee – a spirited, but sickly girl – or a student who gets ragged by mean hostel mates, elicit Pandurang's kindness and empathy. He even feels empathy towards Ramappa, the person in charge of the college canteen, who has most likely misused the canteen funds, putting Pandurang, the acting canteen manager for the year, in a spot by forcing him to beg his father for money: 'I always felt sorry for this pitch-black Ramappa. Love, of a sort. It is my habitude. Immense love for anything.' This rings quite true, since Pandurang seems at his most natural when he is with such people. Going on long walks with friends and getting lost in the hills surrounding his college find him at his happiest; it is the artificial world made by selfish humans where he is a misfit.

One of the most dramatic episodes in the novel describes Pandurang's reaction to news of his sister's death from smallpox at the tender age of five. In passages that have now become legendary in Marathi literature, little details from Pandurang's daily life reflect his loss and depict the absurdity of death. It was a revelation to Marathi readers that acts as simple as Pandurang feeding a stray dog all the milk he has with him could be moving, dramatic constructs reflecting the pointlessness of life.

Some of the most harrowing images of death in the history of the Marathi novel appear in *Kosala*. They create an emotional impact and also give a philosophical disposition to the narrative. Apart from descriptions of Pandurang's sister agonizing from itchy pustules all over her body, or of her eyes going white with smallpox, there are other manifestations of death. A dying cow with a fly-infested hole in its body appears later in the novel:

> How can anyone sleep after realizing how closely death and pain are related? . . . In a way, soul, et cetera, do exist, but basically (metaphysical explanations about life, death, soul, et cetera) should start from the lively eyes of the cow to reach the flies in its wound.

Such surreal imagery was unheard of in 1963.

Pandurang's disrespect for authority, social institutions and norms gives rise to some wry observations in the novel, but these also reflect his rage and frustration. For example,

> A few old men are paid to get together for maintaining the country's accounts et cetera in order (a definition of government).

> It's good that even (good-for-nothing) people like me can find wives. Otherwise, how was one going to win beauties in duels et cetera?

> Find me a wife who will not bear children, et cetera.

> It's just that our ancestors were not destined for impotence.

Hence this birth must be suffered – thanks to our virile fathers.

Pandurang's hatred for his domineering father, for so-called family values (which he finds asphyxiating) and for the hollow patriarchal system are behind this disgust for progeny. This kind of rage against values traditionally considered moral was offensive to some readers and incomprehensible to some renowned critics.

As the novel progresses, Pandurang's natural empathy for the little, unsuccessful people makes the hollowness and the cruelty of all the established, respectable father figures (such as teachers, relatives and other adults) stand out as injustices that make the world so absurd to Pandurang, making him slowly lose his will to live. His yearning for love, truth and beauty ends up making him feel nothing but impotent rage, since he cannot find a world where people can live peacefully by the ideals which, to him, are all that are worth living for. In this respect, Pandurang is like the Byronic anti-hero: intelligent, cynical, flawed and ultimately self-destructive. As perhaps the first alienated protagonist in the Marathi novel, he is closer to Meursault from Camus' *The Outsider*, for whom the inevitability of death makes life absurd. He also resembles the angst-ridden Holden Caulfield from J.D. Salinger's *The Catcher in the Rye* in the way he perceives how 'phony' adults are.

Kosala is also deeply rooted in Indian philosophy, and that is what elevates it above being just a clever imitation of well-known Western alienated protagonists. This makes its appeal universal and not just limited to Marathi readers. Questions about the meaning of life and death are raised throughout the novel. Pandurang's Ajanta visit following his sister's death finds him reminiscing about the Buddha and his outlook on mortality and suffering. Pandurang's all-encompassing compassion can be related to the Bhakti movement or the Mahanubhava tradition. As Pandurang progressively turns inward, the novel turns more philosophical. Here are some examples:

> What is entirely new in this world? . . . Only death is new. It is so fresh and new that its experience destroys the one who experiences it.

> God made a mistake by creating man. Because any man, if he so wishes, is capable of denying the existence of God.

Being a first novel, written in Nemade's early twenties, *Kosala* is not without faults. Despite his rejection of literary conventions, Nemade takes recourse to conventional drama for emotional appeal – while describing the death throes of Pandurang's smallpox-ridden sister, for example. The use of non-standard language in the beginning changes later to a more straightforward narrative without any thematic justification for the same. While the loose structure and the chatty, colloquial style are powerful literary devices that depict Pandurang's cynical, anti-establishment world view as well as his grief and eventual mental collapse, many deviations from standard Marathi do not seem thematically relevant. Such minor lapses do not, however, eclipse the novel's emotional impact.

There are obvious autobiographical references in *Kosala*, so a quick overview of Nemade's life would not be out of place here. Bhalchandra Nemade was born in a village called Sangvi in 1938. (Pandurang's last name 'Sangvikar' means someone whose family hails from Sangvi.) After school, Nemade arrived in Pune and graduated from Fergusson College. Pandurang's college is never named in *Kosala*, but anyone familiar with the premises will be able to identify it as Fergusson College. Nemade went on to earn a master's degree in linguistics and another master's in English literature. The experimentation with form and language in *Kosala* seems deeply rooted in these two fields of his interest.

The lyricism in Kosala betrays the poet in Nemade, so it is no surprise that he wrote poems, which were published in two collections considered seminal in Marathi poetry – *Melody* and *Dekhanee*. *Teeka Swayamvar*, his treatise on literary criticism, received the Sahitya Akademi Award in 1990. He also wrote other novels, the latest of which, *Hindu*, was published in 2010.

One cause of Pandurang's alienation is the difference between the values he holds dear and what he experiences in the changing rural and urban realities as he grows up. Through his fiction and non-fiction, Nemade continued to formalize this concept further into a literary philosophy, known as *Desheevaad* (Nativism).

In his book *Why Read the Classics?*, the renowned writer Italo Calvino has listed a few characteristics of classics, which may prove useful to see whether *Kosala* can claim to be one. For Calvino, a classic is a book that even when being read for the first time gives the sense of rereading something read earlier. Calvino further says that classics come to us bearing the aura of previous interpretations, and trailing behind them are the traces they have left in the cultures through which they have passed.

In *Kosala*'s wake, there is a continuous line of anti-establishment novels written from the perspectives of self-destructive young protagonists who pass cynical judgements on the world around them. This includes the illustrious *Saat Sakkam Trechalis* by Kiran Nagarkar (published in English as *Seven Sixes Are Forty-three*) as well as several more popular novels that tried to imitate *Kosala*'s anti-establishment stand.

Kosala itself has a cult following even today, with people emulating its style of peppering sentences with 'et cetera' and 'for example' on Facebook or on various Marathi Internet forums. Reverent articles and heated discussions between *Kosala*'s fans and detractors can be found on Marathi blogs and forums. The patriarchal and feudal systems that cause Pandurang's frustration and alienation remain strong in India even today, despite many changes in rural and urban life since *Kosala*'s publication. In a world where commercialism is elevated to a philosophy, Pandurang's rage remains pertinent as ever. His observations about the hollowness and futility of our education system are still valid. Therefore, it is no surprise that the novel still strikes a chord among small-town youths and gets regularly listed as a favourite book by sensitive urban people of younger generations. Its popularity and continued relevance seem to have well secured *Kosala*'s place in our literary canon.

RETURN TO A RENEWED TRADITION

Shivaram Karanth's *Marali Mannige*

MRINALINI SEBASTIAN

Long, long ago, a little girl asked her parents why some people who were not wedding guests had come to collect leftover morsels of food from the discarded banana leaves on which the festive meal had been served. It was then that they had given her the Kannada short story 'Hasivu' by Shivarama Karanth. It is a short but gut-wrenching story of a poor, hungry man who was a regular visitor, but never an invited guest, at all festive meals. Annoyed by the constant begging of the poor man for food, the host forces him to eat so much food that he finally collapses and dies at the end of the meal. By making her read this story, her parents had taught her a lesson in questioning received norms and traditions. They had shown her that there was nothing 'normal' or 'natural' about customs and traditions that endorse hierarchies and exclusions in any society. This early introduction to issues of social injustice was an important moment in the life of that girl.

Years later, and after a dissertation on a similar empathetic narration of *Chomana Dudi* (under the guidance of my great teacher and a Karanth scholar, C.N. Ramachandran) and a career in teaching, I know the importance of such literary texts in the lives of ordinary human beings, most of whom become neither politicians nor theoreticians, merely careful and critical readers. Those works of creativity that induce questioning in their readers, listeners and viewers have the power to persuade them to 'unlearn' ways of thinking that they are accustomed to. They have the ability to persuade us never to take for granted the structures and hierarchies in the world around us, a world of which we are an integral part. For those among us whose forebears had suffered at the hands of the landlords and the upper-caste people, a Brahmin author's narration of the story of the Dalits and other marginalized people might appear paternalistic, especially when the movement by the subaltern groups to claim equal citizenship in a democratic nation is stronger than ever, but I would like to recognize the 'Karanth moment' in the history of Kannada literature as an important 'pedagogic' moment in the social and political history of the region. For letting me enter that world, if only as a reader, and for 'sensitizing' me (yes, I'm not afraid of that word) to the hierarchies of our society, I am forever grateful to Karanth, and to those who introduced me to his work.

But it is neither *Chomana Dudi* nor his other writings on the marginalized communities of the society that I wish to give the reader a foretaste of, in this brief introduction. It is the book that is acclaimed as a Kannada classic, a book that has received a lot of critical attention, *Marali Mannige,* that I turn to now. The novel was first published in 1941, but has been subsequently reprinted and translated into many languages. If I were to tell the story in a sentence, it is a book that spans three generations, with the story of the first generation set in the far end of the nineteenth century and that of the third generation in the period of nationalist struggle during the first half of the twentieth century. It is the story of the patriarch Rama Aithal, who is a *Purohit*, the traditional Brahmin who is the chief facilitator in all important rituals connected with births, initiation ceremonies of male children, weddings, deaths, and the ceremonies that mark the deaths and death anniversaries of members of the family in a Brahmin household. He has inherited a piece of ancestral land that is just enough to grow rice and vegetables to sustain his small household of three (the other members being his wife Parothi and his widowed sister Sarasothi). There are no regular labourers tilling his land or harvesting what it yields. It is mostly through the labour of his wife and his sister that the family manages to get food, food that is barely enough to fill the stomachs of three individuals. Or so his wife and sister believe.

In fact, Rama Aithal has managed to save money in the cracks of the walls of his house. We find out later that he has enough money to buy small pieces of land near his property. He can afford to buy a good sari for his second wife (whom he married because Parothi never bore him a child, in spite of the prediction that he would be the father of three children) and has enough money to send his son Laccha (Lakshminarayana) to a neighbouring town to acquire an 'English' education. He hopes that knowledge of English will raise Laccha's chances of becoming an important government officer.

Laccha turns out to be a prodigal son who never returns home. He loses all his money and inherited property, persuades his wife Nagaveni to transfer to his name all the new property that her father-in-law had given her for her own upkeep and that of her son, the younger Rama Aithal, or Ramu. Laccha was never eager to learn the traditional profession that his father had inherited from his forefathers; he was never steady enough to take up even a 'modern' profession, and never willing to stay in one place. He turned out to be an absolute failure in life.

It is the three women in the story, representing two generations, who are as constant as the northern star in their relationship with traditions and the land, which they feel ought to remain with the family. Parothi, who is as surprised as the reader to learn from a conversation between her husband and his friend Sheenu that her husband is going to get married again, her sister-in-law Sarasothi, who is the only woman in the story with the authority to criticize the older Rama Aithal, and the 'educated' Nagaveni, who is an epitome of patience and steadfastness, are the three who make it possible for the men to be what they want to be. They endorse all the dreams of the grandfather, Rama Aithal, give seven times seventy chances to the son Laccha to correct himself (but finally decide not to bother about him), and show great resilience in bringing up young Ramu. The generational differences between the lives of Rama Aithal, Laccha and Ramu do not seem to affect the ideals, the prospects or the goals of the three women, Parothi, Sarasothi and Nagaveni. When Nagaveni returns to the soil, to the land that once belonged to her father-in-law, she also returns to live like her models, Parothi and Sarasothi, frugal and hard-working, never disparaging of physical labour.

In contrast to these ideals of femininity in a society that is rapidly changing, we have the grandson Ramu whose wisdom comes from the fact that he is able to leave the land of his ancestors and live in places as far off as Madras and Bombay. He also receives 'English' education like his father, but is never fooled by the 'evils' of 'modernity' such as betting on race horses, pouring money on women or selling his property for cash. He is a teacher who is also gifted with imagination. He is enthusiastic about transforming traditional ragas into his own musical creations; obsessed about capturing the beauty of the sea in his painting. He is the artist, the future citizen, modern and yet a son of the soil, who knows how to pay attention to the voice of creativity, who never belittles rural life. He has tried out everything and has chosen to go back to the region to which he belongs.

It is in this thick description of a society in transition that we get a glimpse of Karanth's world and his own priorities in life. This novel captures not just the changing realities of the people, their lives and the location, but it also actively constitutes the 'region'. It reflects not just the transformations in the relationship between the owner of the land and the soil, but it also creates an attachment to that land and the region, which cannot be judged merely in terms of pure economics. There is no denying that economics does play a role in this transformation. From being the owners of land that merely sustained their lives, the family of Rama Aithal experience the pleasures of possessing more land, not really necessary for the production of food. It pains them when Laccha, the wayward son, who knows its equity value, converts it into hard cash. They also learn the hard way that land can be turned into cash through its produce – that switching from rice to a cash crop like tobacco could turn land into an investment option, a venture in expanding capital and equity. It is this truth that Ramu, the grandson, finally arrives at. Some of those who possessed the land on long or short leases have no role in this big venture. Or if they do, it is by being at its margins. The ability of the novelist to capture this moment of transformation and to present it quietly and critically is yet another example of his talent. His empathy makes us empathetic in turn, and helps us learn by peering into the world that he constructs. This is a lesson in social history that he welcomes us to view along with him, so that we may unlearn the many things we have taken for granted.

TRANSCENDING BOUNDARIES

Gurdial Singh's *Parsa*

RANA NAYAR

In *Parsa*, Tindi, a low-caste servant, requests his master to tell him an 'interesting story'. On being asked what makes for such a story, Tindi first hesitates and then shoots off a counter question: 'Why are the stories always about kings and princes?' More than a mere rhetorical question, it's the raison d'être of Gurdial Singh's counter narratives. He has consistently and tirelessly tried to put the dispossessed and the dislocated on the central map of his fiction. From a poor, illiterate farmhand to an overburdened rickshaw-puller or a low-caste carpenter, it's always the rawness of human life that strikes a sympathetic chord in him.

Conceived as victims of social and historical tyranny, most of his characters fight back even in the face of imminent defeat. He strongly believes that man's ultimate duty is to fight the tyranny and oppression built into his own situation. This is what often imbues his characters and his novels with a sense of tragic inevitability. And this tragic sense is certainly far more pronounced in his early novels such as *Marhi da Diva* and *Kuwela* than it is in his later works. While Jagsir in *Marhi da Diva* falls prey to the machinations of a beguiling feudal power play, Hira Dei in *Kuwela* stands firm, refusing to cringe before a taboo-ridden society too easily.

However, the heroic or revolutionary potential of his characters began to fully come into play only with the creation of Bishna in *Unhoye* and Moddan in *Adh Chanini Raat*. Unlike Jagsir, both Bishna and Moddan not only refuse to become accomplices in the process of their own marginalization, but also make efforts to rise in revolt against this process. They even go so far as to interrogate the dehumanizing social and legal practices working against them, but stop short of overturning them. It's their lack of self-awareness that ultimately makes failed revolutionaries out of them.

With Parsa, the eponymous hero, a Jat-Brahmin, moves centrestage and the dialectic turns inwards. His consciousness becomes the ultimate battleground. For it is here that social tensions and conflicts wage their most fierce and acute battle. Parsa seeks to overcome the tyranny of caste and class not through exclusion or rejection, but assimilation and inclusion. In his person, all forms of contradictions find a happy resolution. It is in recognition of this fact that *Parsa* (1991) has widely been acclaimed as an important cultural text, a real triumph of Gurdial Singh's lifelong commitment to the art of fiction.

For any writer to make an attempt to reclaim the diverse and complex strands of his cultural memory within the scope of a single work of fiction, with some measure of success, is indeed extremely rare. And if such an example does exist in contemporary Punjabi literature, it is Gurdial Singh's much-celebrated novel *Parsa*.

Almost all his novels are set amidst the shifting contours of the Malwa region – its economic backwardness sometimes obscures

its cultural richness. What is significant is that despite Gurdial
Singh's emphasis upon local colours, sounds and smells, Malwa
manages to become, in his fiction, a microcosm of the world within
which a larger drama of human existence plays itself out.

Gurdial Singh was born on 10 January 1933 in Bhaini Fateh, a
village near Jaito in Faridkot district, Punjab. His father was a
carpenter and blacksmith who crafted wheels for bullock carts.
When his parents refused to fund his education beyond
matriculation, he decided to be his own mentor. He slowly toiled
his way up from the position of a JBT (junior basic training) teacher
to a school lecturer, from there to a college lecturer, and ultimately,
a professor at the Regional Centre of Punjabi University. This is a
saga of courage, a profile in patience and gritty determination,
which reads more like a work of fiction in progress. As one of the
most illustrious exponents of Punjabi language and culture, he has
served its cause for well over four decades now.

Most of his stories were published in *Preetlarhi*, edited by the
redoubtable Gurbaksh Singh, the eminent Punjabi novelist and
short story writer. Singh tasted success as a novelist when he
published his first major, path-breaking work, *Marhi da Diva*, in
1964. Translated into English as *The Last Flicker* (published by Sahitya
Akademi in 1991), it was hailed as a modern classic soon after it
appeared in print. The significance of *Marhi da Diva* lies in the fact
that for the first time ever in the history of Punjabi fiction, a social
and economic outcast made it to the centrestage of fiction.

This early success was followed by equally powerful and
significant works of long fiction such as *Unhoye* (*The Survivors*),
Kuwela (*The Inauspicious Hour*), *Adh Chanini Raat* (*Night of the Half-
Moon*), *Anhe Ghore Da Daan* (*Alms in the Name of a Blind Horse*), *Parsa*
and *Aahan*.

The title *Parsa* reminds us of the mythological character
Parashurama, a Brahmin who declared himself the sworn enemy of

the Kshatriyas and vowed to eliminate all Kshatriyas from the face
of this earth. Why did Singh extend the cultural frame of his novel
beyond history, into the realm of mythology and folklore? To put it
simply, he sets up a frame within which cultural history becomes
not just an alterity, but perhaps the only discourse available within
the novel. Moreover, it has definite implications for his
characterization of Parsa.

Parsa has been conceived of as a complex figure, a product of
both mythology and history, a Brahmin by birth and a landowning
Jat by profession. In fact, it is by invoking this context that Singh
reconstructs a specific notion of the cultural history of Punjab,
within which transgression of caste divisions is as real as the
transgression of the boundaries between discourses. Singh needs
such a framing device to situate or locate his vision of the syncretism
of Punjabi traditions where Hindu, Muslim and Sikh identities are
not constituted separately but are caught up in a melee of time and
history, constantly shaping and reshaping one another.

Singh presents Parsa, the main protagonist, as a witness to the
processes of history as well as an active participant, both as a
worthy inheritor of the cultural memory and tradition, and also its
worst denouncer and critic. This dichotomy is built into the very
conception of Parsa's character and is evident in the way in which
he is located. Singh locates him not in the actual physical, social or
moral space but instead within the plural, folk and amoral cultural
space where rigid caste boundaries are as irrelevant as the material
and historical contingencies of his situation. He manages to establish
the fact that cultural history neither supports nor legitimizes caste
divisions, which in any case have become irrelevant and
unsustainable.

The sociology of such caste distinctions in our contemporary
society, he suggests, is far more complex. As the division of labour
and the principle of specialization have now long ceased to be the

determining factors, there is much greater intra-mobility among
and across different caste formations (both in Indian and Punjabi
situations), though this fact is not widely accepted.

This redefinition of caste boundaries allows Singh to combine in
Parsa's character the proverbial Brahmanical memory – which is
traditionally regarded as the result of the long-established practice
of memorizing the Vedas, but in Parsa's case, the result of his
inheritance of the eclectic folk tradition of Sufism – and the
rebelliousness, non-conformism and the intransigent, self-willed
rigidity inherent in Jat identity.

If Parsa refuses to live by any code other than the one he defines,
it is because he posits himself outside the framework of conventional
social morality. His refusal to accept or honour any social, moral or
religious code testifies to his status as an archetypal rebel, an
eternal outsider who lives life purely on his own terms.

The influence of folk cultures is another aspect of Parsa's character
that deserves closer scrutiny. He has had no formal or informal
education, but the entire folk tradition not only lives inside him but
is also readily available to him. In his moments of intense pain or
joy, Parsa often breaks into snatches of poetry – verses that he has
neither heard nor read. A closer look reveals that the lines he
recites are the eternal words of Farid, Guru Nanak, Bulleh Shah
and Waris Shah, sung in a highly inflected, even conflated style.
Significantly, his attempts at reclaiming cultural memory are
intensely personal as he often improvises on the Sufi songs, the
most precious collective heritage of Punjabis even today.

If there is any creed that Parsa either believes in or subscribes to,
it is the all-embracing mysticism propounded by the Sufis who look
upon both life and death with unconcern, indifference and
detachment. When his wife passes away, Parsa performs her
cremation without any fuss and blatantly refuses to go through
rituals or ceremonies, none of which he personally believes in.

Though he brings up his three sons single-handedly, he neither has great expectations of them nor does he try to control or run their lives in any way. When his elder sons leave him one by one, he simply acquiesces without protest. When his youngest son Basanta joins the Naxalite movement and leaves home, he makes no effort whatsoever to either wean him away or dissuade him. He remains impassive when he gets news of Basanta's death in police custody and goes through all the formalities as if it were someone else's tragedy.

This is not to suggest that in Parsa, Singh has created an emotionally vapid or atrophied character, someone who is reminiscent of Meursault, the indifferent and emotionally detached central character of Albert Camus' *The Outsider*. In contrast, Singh has bestowed this character with a rich array of emotions. Parsa believes in their worthwhile 'investment' and refuses to squander them away. That he is capable of both emotional plenitude and its rich investment is evident from the way in which he takes moral responsibility, initially for Mukhtiar Kaur and then their young son, though he could easily have discarded them both.

His decision to start his life all over again with Savitri and the son he had with Mukhtiar Kaur is testimony to his personal philosophy – that human beings too must seek renewal and reconstruction almost as naturally as nature does. He sees no contradiction between the human and the natural worlds, and his acceptance of life as well as destiny essentially springs from this understanding.

Singh has managed to create a narrative space within which cultural memories/history and/or caste hierarchies can effectively be subjected to a process of renegotiation.

It is important to stress here that Singh's vision in the novel is not located so much in the exclusionary or dominant Hindu view of life, as much as it is within the eclectic and egalitarian notion of Sufi mysticism, popular in folk consciousness. In *Parsa*, he has created a novel that transcends the narrow boundaries of caste and class, the dominant and the marginalized, and the high and the low. The novel moves towards a more integrated vision of human consciousness where dualities of all kinds simply cease to exist.

MOTHER TONGUE SET FREE

Upamanyu Chatterjee's *English, August*

SIDDHARTH CHOWDHURY

When *English, August* was first published in 1988, no one noticed it much in India. To be sure, it got good reviews in the British and Indian press but nobody could have then predicted that within two years of its publication it would become the cultural phenomenon it is now. I bought a Rupa/Faber & Faber paperback for Rs 30 in 1989 and read it in a fevered rush. As soon as I finished the novel, scarcely believing my own eyes, I read it again. It was then taken out of my hands and soon, like a talisman, passed through the hands of my tenth standard classmates in Patna. What added to our pleasure immensely was the fact that Upamanyu Chatterjee was born in Patna in 1959. I would eventually lose that copy in Delhi University in the early 1990s but by that time hundreds of young Bihari boys and girls had read that novel and quite a few of them would eventually become writers. A mortifying thought, no doubt, for the patrician Chatterjee. It is a fantasy of mine that one Sunday morning in the Daryaganj pavement book market that magical copy of the volume will be restored to me.

Close to a quarter-century after its first publication, *English, August* remains as fresh and irreverent as it was when it first came out. An intensely Indian novel that could only have been written in one Indian language: English. In any other Indian language it would be condemned outright for being decadent and pornographic. I can't even begin to think about the kind of outrage that *English, August* would have caused if had been first published in Hindi or Bengali in the deeply clannish and conservative world of bhasa publishing.

Agastya Sen (also known as August) is in his early twenties and is an Indian Administrative Service probationer going through the first year of his training. He is bearded, 'athlete slim', listens to Keith Jarrett, reads Marcus Aurelius and the Gita — 'the mind is restless, O Krishna' — masturbates, and stones on ganja to eliminate his sense of total dislocation. Though not necessarily in that order.

Brought up in upper-middle-class privilege, the son of a governor and now part of the elite IAS (like Chatterjee), one would expect, as would all of middle-class India, that this young man had been set aloft on the wings of angels and is destined to live a charmed life. But no, 'the mind is restless, O Krishna', he is bored. And this novel is about that monumental boredom. For that reason alone it could have been written only in English. In any other Indian language, this would have been a bright-eyed, middle-class chronicle of an earnest young man trying to fight his way through a venal bureaucratic system in socialist India.

In Madna, Agastya finds many educators. There is Srivastav, the collector of Madna, who is fully satisfied with his lot and is probably the most well-adjusted character in the novel and is frankly perplexed as to why such a bright young man like Agastya is such a slacker. That Srivastav is not bothered by the class divide between them also adds to his bourgeois charm. There is Sathe, the joker of Madna, who leads a cynical and stunted existence as a rich man who provides diverting company for Agastya. Shankar, the alcoholic engineer and thumri singer and Agastya's neighbour at the rest house. The Godot-like sarkari artist Tamse, whose monstrosities are strewn all over Madna in the form of paintings and sculptures of Gandhi and is a constant reminder to Agastya of the half-baked nature of provincial critical faculties. In the name of art anything goes in India. And oh yes, there is Dadru the frog, who provides August lessons in transcendental calm. There is also John Avery (and his Indian wife), who wants to locate the exact place where a tiger killed his grandfather, an ICS officer in the Raj, and provides Chatterjee the perfect set piece to send up the Raj nostalgia of the British.

But what Chatterjee sends up endlessly throughout the book is Agastya and thousands of honourable schoolboys like him: their refusal to grow up and face up to the reality of India and their instinctive distaste for it. But as Chatterjee shows, despite their endemic dislocation, these head boys are as Indian as they come.

With *English, August* Upamanyu Chatterjee effected a much needed image makeover for the Indo-Anglian novel and novelist. From a staid tweedy Brahmanical reticence to a full-throttled rude-boy flamboyance. Chatterjee would go on to write far more complex novels like *The Last Burden* and *Weight Loss* in the future and cement his reputation as one of the most fearless and inventive writers of Indian fiction, but it is still *English, August* that makes him a rare phenomenon in the world of Indo-Anglian fiction: a bona fide home-grown rock star; one who is actually read in his own country.

Written with corrosive wit and candour, *English, August* is a social realist novel of the first order. Read it again.

REINVENTING FAMILY MATTERS

Krishna Sobti's
The Heart Has Its Reasons

CHARUMATHI SUPRAJA

Krishna Sobti's *The Heart Has Its Reasons* sets off my deepest doubts
on the Family dancing. Why does this institution use its capacity to
scar people for life more often than prepare or protect them? How
does the nurturing space turn into a cruel, intractable force in
practice? Can't the clay be helped to spin along on the wheel into a
shape it feels within; should it succumb completely to the fingers
guiding it? And where do they stand, who do not have a Family
banner backing them?

Most of the action in Sobti's closely crafted novel takes place at
two ends of Chandni Chowk in Purani Dilli of the 1920s. One site
is noisy, bright and bold while the other is shabby, curtained off and
holds heavy silences.

Haveli Charburzi is filled with people, ancestral wealth, hatred
and pride. The daughters-in-law of the Haveli bow before a diamond-
studded walking stick, originally belonging to Vakil Kripanarayan's

great-grandfather, on all festivals observed by married women. Cheeky children run from one set of rooms to another, spilling secrets in return for *meetha saunf* or *aam paapdi*. Kutumb Pyari, Vakil Kripanarayan's bedecked wife, seethes in this Haveli and demands redress for her husband's betrayal, despite her having produced three sons for the Family. Farashkhana, Vakil Kripanarayan's other establishment, is peeling and dilapidated.

This is where the incomparably beautiful Mehak Bano and her two children, Masooma and Badruddin, live with many questions. Mehak Bano barely refers to her position or the lack of it, as she graciously entertains Vakil Kripanarayan — her mother's erstwhile lawyer — whenever he chooses to visit her here.

Yet, Sobti makes it clear early in the novel that Mehak Bano is no pushover. She gently asks Vakil Kripanarayan the whereabouts of her mother's priceless jewellery and extensive property. She gets a curt reply that the jewellery is very safe in his keeping and that much of the property was sold to fund the court case. Dazzling Mehak Bano is practically invisible in the eyes of 'respectable society' though she is the subject of many whispered conversations. To me, she truly comes to light in Sobti's description of how she views her lover: 'He was not of flesh and bone, just a musty dungeon filled with old court papers and legal information.'

The same lawyerly felicity with argument and tangential sense of justice infuriates Kutumb. When her husband's extramarital relationship is proved beyond doubt by the birth of two children, a raw and raging Kutumb confronts him to be told that 'Society gives this status to men . . . Cursing is useless. Every man has a net in his hand. It is up to him to catch as many as he can with his daring and manliness.' Kutumb receives recurring messages on male privilege from all sides of the Family: accept the situation dignifiedly — there are children from that relationship now; cursing someone day and night is causing your facial skin to sag; he will come back to you when he is ill; what has happened to you is no different from what happens to women in every house. Bauaji, Kutumb's mother-in-law, consoles her Bahuji lovingly and sighs that Kripanarayan is only following in the footsteps of his illustrious forefathers.

So strong is the influence of the forefathers that Vakil Kripanarayan develops his own moral code, as it were, to discriminate between the entitlements of wife and mistress. He repeatedly reminds Kutumb of her privileged position as his wife. He makes love to her, staring with fascination at the sindoor streaking the parting in her hair. He orders her to dress as befits his status, heaps her with gold, even if to buy her silence, and caters to her whims, when he sees fit. He also constantly reminds Mehak Bano that he is obliged to provide only in a limited manner for her and the children. No words of retribution flow out of Mehak Bano's lips but her eyes and gestures shoot many barbs. She is mostly that personification of dignified acceptance that everyone seems to want Kutumb to be. And Mehak Bano is decidedly more popular for it. From Munshiji to Chunna Bua, Vakil Kripanarayan's widowed sister, all favour Mehak Bano.

Chunna's bickering banter with Kutumb is in sharp contrast to her affectionate response to 'Mehak Bhabhi' and her children. As clever as her brother and able to 'endlessly split hairs' like him, as Kutumb grumbles, Chunna claims her space in the story and Haveli as none other. She gets the best set of rooms; refuses to give up her jewellery to her in-laws; will not stay in her room till late morning so those setting out on auspicious duties can be protected from her 'inauspicious' face; knits, sews and sings as she pleases and – worst of all – does not adhere to the dress code for widows.

She decides to get educated further and even to remarry. Chunna is supported in all this by her brother but when she extends her heart and hand to Mehak Bhabhi at her worst moments, the brother feels threatened and tries to block the sisterly synergy.

Sobti's revelation of the way behaviour patterns replicate themselves from one generation to another, especially from mother to daughter and father to son, is riveting. Mehak Bano's daughter Masooma watches her father with guarded eyes and receives or asks for nothing unless Badru, her brother, reminds their father of her existence. She senses the awkward nature of her parents' relationship and their own fragile status, as astutely as Badru denies it. She is the one who loudly points out her father's hypocrisy when the bangle gifted at Badru's birth by Bauaji is later demanded back by Kutumb. Yet, the pull of her youthful desires is too strong for her to refuse the conditional offer of marriage that will sever her connection with her mother forever.

Similarly, Rajjo, Kutumb and Kripanarayan's firstborn, is not unlike his father in his inability to register his mother's anguish. He takes to Badru and draws him, well and truly, into the Haveli's fold.

Sobti's novel, in which every character determines his or her own position, goes far beyond an account of man, woman and mistress. It documents the conflicts and patterns that only families can foster over the years. To me, it speaks of something that has always puzzled me about the human condition — man and woman play with each other's bodies with flair but when it comes to touching each other's spirit, they stumble and bungle about.

Sobti is equidistant from all her characters and treats each one with respect and objectivity, freeing them even of her imagination. I wonder if this is what makes them appear so real. She seems to have grasped a need for 'neutrality' and 'detachment' in the writer's approach through her own life experiences.

Krishna Sobti was twenty-two — a student in Lahore — when her place of birth, Gujrat (West Punjab), suddenly became part of a newly formed country. She happened to be holidaying in Delhi in 1947, when relatives from villages and cities in 'Pakistan' started arriving at her father's house.

This was when Sobti wrote her first 'important' story, 'Sikka Badal Gaya'. The story was based on her maternal grandmother's experience of being 'rescued' from her own Haveli and lands by a Muslim friend who knew that much as she wished, she could not stay on there and be safe. 'We didn't hear from her for months and then got to know that she was in Delhi after having walked for three months with a kafila or caravan of people.' '*Thande dimag se* (with a cool, calm mind),' she says she wrote the story, though the subject itself was 'too dangerous to be remembered and too difficult to be forgotten', and what they were going through was anything but a phase of calm.

'There was no time to ask why this Partition had happened but I wanted to capture – in text – how it had affected a change in people's perspectives. A political assertion by the leaders changed the lives of the people with such finality' (Hindi Urdu Flagship). When Sobti saw her story published, without a single word altered, in *Prateek*, a prominent magazine of that time, she felt she should take herself seriously as a writer.

During that time, she remembers that a distant uncle arrived alone, looking like his 'own negative'. The unspoken rule in the household was that no questions be asked of those who turned up. He announced that he was going back to the refugee camp and she followed him to the bus stand. She recalls being trapped in 'a voice of hatred' for an instant, when she noticed that there was something wrong with his legs. '"That was the first and last time I lost that neutrality. I was losing my faith in humanity. But then suddenly I got an image of a young girl in my head." This was to become Pasho, the protagonist of *Daar Se Bichhudi*, Sobti's first novel, set in the strife-torn Afghan wars' (*The Hindu*, 27 September 2007).

She went on to write many other novels – *Mitro Marjani*, *Surajmukhi Andhere Ke*, *Zindaginama* (winner of the Sahitya Akademi Award, 1980), *Ai Ladki*, *Hum Hashmat*, *Yaaron KeYaar*, *Teen Pahad*, *Badalon Ke*

Ghere, Sobti Ek Sohbat and *Samay Sargam*. She read English, Hindi and Bangla writers.

Her works reflect her interactions with historic events of transition – Partition, Independence, the search for a national identity – as they were happening. Sobti records the human implications and impressions of these events. She brought more to the story by stepping back and giving 'spiritual space' to her characters. Mitro – the protagonist of her second novel – left her 'impressed' by the nature of her language and lack of scruples (www.katha.org).

The writer writes even when not writing, asserts Sobti in an interview (Hindi Urdu Flagship). She holds that the simmering of experiences and responses to life, in the writer's deepest consciousness, is as much a part of the creativity process as the actual writing of the work. A great believer in the freedom principle, she chose not to accept the Padma Bhushan from the Government of India in 2010. She finds it necessary to keep 'a distance from the establishment' (*Indian Express*, 9 February 2010), as a writer needs 'a vast sky' to express herself (*Hindustan Times*, 11 April 2006).

Writing as an 'ardhanarishwar (half man and half woman) of sorts' helps to create more fleshed out male and female characters in a novel, says the author who claims her space and preference to write through the night in her Delhi flat. 'As a writer, sometimes you need isolation; but when you sit down to write at night, the whole world must be with you at your desk' (*Tehelka*, 19 September 2009).

The Heart Has Its Reasons (*Dil-O-Danish* in Hindi, translated by Reema Anand and Meenakshi Swami) is one of Sobti's later novels. Sobti writes that 'it is inspired by Begum Samru ki kothi – an old mansion . . . one of the grandest houses in Old Delhi . . . currently the site of an electrical goods market' (*Outlook*, 15 January 2008).

This novel underlines for me the politics of what many would dismiss as the petty struggles of daily life. It affirms that we all begin our basic education — learning to spar and survive — in the family. Arranging personal relationships in ways that satisfy and secure could go a long way in changing the world, yet, this is a much neglected task. Our feelings and relationships drive and shape us, yet, they are hardly acknowledged.

If we look beyond the babble and strife of human relationships, maybe we will discover that everyone wants the same thing — to love and be loved. Sobti's beautifully detailed book makes me certain that the Family needs to be re-imagined and that the writer has a crucial role in this process of reinvention.

THE GOSSAIN OF MRITYUNJOY

Birendra Kumar Bhattacharyya's *Mrityunjoy*

MITRA PHUKAN

Birendra Kumar Bhattacharyya (1927–97) is recognized as being one of the stalwarts of Assamese literature. He was prolific as an essayist, novelist and poet, and also as a journalist. As editor of the iconic literary journal of the 1950s, *Ramdhenu*, he was instrumental in shaping the contours of Assamese literature of the time. Indeed, he is credited with having shaped an era in Assamese literature, which is today named the 'Ramdhenu' era. Recipient of numerous awards and honours, his novel *Mrityunjoy* was awarded the Jnanpith Award. Before this, another novel, *Yaruingam*, a path-breaking tale set in the Naga Hills during and just after the Second World War, was awarded the Sahitya Akademi Award in 1961.

Most of his novels are based on the complexities of political issues of the time, but they are leavened with his deeply humanistic and compassionate approach. His characters, though often flawed, display a lifelike complexity that is bathed in the author's humanism.

His work rises above politics to show the joy, pathos, sorrow and wonder of the human condition.

Mrityunjoy (Conquering Death) was first published in 1970. Based on a true incident, the novel is set in the 1940s in the sleepy Nowgong district of Assam. The freedom movement provides the riveting backdrop to the story.

After the arrest of many of the main leaders of the Congress subsequent to the Quit India movement, there was a violent upsurge throughout the country. This was expressed in all kinds of guerrilla activities, which included sabotage.

Mrityunjoy explores the various strands that were part of the nationalist movement. The plot details the derailment of a train carrying imperialist soldiers. The narrative is straightforward and linear. The clarity with which the story is told brings into relief the complexities of the motives of the main characters. Indeed, it is the interplay of the motivational forces of these people who are behind a violent act within the broader canvas of a non-violent movement that gives the story its tautness and its philosophical edge. As the group moves ahead with its plans, the growing camaraderie and feelings of kinship between the various members are sensitively shown, in contrast to the dehumanization of their minds as they plot the terrorist act.

Paradoxically, the leader of this sabotage is the anointed head of a Sattra, a Vaishnavite monastery, who joins the freedom struggle as a Congressman and a Gandhian. The pure devotion and peaceful beauty of his religious background are in sharp contrast to the violence of the act that is central to the story. His beliefs as a Gandhian are gradually pushed into the background as he plans the execution of the horrendous deed.

His followers are a diverse group of people, with their own personal and political motives. The reasons for a Sattradhikar's taking to violence as a means to attain freedom are sensitively explored. But this journey is not a peaceful one by any means. His is a tortured soul, with the polarities of his beliefs creating a great deal of tension within him, and through him, within the reader. His religious background, coming from a world of effulgent devotion and peaceful surrender of the soul to the Deity, is portrayed in lyrical terms, contrasting with the harshness and cruelty of the violent deed that he has committed himself to. There is also the anguish of the conscientious leader who sees his followers falling prey to bullets. Naturally, he feels responsible for the pain that this causes his followers and their families and loved ones. His own frail body is in any case unequal to the rigours of this kind of harshly demanding physical work.

Mrityunjoy has all the qualities of a great novel. Grippingly plotted, its large cast of characters is well delineated. Even the smaller characters are nuanced and as multidimensional as their role allows them to be. The main characters are highly idealistic, capable of great goodness, but also capable of unspeakable acts of cruelty against fellow humans who are on the other side of the political divide. It is a novel where questions of morality and philosophy are raised, where beliefs are questioned and long-held convictions are shattered. Unlike many contemporary novelists who tend to glorify terrorism at times, the author here quite clearly shows that what is being planned and executed is not an act that can be glorified in any way.

And yet all this is done within the format of the novel, without degenerating even for a moment into preachiness. The style is taut, with the dramatic climax peaking masterfully. The descriptions of the lush land- and riverscape of Assam are beautifully written. The peace of the countryside contrasts sharply with the brutal realism of the aftermath of the terrorist act.

Mrityunjoy is a book that is even more relevant today than when it first came out. It is a book whose thoughts and questionings have had an ever deeper significance in the society in which its author was born. Assam, for the past twenty years, has been torn asunder with violence and conflicts. The incident that forms the core of the novel is now replicated in numerous similar occurrences across the length and breadth of this once peaceful land.

The questions that plague the Gossain (the priest) of *Mrityunjoy*, as he moves away from the luminous tranquillity and peace of his Sattra to the violence of his terrorist act, are even more pertinent today than they were when the book was first published. The 'ends versus means' debate continues to be as important today as it was then. Just as the peace of this verdant land on the banks of the vast Brahmaputra was shattered by that act so many decades ago, bullets continue to rip through the land that yearns for peace till this day.

'WHAT SHALL I DO WITH THE BODY OF THE GOD?'

Mahasweta Devi's *Aranyer Adhikar*

RIMI B. CHATTERJEE

Mahasweta Devi began her writing career in 1956 with a biography of the Rani of Jhansi, followed by her first novel *Nati* (*The Dancer*) in 1957. Her time at Visva-Bharati as a college student sensitized her to the world of tribals in West Bengal and her interest led to a programme of study of and interaction with the tribes that many scholars find hard to sustain. She channelled all this intellectual energy into her stark, terse and incredibly moving stories. She is unique among Bengali writers in her ability to enter into the worlds of others far removed from her own world, and she projects a compelling empathy with people whose culture, language and very existence cling to the edge in every sense. *Aranyer Adhikar* was first serialized in the Bengali journal *Betar Jagat* in 1975, and later published as a book in 1977.

The book is a novelized biography of tribal hero and freedom fighter Birsa Munda, and has never been translated into English, in

spite of it having won the Sahitya Akademi Award in 1979. The
forest tribes of India, particularly the Cheros and the Mundas, have
been a political force in India throughout recorded history. Sher
Khan's entente with the Cheros was instrumental in his campaign
to win Bengal and then Delhi in the sixteenth century. During
British times the Santal Parganas were officially 'subdued' in 1765,
and soon after, the forest tribes began a 'hul' or rebellion against
foreign rule, of which they had a particularly intimate understanding
because of the activities of European Evangelists. The bloodiest and
most widespread of these revolts was the Santal Hul of 1855, led by
two brothers of the Murmu sub-tribe. Around the time of Birsa
Munda's birth in 1875, the Kherwar movement was active; its
followers are the 'sardars' referred to in *Aranyer Adhikar*. Birsa
himself called his movement the 'Ulgulan', which climaxed in
1899 with a pitched battle with the British in which roughly 460
Mundas, including Birsa himself, were captured. Some months
later, while the show trial was still on, Birsa Munda died in jail in
June 1900, and his body was cremated with suspicious haste.

Mahasweta Devi chooses the moment of Birsa's death to open
the story. We are thrown without ceremony into the scene of his
last moments in the jail cell in Ranchi. Birsa is unconscious but he
seems to be able to see the whole panorama of the Mundas' past,
present and future. As he lies dying, we hear the Munda prisoners
singing a song mourning him. The British Superintendent Anderson
is in a tearing hurry to complete the formalities of his death, and he
has an exchange with the Dom of the post-mortem room that is
almost stichomythic in its terseness:

(Dom): What shall I do with him?
(Anderson): Who?
(Dom): The god.
(Anderson): The god? Is he your god? Are you a Munda?

(Dom): No.

(Anderson): Then don't call him god.

(Dom): Very well, huzoor, I shall not call him god.

(Anderson): Good. What did you want to know?

(Dom): What shall I do with the god?

(Anderson): Shut up!

(Dom): Yes sir.

(Anderson): Speak properly.

(Dom): What shall I do with the body of the god?

This repetitive, incantatory kind of speech recurs throughout the book, giving it the elegance and inexorableness of a Greek tragedy. All that is left to the oppressed is this kind of dumb defiance. Defiance of another sort comes from the 'Deputy Babu' Amulya Roy, who carries out his orders to the letter, but in fact has a history of his own: he was Birsa's classmate at the mission, where Birsa predicted he would become a 'diku' or 'outsider', in other words an enemy of the Mundas. Amulya informs Birsa of the government's plans, in effect spying for him, but is unable to save him. The scene then shifts to Birsa's fellow Munda prisoners captured during the Ulgulan. As they mourn their 'Dharti Aba', their earth father, they retell the events of his life as they wonder what their own future holds.

Through their sometimes disjointed recounting, we unravel the events of his tragically short life. Ironically, through their retelling, we see that Birsa was anything but a god. In fact, his calling himself the 'son of god' seems to have been the result of his study of the revolutionary implications of Jesus, a fact reflected in the reluctance of the British doctor to declare him insane on the grounds of his claim to 'divinity'. Many tribals considered themselves to be both Christians and adherents of the tribal religion. Mahasweta Devi also gives another explanation: when Birsa is under trial at the

Khunti court, she shows a deputation of Mundas coming to petition Deputy Commissioner Gordon for permission to see their 'god'. When Gordon denies that Birsa is a god, the assembled Mundas tell him that ever since Birsa has been put on trial, they have fasted, abstained from all pleasures, and that they must die or live with him. This is what is adduced as evidence of his godhead: their devotion. They further clarify that he is their 'guru, god and leader'. Thus, as is often the case in small, close-knit societies, the religious, political and personal charisma of the hero is bundled up in a single category.

There is another story involved in this book: that of Kumar Suresh Singh, the anthropologist whom Mahasweta Devi acknowledges in the introduction. Singh's beautiful account of how he heard some Mundas singing about the Ulgulan, leading him to rediscover Birsa Munda for the world, is told in his book *The Dust Storm and the Hanging Mist: A Study of Birsa Munda and His Movement in Chhotanagpur, 1874–1901*.

Birsa Munda was, as Mahasweta Devi says in her introduction to the 2009 edition, a 'modern man', a concept so removed from Munda experience that Birsa's exploits seemed supernatural to them. But we, the educated readers, read his story very differently. In a practical sense, Birsa Munda was modern because by the standards of the Mundas he was educated: he had been to primary school under Joypal Nag, and later he studied at the mission school in Chaibasa. Birsa was, however, one of those rare minds that need only a very superficial exposure to anything in order to understand it down to its roots. Mahasweta Devi shows us how his brush with education radicalizes him further, because he comes to understand how society conspires to rob his community of everything they have. For Birsa, as for all the Mundas, the fight for freedom was not just about freedom from the British: it was, and is, the dikus, the moneylenders, the landlords, the colliery owners, the hirers of itinerant labour and the corrupt petty officials who were and are their oppressors.

Mahasweta Devi shows how Birsa's early radicalism is influenced by his interaction with the forest, when as a child he works as a goatherd, a job he did very badly, since he was continually distracted by his own thoughts and his burgeoning understanding of the forest and the Mundas' reliance on it. As he grows older, he begins to experience and comprehend the many forces that are conspiring to deny the forest and its rights to him and his people, in effect denying them their very existence. In tandem with this knowledge, his anger grows. He speaks of it, and all the tribals who hear him feel its echo in their hearts. In a short while he becomes a charismatic leader, and the government reacts by jailing him in 1895, then releasing him. His response is to begin the Ulgulan in full force, and the Mundas start agitating for their rights. Reprisals begin, the army raids the Munda villages, and from this point on Birsa's fate is more or less sealed. In spite of the efforts of Barrister Jacob to have the flimsy and incoherent case against him and his followers dismissed, it is clear that the animosity of the British government will find a way to finish him off. Birsa's death is thus brought about by his innocence: there is no other way the rulers can defeat him.

One is left with a sense of cold anger after reading this story, and not just against Birsa's killers. It is a fact that most histories of the Indian freedom struggle usually ignore the long record of tribal resistance to foreign rule, or ghettoize it in a separate chapter as if it were different from the predominantly urban, middle-class and mainstream freedom movements that got better press and thus more safeguards for their leaders. This is consonant with mainstream India's continuing indifference to the concerns and problems of the tribals, who are still seen as a 'law and order' problem or at best an inconvenient anachronism, and whose rights to the forest are threatened on the one hand by draconian laws governing 'reserved

forests' and on the other by corrupt mafias and corporations who
wish to exploit the rich natural resources of their homelands.
Mahasweta Devi's book is an attempt to redress this injustice, and
to bring Birsa's life and work to a larger audience.

MY FATHER AS A READER:
IN PRAISE OF DISINTERESTED
LOVE

V.S. Naipaul's *A House for Mr Biswas*

PADMAJA CHALLAKERE

'Mohun,' Seth said at last . . . 'you been eating well?'
Mr Biswas thought about the miserable meals, the risings of his belly,
the cravings which were never satisfied.
'Yes, I been eating well.'
'You know who provide all the food you been eating.'
Mr Biswas didn't answer.

—V.S. Naipaul,
A House for Mr Biswas

And there lay the essential differences between reading and rereading
. . . The former had more velocity; the latter had more depth. The
former shut out the world in order to focus on the story; the latter

*dragged in the world in order to assess the story. The former was more
fun; the latter was more cynical. But what was remarkable about the
latter was that it contained the former: even while, as with the upper
half of a set of bifocals, I saw the book through the complicating lens of
adulthood.*

—Anne Fadiman,
Rereadings

Rereading Naipaul's autobiographical novel *A House for Mr Biswas*
(1961) through what Fadiman calls 'the complicating lens of
adulthood' brought my father's spirit closer to me. The book
turned into a looking glass. In its clear depths, I saw my father's
kind, world-absorbing eyes and their weariness, felt in my nerves
his fastidiousness and horror of vulgarity, and smiled at the memory
of his quick recognitions and shatteringly precise observations. The
mirror did not hide his distress or his melancholy or his fears or his
struggles and fragility but, oddly enough, these memories did not
bring on hot tears; they consoled me. The book filled the gaps in
what had been incomplete, leading me to understand and reimagine
what was painful. I laughed hard at Mr Biswas's scathing remarks as
I recalled my father's mordant humour and his many irritations
with middle-class posturing.

There is a moment in Naipaul's novel when a heedless, snobbish
doctor has rudely certified Mr Biswas's mother's death. This is the
final blow to a woman who has suffered all her life and Mr Biswas
grieves, refusing to go to work, and sits on the bed, writing letter
after letter to the doctor, which he keeps tearing up. Finally he
seeks young Anand's help, and together they collect the most
telling quotes from *Measure for Measure*, the New Testament and the

Gita, which they use in their letter to the doctor, which runs to eight pages. Anand is thrilled to imagine the doctor's reaction when he receives such a letter from the son of a woman who, in his reckoning, 'is a peasant'. This doctor needs to be shaken out of his smugness and Mr Biswas and Anand spend a fortnight writing and rewriting this letter till it moves from 'a hysterical and libellous' draft to a 'broad philosophical essay on the nature of man'. I think my father would have understood this perfectly. A new-fangled psychology word like 'over-reaction' would scarcely be conceivable to him!

Rooted in the author's father, Naipaul's autobiographical *A House for Mr Biswas* has long been one of my favourite mega novels; certainly my favourite Naipaul book. It is funnier, finer, more layered and resonant than Naipaul's later fiction to which it is linked, *Enigma of Arrival* and *Half a Life*, and markedly different from Naipaul's non-fiction, whether it is *Area of Darkness*, *In a Free State*, *India: A Wounded Civilization*, *Among the Believers*, *Finding the Center*, *A Way in the World* or *Beyond Belief: Islamic Excursions Among the Converted Peoples*. As Vivian Gornick helpfully explains in *Situation and the Story*, it has crucially to do with the kind of narrative persona that Naipaul is able to pull out of himself in this early novel: 'a narrator who the reader experiences as reliable, the one we can trust will take us on a journey, make the piece arrive, bring us into a clearing where the sense of things is larger than it was before.'

The novel's plangent humour is far richer than those quick comparisons with Dickens suggest, because the descriptions here are not just coldly detached, external or scornful. It seems to me that the novel's quality of attention is more Chekhovian than Dickensian, its humour closer to sadness and disappointment than to unsympathetic satire. Story One is about Mr Biswas's helplessness, entrapment and struggle for self-definition in the Tulsi family. The Tulsi 'joint-family' household, like the Chancery in Dicken's *Bleak*

House, is an institution as much as a domestic space, requiring complete obedience to its norms and protocols. The minute the narrator arrives into the shop-owning Tulsi extended family, an existential alarm sets off inside, and he discovers his need to resist and escape. Shama, one of Mrs Tulsi's daughters, had been the addressee of a half-hearted love letter written by Mr Biswas when he paints a sign for the Tulsi store. Before the week is up, the family blackmails young Mr Biswas into marrying Shama and Mr Biswas feels that he 'had committed himself in every legal and moral way'. Although penniless, Mr Biswas is a Brahmin, and the Tulsis, who are clutching at their Hindu identity in Trinidad, believe they are rescuing him. But Mr Biswas, 'although he has brought with him nothing other than what can fit on a one-inch nail', is different from the other sons-in-law: Govind, the former 'crab-catcher' who industriously transforms himself into a suit-wearing cab driver, and Hari, the dutiful pundit who does all the family pujas.

Mr Biswas's destitution does not make him a 'viable' Tulsi. First, there is the unembarrassed love of reading, and worse, there is his refusal to be responsible or useful. Then there is the ingratitude, and worse, the insults, which Mr Biswas learns to polish into a fine-honed weapon of vengeance. When the Tulsis have had enough of his insults, they send 'Biswas-the paddler', as they call him, to manage a store at Chase, one of the Tulsi estates. The store and his first home away from the Tulsi household is 'a short, narrow room with a rusty galvanized roof that leaks, a concrete floor barely higher than earth'. While the puja ceremony is under way, Mrs Tulsi compliments Mr Biswas on his 'nice bit of property'. Here is a small sample of Mr Biswas's developing skill of the ironic put-down:

When Mrs Tulsi tells him with bright optimism that he does not need another room but can easily make do by 'hanging

some sugar-sacks in the gallery for extra-room,' Mr Biswas
tells her with a dead-pan earnestness, 'Just send me a coal
barrel':

'I don't know why they still building houses . . . Nobody
don't want a house these days. They just want a coal barrel . . .
Whenever a baby born, just get another coal barrel. You
wouldn't see any houses anywhere then. Just a yard with five
or six coal barrels standing up in two or three rows.'

Mr Biswas's satirical salvoes are sharp and scathing. He observes
things and makes poetic associations, and more importantly, he is a
seeker. He knows that while the Tulsi house offers security, he, his
wife Shama and their four children will count for nothing there.
Mr Biswas's struggle is not just a search for shelter or privacy or the
struggle to build a house for his family. Rather, the novel poses the
question of family and designates it as the object of struggle in a
way that is non-Western, in a way that is international rather than
Western cosmopolitan. Mr Biswas is not exactly the alienated
existential hero in the tradition of Camus' 'outsider', turning down
family or fatherhood, but he clearly revolts against (and is revolted
by) the Tulsi family tutelage in worldliness, failing their tests again
and again, almost by instinct. My most intense identification with
the narrator has to do with his struggle to hold his own against the
commercial straitjacket of the Tulsi family on the strength of
something as thin and precarious as his 'love of reading'. To me, it
evokes an entire generation of Indian fathers, or at least people like
my own father, who out of integrity, decency and a sense of
aesthetics, refused the worldly-wise identity on which their very
survival depended. This refusal expressed itself as a sort of crisis of
energy, even a sort of decadence, which refused the sour and harsh
economies of upward mobility. When Mr Biswas sees a beautiful
wooden dollhouse, he spends a week's income to buy it for his

daughter Savi. On another occasion, when the Tulsis relocate to
Shorthills, Mr Biswas thinks he is being worldly-wise when he
steals six oranges from their orchard every morning in the
hope that he can sell them in the city. But he is no match for
the other sons-in-law of the Tulsi family; no match for W.C. Tuttle
who has been felling all the trees as huge trucks arrive daily
from the logging companies. The novel defends Mr Biswas's refusal
to be coerced into the stupidity of such plunder. It is W.C. Tuttle's
new gramophone rather than his sturdy house, Mr Biswas most
envies:

> He had grown to look upon houses as things that concerned
> other people, like churches, butcher's stalls, cricket matches
> and football matches. They had ceased to rouse ambition or
> misery. He had lost the vision of the house.

But like Godot in Beckett's play, Mr Biswas never stops 'waiting'
to build his house, and during this waiting, he learns to read, learns
intimacy and learns to write by taking a correspondence course in
journalism. Financial pressure is his only reality and his four children
are growing up in the folds and pleats of the Tulsi household. There
is nothing he can do about it except teach them whenever he gets a
chance. Seated on his Slumberking bed, surrounded by the pieces
of accumulated furniture, Mr Biswas writes, building the habit of
writing. He gets a job as a reporter for the *Sentinel* where he writes
reports: whimsical, inventive and shocking, while at home he
writes his 'Escape' stories and broods over Anand anxiously as
Anand prepares for the Exhibition exam. Anand has been given
'unlimited credit' at the school canteen and money for 'prunes and
milk' and Shama's accounts are now permanently beyond repair.
Mr Biswas has 800 dollars saved up for the house. And at the end of
his life, the house happens. A solicitor's clerk is able to palm off 'a

jerry-rigged, rickety, uneven, overpriced house in Port of Spain on Mr Biswas. In this house, away from the Tulsi house at last, he dies owing 2000 dollars on the house.' It had looked perfect on that rainy evening but on the very day the family moves in, they are able to see the glaring flaws in it — 'the dangerous staircase and the sagging upstairs' — but they accept the inconveniences and live there. The pathos of the novel inheres in this rescue operation, in the fact that it is an adequate rescue.

In this house, Mr Biswas plants a laburnum tree and writes long letters to Anand, who is at Oxford, and whose letters home are 'gloomy and tinged with a hysteria, which Mr Biswas immediately understood'. I found this book more funny and poignant on rereading: a sympathetic meditation on vitality, humour and the importance of failure. This is the least self-absorbed of Naipaul's books. The world he creates here is not just vivid and satiric but rich in community. The novel poses the question about our social and ethical obligations: 'Why should we care for other people?'

Encoded into the interstices of Story One are the predicaments of Mr Biswas's adversaries: Seth, Mrs Tulsi and Shama, Mr Biswas's wife. Seth, the family insider — the 'loyalist' tough guy with the 'thick, bruised fingers' and hardened palms — does not fare any better than Mr Biswas 'the outsider'. Seth is expendable precisely because he has been such an obedient Tulsi. Mrs Tulsi — Mr Biswas's vampire — entrenched in the Blue Room enjoying everybody's unending attention as she enacts scene after scene of dramatic bodily suffering, is miraculously cured of her fainting spells as soon as she moves away from the Hanuman House. Similarly, within this secret story, the reader sympathizes with Shama's despair over Mr Biswas's unaccommodating nature and is able to see her as someone who supports him intelligently and proportionately; with courage, resilience and humour.

In this age of the rise of money and ugliness when people are 'economically minded' and 'money-smart', the garbage it has produced both commercially and in the life of the mind is terrifying. My memory of that generation of men for whom graciousness was a real word, men who allowed themselves to be taken in by speculators because they were decent and delicate and believed in the beautiful rather than the useful, fills me with affection. Like Mr Biswas, my father was not pragmatic or what these days we call 'a realist'. Mercifully, everything he has taught me came from his impractical side.

THE BOOK OF LAUGHTER AND REMEMBERING

Lummer Dai's *Prithibir Hanhi*

ATREYEE GOHAIN

These people are known to me. But they never approached me; on the contrary I drew close to them. I had no lofty ambitions. My aim was to draw a picture of them, as they are, and they permitted me to do so. I drew the picture — and engraved it in this book.

Lummer Dai sets his novel *Prithibir Hanhi* (1963) or *The Laughter of the Earth* in the world of the Adis, a tribe from Arunachal Pradesh in north-east India. An Adi himself, Dai incorporates the rituals and customs that are such an integral part of Adi culture in his book, with the loving engagement characteristic of the insider. The novel is a repository of information on Adi festivals, weddings, hunt and trade, and has indirect historical value as the picture of an indigenous society prior to urbanization.

In his interest in foregrounding an indigenous culture, Dai is not alone. As early as 1894, Rajanikanta Bordoloi, one of the pioneers of modern Assamese literature, published *Miri Jiyori* (*Daughter of the Miris*), a tragic love story of a young couple which unfolded in a society of Miris or Misings, an ethnic group of Assam. Like Gopinath Bordoloi, Bishnuprasad Rabha, Birendra Kumar Bhattacharya and Medini Choudhury before him, Dai belonged to a tradition of Assamese writing that centred around indigenous characters, allowing the reader rich glimpses into an indigenous way of life. The writer's ethnic identity is only one of the reasons behind the novel's tilt towards ethnography. The other is Dai's language of expression. Though an Arunachali, he wrote in Assamese.

The medium of instruction in Arunachal Pradesh was Assamese for a long time, before a policy change by the Central government replaced it at one stroke with Hindi. Dai belonged to the early generation of Arunachalis who were fluent in Assamese. Besides educated Adi readers, Dai's works were likely to be read by Assamese readers who were not as well versed in Adi culture, and the writer felt keenly the responsibilities of representing his culture truthfully to the latter group of readers. The ethnographic details were necessary to authenticate the fictional world that he created for his readers.

Prithibir Hanhi, says the publisher's blurb, is a 'heart-warming novel based on the lives of a group of young men and women, nourished by the culture of the Adis'. While it is a narrative made up of several smaller, intersecting narratives, *Prithibir Hanhi* is primarily the story of Kardug, the handsome and arrogant son of the most influential man in an Adi village, and a young woman, Gosi. Kardug and Gosi are attracted to each other and Kardug's father decides to get them married. However, Kardug mistakenly suspects Gosi of having an affair with another village youth, Bangkong. Gosi, on the contrary, is only interested in Bangkong as a potential groom for her friend Karpung. Hurt and betrayed, Kardug violently rejects Gosi and decides to break the alliance, without letting on that he has been 'cuckolded'. How he proceeds to execute his plans makes up the rest of the story. On the face of it, this is a simple enough tale of love and heartbreak, but as we read on we find that there is more to Kardug's betrayal than meets the eye. Dai's story takes many an unpredictable turn, the characters driven by passions darker than they first appear.

Prithibir Hanhi negotiates the spaces of ethnography and fiction with poise. The reader is not assaulted by the ethnographic details – these are woven intelligently into the plot. For example, Kardug, tormented by Gosi's supposed infidelity, retreats to the shelter of the *mosup* or the traditional dormitory for village youth, and Dai takes this opportunity to slip across to the reader the importance of the mosup as part of a rite of passage for young Adi men. Kardug recalls: 'Our term as *mosup* young men will end in five years. Younger boys will then become *mosup* young men. We would still be able to sleep in the *mosups*, but will not have the influence of the *mosup* young men.' A deer hunt reveals the innate compassion of Libo, another young man, but it also gives us a glimpse of the deeply masculine and patriarchal Adi society where a man is compelled to hunt and kill if only to reaffirm his masculinity. The *delong* dance – 'a dance performed by men. Its rhythm rises like waves in the bodies of the young men' – provides a lovely and colourful backdrop to the drama ominously unfolding in a corner of the village, where Gosi's secret meeting with Bangkong to persuade him to marry Karpung causes tongues to wag. And the novel's climax takes place in the mosup, in front of the *kebang* or the village council comprising village elders who have judicial responsibilities.

What also helps *Prithibir Hanhi* successfully tread the fine line between fiction and ethnography is a layered plot and thoughtfully conceived characters. Dai is a master storyteller who never allows his reader to settle into an easy complacence, raising expectations only to thwart them. Kardug, in particular, is a triumph in characterization, with motives that are opaque and actions that provide room for endless speculation. Is his interest in Gosi purely carnal? Does he abandon Gosi because he becomes infatuated with her vivacious and spunky friend Liyi? Or is it because his pride makes it difficult for him to retract his judgement on Gosi's (in)fidelity?

The other characters are no less compelling and well fleshed out and it is interesting to see how Dai resists idealizing or stereotyping his Adi characters, flashes of which we see in his preface ('The people in this book are people of the earth. Their laughter is a gift of the earth'). There is Gosi, who balances a trusting innocence with dignified strength; Karpung, who carries her mysterious burden of guilt and shame; and Libo, who is a paradoxical blend of naiveté and wisdom. With Libo, Dai rewrites the stereotype of the simple tribal man, investing the trusting and gullible Libo with moments of introspection that his shrewder brothers lack. ('You know, Kardug, I am Yama. I unjustly killed an animal that, like a child, does not even know what it is to harm. I am Yama himself.') Ironically, Libo is gulled by a fellow Adi. The non-Adi characters in the novel that he meets, like the waiter Ramesh and the ticket checker, treat him with understanding and compassion.

The novel's conclusion, dramatic and open-ended, is of a piece with the narrative. In the final chapter, Liyi takes the measure of the kebang in her fiery indictment of the council ('Why are you so silent? What is the meaning of this silence, this muteness? Is this truth? Is this justice . . . is this called the kebang?') and possibly pays for it with her life when Kardug brutally beats her up. The novel concludes with the line: 'The kebang broke up.' But has justice been done? Does Kardug get his just deserts? Dai is curiously silent on the possibilities.

Throughout the novel, Dai offers a critique of the kebang in the voices of various characters, indicating a society in transition where traditional institutions like the kebang were gradually losing their validity and influence among people. The breaking up of the kebang in the last line may signify its dispersal, but it may also refer to its collapse. The kebang breaks up because it is no longer effective. The laughter of the earth, Dai seems to say, is poignant.

Dai's narration is heartfelt, bordering on the poetic at times. His characters' words thrive on lush natural imagery. 'Now her face lights up,' says Karpung about Gosi, 'never found out when the clouds on her face lifted.' 'She [Oyi] is a star, a twinkling, live star,' Kardug thinks. 'She is the full moon, the full moon glowing with silvery light. She does not weep even if the earth weeps.' (My only quibble about the book is the long bouts of introspection some of the characters are given to, which can be a tad demanding on the reader.)

But there is no denying that this is a novel marked by powerful scenes. A personal favourite is the scene where Kardug callously abandons Libo at the railway station. The impact of the scene is heightened because Dai resorts to showing instead of telling and we are not privy to Kardug's thoughts, to which, in any case, we have had intermittent access. We see Kardug fretting as the time for the train to leave draws closer. The whistle blows, he casts a quick look around and then leaps into the train. The train pulls away just as Libo runs into the station, out of breath. Libo picks up his bags, which Kardug had discarded on the platform, and starts running after the train, his gaze fixed on Kardug's face, pleading with him not to leave him behind. I shared Libo's sense of shock and helplessness as the train chugs away, carrying his only link to home in it, leaving him alone and penniless in an alien city where he does not even speak the language. Such are the touches that set the novel apart. Though set in a distant Arunachali village and written almost half a century ago, *Prithibir Hanhi* retains its freshness for the contemporary reader.

Lummer Dai's literary career spanned a little over forty years. His last novel *Upor Mohol* or *The Top Storey* was published in 2003, a year after his death. A high-ranking bureaucrat, he was also a successful journalist, founding and editing Arunachal Pradesh's first English daily, *Echo of Arunachal*. *Prithibir Hanhi* was one of his earliest novels, published when the writer was in his twenties, and the sparks of brilliance that he showed here would light up his later works like *Kanyar Mulya* or *Bride Price*. Dai's works, including the present novel, gave the marginalized populations voice and visibility; his thoughtful and sensitive representations could foster an understanding of the indigenous people of the hills in the plains of Assam.

LOST LOVES

Amrita Pritam's *Pinjar*

MITA KAPUR

I wondered what it would be like to read Amrita Pritam's work after a gap of twenty-seven years. In college, her poetry had become sustenance. She was what each of us wanted to be — a free spirit with volatile energy that trembled in its own strength, that plunged into romantic depths and quivered to lift itself up. Freedom and creativity, existence and romance, writing and Amrita were one. When I read *Pinjar* again, I found that I felt the same way about her writing. It made me stop and wonder if I had stood still against evolution. Why were my responses the same as they were more than two-and-a-half decades ago?

Twenty-seven years later, each word drips with Amrita's gamut of feelings — love, loss, yearning, regaining and moving on. What she wrote then still reads fresh, still exudes the same vitality — perpetual, relentless and alive. The freedom that Amrita stands for and her inflamed concerns for the societal pressures on a woman's identity strike right through, piercing the consciousness even today.

The story in *Pinjar* (1950) is largely one woman's tale: Pooru. Leading a sheltered life, she is to marry Ram Chand and weaves happy dreams about her future. Rashid, a Muslim out to avenge his family's honour for a misdeed committed by Pooru's forefathers, kidnaps her. Pooru's life fills with hatred and bitterness – once touched by a Muslim, she simply ceases to exist for her parents. There is a continuous stream of the sense of loss in the story, physical loss that makes life a hellhole for Pooru. Rashid marries Pooru and is in love with her but his love remains unreciprocated till the end. Pooru cannot feel any more. Her heart is a vast barren space of nothingness save rancour, which is stifled and can be felt only beneath the skin.

The colour grey dominates *Pinjar*. The cesspool is a symbol of Pooru's life. A sense of foreboding breathes heavily down the reader's neck right from page one. Suppressed aggression takes the overriding tone of the story forward. The baby growing in her womb makes Pooru want to 'pick it out with her nails as if it were a thorn – pluck it off as if it were a maggot or a leech'. Pooru had been plucked out herself from the safe cocoon of her home. This was step one in the process of a woman losing her identity, set against the socio-political milieu of the Hindu-Muslim riots during Partition.

The next step in the continued displacement of her own self is when the name Hamida is tattooed on her arm. The harshness in her mind is startlingly still, stemming from deeply set melancholy. As Pooru harks back to her home, 'Hamida had no tears left in her eyes. She simply held her head between her hands and remained where she was for a long time.' She listens to the songs of revelry at the time of Baisakhi and wonders why they were all in praise of pretty girls when most of the girls faced dismal predicaments like herself – her thoughts run like a social commentary of the times.

Pritam's powers of weaving elements of gross reality that repel and make the heart shudder, go deathly still and pensive, are as pulsating now as they were when I first read *Pinjar*. Pooru in her strongly defined mind cannot bring herself to love her child since he was a human being born not out of love, but force and abduction. Just as natural and instinctive is that one brief moment of rising emotion when she does feel a mother's love for her child, but it is like a flash of lightning. She thinks, 'Men gnaw a woman's body like a dog gnawing a bone . . .' Don't we still face similar reactions when we read of gang rapes or dowry deaths?

Pooru and Hamida live side by side within one body. Love and hate equal conflict. There are other characters in the story, like Kammo, a neighbour's deprived daughter. Pooru almost adopts her and showers her with affection. Kammo blooms under her care but such happiness is not to last in any woman's life. Pritam, the writer, makes sure her women characters remain rooted in the reality of the life they were decreed to live according to the existing patriarchal dictates. Politics and religion are naturally the essential elements in *Pinjar*. Taro is another character that Pritam sketches to reflect on yet another sad subtext of the plunging indignities pushed upon women, which once again invokes the same reaction from the reader — have we really evolved as a society? What is human dignity? Where is the right to freely choose how to live the way we wish to? Taro has the noose of a forced marriage around her neck. She is another *pinjar* — yet another skeleton. The symbolism and imagery remain steadfastly faithful to the grey shades of the story.

The naked insanity of the nameless woman who dies while giving birth to a child under a tree works as a reflection of all social evils — she had lived an undead life, which in some ways Pooru also lives. Which in some ways even Kammo lives. The poignancy floats over and settles like a shroud — they all move like skeletons with a pulse that refuses to let go of them. Pritam's pen persists — tragedy takes on new overtones and roles. Hamida nurtures the motherless newborn, but the interplay of superstition and casteism vomits its wrath – the gurgling baby is taken away from her by the Hindus, only to be returned when he is about to die. Pooru remembers how she was taken away by Rashid, her husband. With the child being returned, was Pritam as a writer being hopeful that there is a chance we may lift ourselves out of our depraved conditions? Yes. Maybe. I don't know.

As riots, violence and displacement strike, Partition is announced in Punjab. Pooru's past revs up again. Lajo, Ram Chand's sister, now also married to Pooru's younger brother, is abducted by a Muslim. Pooru finds Lajo and helps her escape. This is the only part in the story where I felt that Pooru as a woman took a stand. She pretends to be a woman selling durries and through her guile manages to help Lajo escape. She makes sure Lajo does not become another Pooru. That identity and human dignity can be restored offers hope for a woman's life. She reconnects with her past, tears flow as if to drown it away. Pooru's brother hints that this is her last chance to go back to India to her family. But she stays. She accepts her life as the weight of a ton of bricks she must carry.

The prose is as strong as Pritam's spirit as a writer. Pooru is a figure who stands solidly like a rock. Rashid, her husband, obviously loves her while Pooru remains inanimate towards him. She meets Ram Chand but keeps her boundaries, quelling her emotions. The story leaves the reader shaken, questioning, probing, seeking and admitting to hard-hitting truths.

To search for what drove Pritam to write of lost loves and displacement, to find the source of her life force, I picked up the book of letters, *Amrita and Imroz: In the Times of Love and Longing*. They too told a story – in fact many stories. The letters don't follow any rules; they are raw, naked, pulsating expressions of the moment they are being written in. The openly bared honesty brings out the grain of the writer – what went through her mind, her love for her pen, her preoccupation with the social milieu, her surrendering unabashedly to her heart. Her wish to fly untethered and feel the wind beneath her eyelids and how that feeling fuelled her creativity as a poet and a novelist.

A melancholic tone runs through the letters and there seems to be no mention of some of the happy moments spent together – their happiness is always spoken of as a dream they dream of, aspire to and live for. Is pain their only source of energy? There also runs a questioning and bitterness at how society looks upon their relationship – they are not a married couple and the difference in their years is not acceptable so the language accorded to them is 'bitter, sarcastic and scathing'. And as if in answer to this, Pritam writes: 'I crave for you because I discover the meaning of my existence in your creations.'

Beyond her writing, everything else is superficial to Amrita. The woman in Amrita is like a secondary identity. She is first and foremost a writer. But when the woman in her rises, she scales and soars and lashes through the indignities borne by her kind.

When I moved into your bed
I was not alone – there were
two of us
A married woman and a virgin
To sleep with you
I had to offer the virgin in me
I did so
This slaughter is permissible in law
Not the indignity of it
And I bore the onslaught of the insult
The next morning
I looked at my blood stained hands
I washed my hands

But the moment I stood before the mirror
I found her standing there
The one whom I thought I had slaughtered last night
Oh God!
Was it too dark in your bed
I had to kill one and I killed the other?

The writer and the lover in Pritam are inextricable. Her journeys to different countries heighten her writer's instincts and make her travel within. Observing what is around her, she evolves as she reacts to every scenic or social change, grows and reflects deeply. Normality is escapism, to be oneself is the only way to be. She sees perfection as stagnant and cold and progress as moving and palpable — just as her writing is — fluid, oozing universal sensitivity. The poet belongs to every country where there is freedom and to every language that touches the heart. It is evident not just in her poetry but also her short stories and her autobiography, *The Revenue Stamp*. The thought, the feelings, the characters are fresh, multidimensional and alive even today. A little bit of Pritam can be seen in each of the women characters in *Pinjar*.

DICK WANTS (TO BE) CUNT

Charu Nivedita's *Zero Degree*

CHANDRA SIDDAN

Zero Degree is a pool of ejaculate, in which spermatozoa of competing perspectives desperately pullulate and thrash about romancing that glorious egg, your mind. No sooner than a few pages in, the reader is overwhelmed by a sea of words rising neck-deep, higher, through which the writer's head bobs up sputtering more urgent words, endless words, chained close, forming a snake, rather an endless dick, like the one wrapped around the shoulders of one of his characters. Oh, hear that? The dick head is insisting that this book I hold is his ejaculate, his cum, his man juice: a result of masturbation, of copulating with his own shadow. 'Here, smell my word. Can you smell my blood in it? Can you taste it?'

I close my eyes to do justice to his lonely exertions. When I open them he has donned a Helene Cixous mask, intoning: 'Erase the difference between me and you.'

Zero Degree (1998) is a hydra of a novel, each head clamouring its own narrative, fighting against erasure, characters appearing and disappearing at a psychedelic rate, threatening its own boundaries, the patchwork fraying right before your eyes under the stress of its polyphonous ambition. It is perhaps best approached as a cross between a novel, a collection of stories and an epic poem, its thematic range encompassing . . . oh, I hear you groaning 'oh god, epic poem', but trust me, it is one where the fun never stops. It is full of jokes, many pretty macabre. But then the names Charu Nivedita drops should be enough warning: Henry Miller, George Bataille, Kathy Acker (the English translation is dedicated to her), and a number of Latin American authors. Nivedita places himself firmly in the counterculture of the global literary world wearing his pretentions on his sleeve. There, spit on him if you must, and he (or Muniyandi, the closest resemblance to Charu in the book) stands with his mouth open, already spat on by a number of characters.

Here is a book that was written for me: a lady reader! The very first chapter is addressed to me, or you. And we also appear as a character in the book critiquing one of the narrators. It is a dick novel justifying itself to the cunt reader. Let me simplify: in a book that is nearly half the time about itself, a host of narrative masks tell a number of stories in different voices and styles. This master scheme allows the book to rush any subject on earth with the trepidation of a fool, slash at literary nationalisms/parochialisms, grieve at global genocides, muse on the origins of time, space and life, double-back to Tamil soil on why Tamil women have eschewed the sari for the salwar kameez and take recourse to pornographic phone chats.

But amidst newspaper reports, interviews, letters from Rwanda, descriptions of torture sessions in Tamil police stations, recipes for charms, book reviews, film songs and guided instructions for successful masturbation to middle-class women, in Chapter 21, a character, a lady reader (you!) says, 'Just where is this story headed?

A proper story needs characters, and character development!' To which the author, or at least one of them, throws up his hands: 'But who will create them? I live in a godless world. I live in a world full of injustice . . .' and points to baby chicks carried away by kites, male crickets falling dead upon mating, and other such magnitudes. How can he be a god of this world you are complaining about? In fact he is dead. And, as on earth, in this novel chaos reigns.

All the same, there is some overlap and occasional coherence in terms of characters and their stories even if they seem like simple devices to drag you through the textured gunk of (predominantly) Tamil underclass existence. Plots rush along presented in shorthand with nary an attempt at bourgeois, finely crafted good-writing. It is not so much characters that matter here than certain broad thematic concerns which include: women and pain, prostitution, the impotence of writers, the body and its infinite vulnerability to the whole gamut of sensations from orgasm to torture, the abuse of the poor by the poor and those above, the degraded and demoralized body politic, the human impulse to genocides, the expendability of life in nature, all cemented together with a good quantity of smut.

Let us start with the male narrators grabbing each other's pens, bad-mouthing and furiously editing one another: Charu Nivedita, who editorializes; Surya, who editorializes and writes the master narrative (which is apparently a letter to his daughter); Muniyandi, who makes corrections in Surya's notes; Misra, who committed suicide in page 144 of *Existentialism and Fancy Banyan*, an earlier book by Charu Nivedita; and a ghostly 'Ninth Century Dead Brain'. And there are also Fuckrunnisa, an ethereal courtesan; Nina, her daughter who descends from gutter prostitution to marriage rising again to prostitution; Avanthika, Surya's lover; a Rwandan theatre actress and Riyyo and Kiyyo, science fiction authors. Misra's Hindi, Muniyandi's English and Surya's Tamil notes are interpolated by Charu, who invites his lady reader to add to the growing patchwork

of inauthenticities. Surya apologizes to daughter Genesis that the
chapters have got shuffled and that may be because he loves Misra
and hates Muniyandi. It works to read chapters at random. In fact,
this book would make a good interactive, online novel which
infinite number of people could add to and edit. Let's call it 'Zero
Degree Live'. (The Sahitya Akademi should do something about
that.) But it helps for the sake of coherence to see the whole novel
as a letter from Surya to his daughter Genesis, a legacy of an
impoverished self-exiled father to the feminine future.

Initially the narrative is dominated by the degraded state of the
body politic, be it Tamil, Indian, Peruvian or Rwandan. Notes from
Misra's historical novel about the long-standing mutual butchering
of Kasarmenians and Karmenians trails into two streams of narrative:
one a trading of insults between two film actresses and the other a
report on bonded labour. 'When the villagers protest the police are
called, false charges are filed, and the village women are raped. Of
course if I continue to write like this you will call it newspaper
reportage. But you celebrate an American who does the same as a
writer of New Journalism.' This last must be Muniyandi because
another writer (Ninth Century Dead Brain) pipes up to critique
Muniyandi's novel, which celebrates the looting of a textile
showroom in Nagercoil as a modern-day Santal revolution.
'Muniyandi does not seem to grasp the difference between righteous
rebellion and everyday poverty driven crime,' he points out, pitying
the shop owner who is a father of nine and the policeman who died
during the atrocities.

Besides stylistic prestidigitation, what might these constantly
changing masks between the male writers be good for? For ensuring
diversity of voices and opinions, of course, since we also find out in
a third account (by Surya or Charu) that the textile shop owner has
many beedi factories where bonded children work for nine rupees
a day. We are told about the slavish conditions of their work, and
the reasons of their pledging: wedding expenses or temple tourism.

The women's narratives, however, are not mutually competitive — instead they reiterate a relentless history of pain. Some pleasure too, but mainly pain. Let us take Aarthi, for example, Surya's sister, whose ongoing fights with her husband, the unsuccessful pickpocket Kamalnathan and her mother-in-law-cum-aunt, Kamachi. His unrequited love, their poverty and endless fights are only relieved by the kindness of Papamma whose liquor-running business runs dry when prohibition is lifted. Here is a view of poverty sans any fig leaf — poverty not just of money but also of kindness or any liberating vision. A homeless pregnant Aarthi goes looking for her parents, who accept her back, but fights ensue between the families: 'May you be ruined! May your daughter become the whore of this town! May your womb rot', etc. A cure for bourgeois high-mindedness.

It makes sense to see *Zero Degree* as a storming of the Bastille of high-mindedness, particularly Indian high-mindedness, which, you will agree, is pompous to the extreme. It is a fall, an orgiastic descent into base materiality (if I may take recourse to Bataille) of life. The poor, lacking any alibi or pretensions to higher truths and transcendent realities, descend without end, but I must add, without the revolutionary moment anticipated in Bataille, which unleashes the radical expenditure of the poor seizing the wealth of the rich. Is this a deep philosophical flaw of the book *Zero Degree* or a realistic cynicism of the author in the face of the aforementioned demoralization of the body politic? The endless self-parody of the wretched underclass and the lower-middle class, the dehumanization of the poor by poverty and by those above spitting and shitting on those below . . . it is an acknowledgement of the cremation grounds we are on without the call for action. The acknowledged homage to Bataille, in the story where Deepti, a middle-class woman, is seduced and killed by presumably Muniyandi, is definitely problematic. He risks losing his lady readers there most of all . . .

but it is perhaps best to see the provocations rather than the imperfections. This is a dick written book and one where the dicks love the cunts but I am waiting for a cunt written (or a genitally diverse) answer to *Zero Degree*. Let's hope to see a few examples in the next decade!

(Talking of the gendering of authors, when I went to meet Charu Nivedita I was expecting a woman I'd want to snuggle close to, a shoulder to put my head on, a soul sister. The book had just exploded upon my consciousness like an incendiary love letter that had changed everything. I was so excited! But he was a man. I forgave him, though. We whispered of Bataille, Acker, Cixous. He showed me his scar from the rape of the surgeon's knife . . . and I remembered the book itself, a hardening shell of an oozing wound constantly threatening to crack . . . and we melted into a pool of love.)

To celebrate one of the best Bataillian moments in the book, 'the bastard will fall sick excrete deteriorate further when will you die donkey you dirty bitch Mudevi unwashed Mudevi bitch in heat working through the day singing and dancing when he arrives he will start to dance and oh what a dance he'll put her on his head and twirl ecstatic demented frenzy they will melt into each other like sugar cubes what's this? Why did these lines intrude into the story, only to generate confusion? Forget it.' If there is any hope for humanity caught in the nets of misery it is in such eruptions of sex, gesturing towards that ever present zone of sovereignty.

Claiming equal space in the novel, however, is torture. Both men and women undergo a variety of it without any hope of escape from the materiality of existence. Whether it is what the Hutus did to the Tutsis or what the Tamil Nadu police do to comrades in Tamil prisons or events of Avanthika's life that include exorcism through rape, beatings while pregnant and repeated D&Cs.

To pick up Aarthi's story, she succumbs to the love of a neighbour whose upper-caste upper-class family humiliates Aarthi's retired schoolteacher father and drives the family out of town to Aarthi's aunt's village, where her father attempts suicide in shame. 'But, of course, he failed in that too.' Long story short, Aarthi abandons her son and takes to prostitution in Trichy, where she proudly shows family photos to customers. 'Somehow this reached her uncle, who sent rowdies to chase her out of Trichy.' If the story ends there it is not because things reach an unplumbable low – there is no such thing – it is simply because Aarthi has disappeared from the radar of even the most fervent researcher.

The impotent author grieves: 'I was no help to her. How her heart must be grieving, as so many strangers lay their bodies on top of hers.' The impotence of writers and writing is at the heart of *Zero Degree*. Muniyandi is called a eunuch by the fortune-teller's parrot and his manuscripts get pissed on by an angry prostitute. Words disappear at a rapid rate. 'Like ink on blotting paper, the past dissipates from the pages of my memory . . .' Why write then? Why indulge in this cry of protest against history, human nature and nature itself? This scream of anger and despair with nothing to stand on?

The narrators of *Zero Degree* are simply doing what a character called Kottikuppan did while escorting children through the cremation grounds: keeping up a chant of words to keep their existential angst at bay. Perhaps that is why we write and why we read. It is not a luxury, it is a necessity. Ariadne's thread in the labyrinth. These are hasty notes of reminder that we keep writing to remember who we are.

In some accounts Genny, the recipient of this novel-letter, is alive and separated from her father by a cruel mother. In another she is born dead. A father's immeasurable love denied personal expression spends itself on poems, stories and letters. Appropriately, a patchy novel at war with itself precipitates into a shower of poetry, while

the misanthropic Himalayas-headed author doubts everything but
the truth of his love. Daughters have a special place in this book.
Avanthika too says she could not have survived but for her daughter
Nitya. Daughters unlock that wealth of love that makes the
unspeakable horrors of life not only bearable, but necessary to
acknowledge. To echo what was said earlier, it is an abdicating
father's legacy of a violent past to the feminine future.

The novel ends in mid-sentence, almost. Like Fellini's *Satyricon*.
In other words, there is no ending. You can dip in anywhere, read
the chapters at random or backwards, not even finish it, for it will
have done its damage. For a novel this slim it is many novels in one,
sampled in fragments, a shattered sphere, each shard reflecting a
different world, a Borgesian Book of Sand with neither beginning
nor end.

EVOKING A TREASURE

Attia Hosain's
Sunlight on a Broken Column

VIJAY NAIR

'The final test for a novel will be our affection for it, as it is the test of our friends, and of anything else which we cannot define.'

—E.M. Forster

The book was a secret treasure for a long time. Whenever I brought it up with other writers, friends who should have understood my enthusiasm if not my love for the work, I drew a blank. I learnt to be smug about my knowledge of *Sunlight on a Broken Column* by Attia Hosain and enjoy the confusion on the faces of others every time I brought up my favourite novel by an Indian author. It helped that the book was not in print for a long time and I had to request the author's daughter to claim a copy. I had chanced upon the book in a second-hand store in Calcutta many years ago. But in the transit to Bangalore, it mysteriously disappeared.

Ruskin Bond spoilt it for me. When I asked him about his favourite writers in an interview, he mentioned Hosain among a few others. Just as I was recovering from this setback, a friend who had returned from the US after completing her PhD turned indignant when I shared with her how obscure the book seemed to have become in present times. The novel had been part of her research and she provided half a dozen links on the Internet where the book was being discussed. I was told somewhat sternly that the book is a prescribed text for the students of MA in literature at Delhi University. Buoyed by all the renewed interest in the text perhaps, the publishers have reissued the book as a modern classic with a new cover.

Sunlight on a Broken Column, Hosain's first and only novel, was published in 1961, when she was forty-eight years old and living in London. She seems to have carried a remarkable legacy with her to the foreign shores, being the first woman to graduate among the privileged Taluqdar families into which she was born. Other recorded facts about her tell us she was in the thick of the nationalist movement in the pre-Independence era as well as a leading member of the Progressive Writers' Movement that was set up afterwards. Her family was one of the victims of Partition, forced to make the choice that they would rather not have made, like millions of others on either side of the border. The tragedy experienced first-hand is very much part of the novel.

The inspiration for a novel is intrinsically linked to its writer's sense of self. It either derives from what the writer is or it is about the writer. Literature's worst-kept secret is that most first novels are autobiographical. Authors may start by creating a separate reality while attempting works of fiction. At some point of time, however, they begin to draw upon their experiences not just as a spectator or participant, but as a writer.

Laila the protagonist seems to derive from the life as well as the politics of her creator, thereby creating an impression that the work is a fictionalized autobiography. The biographical elements do not in any way impinge on the story. On the contrary, elements of her own life that Hosain may have chosen to bring to the novel add to its accessibility and historical significance. The familiarity she had with the context plays a significant part in making real the turbulence against which the story unfolds.

The work is suffused with romance although to cubbyhole it in that genre would be grossly unfair. In recording the triumphs and travails of one feudal family, the novel acts as a mirror to the social and political upheavals of an entire country. Laila grows up fighting conventions and stereotypes in her paradoxical life. She is born to affluence, but loses her parents as a child. She lives in a palatial house with a retinue of servants. The financial prosperity in no way compensates for her psychological deprivations. Her early life is about negotiating landmines around the politics of a large joint family. Being an orphan gives her a unique advantage. She can be a spectator to the lives of the uncles, aunts, cousins and servants she finds herself surrounded by and she can also view her own tribulations with a wry sense of humour that is as liberating for the character as it is for the reader.

The anger that builds up in Laila helps her challenge the biases not just specific to her, but to her gender and class too. It also helps that Hosain's protagonist is perceptive enough to understand the follies of her own class as well as all the classes and categories of people she must encounter to arrive at her personal truths about life and living. She is a traditional hero in the classical mould. There are times when she is defeated by the forces inside and outside of her, but she remains undaunted.

The novel also profits because of its evocative style. Beginning with the title, everything about the book is designed to induce nostalgia. The background against which the story unfolds may seem wrong to the contemporary, politically correct reader. Laila belongs to a feudal patriarchal family where women and servants vie to be exploited and abused, and yet there is something in the way Hosain humanizes her characters that you feel for even the most fiendish of Laila's uncles.

The other remarkable aspect of the novel are all the stories within stories that come together to enhance the central plot. The book is not just about Laila. It is as much about Baba Jaan. And for that matter about Abida. And Zahra. And Hakiman Bua and Nandi. As well as Nita and Sita. Hosain has a unique gift. She magically transforms each character, minor or major, into a metaphor for something larger, something precious that the reader sees as a way of life that can never be brought back and therefore becomes all the more luminous. There are the occasional lapses to sentimentality but who can avoid the trap fully when it comes to recording and storing stories that derive from the family.

Hosain was writing her novel at the same time as the two leading luminaries in Urdu, Ismat Chughtai and Qurratulain Hyder, were setting up their literary milestones. The Indian English novel had not gained the readership it enjoys today and the influence of the book remained confined to select academic circles. The new edition should change the tide for this literary marvel.

Hosain is a great storyteller. Her style is unique and distinctive and the narrative acquires a distinctive flavour because of the pungent and incisive dialogues. *Sunlight on a Broken Column* is essential reading not just for aspiring novelists, but also students who must explore a novel to come at the craft that lends it form.

The story of how the novel was conceived is as fascinating as the novel itself. Apparently, the invitation came from the publishers, and for a long time Hosain despaired. She felt she could write a short story, but a novel wasn't quite her cup of tea. She was in England and dreadfully homesick. So some parts of it were written in the wild frontiers of Pakistan. And then she wrote a bulk of it in Nepal, when it wasn't the tourist destination it is now. She was a guest of the Indian Ambassador and requested him for complete privacy to write her book. She began the work by wanting to write a novel on the 'agonizing heartbreak' of a family falling apart because of the partition of a nation, but ended up with this work that she was dissatisfied with. Cecil Day Lewis, who was later designated the poet laureate of Britain, was handed the manuscript to edit and nurture. He suggested a great deal of editing and Hosain obliged, not very happy at the prospect of chopping what she considered to be relevant. The collaboration paid off, with Lewis editing the work with a poet's sensibility. We don't know whether Lewis also played a part in naming the book after a line from Eliot's 'Hollow Men' but the evocation is a perfect complement to the lyrical text.

Hosain was unarguably a pioneer as far as writing fiction in English in India is concerned, a position that is falsely arrogated by many of the writers who came *after* her. She never wrote another novel, although she received only praise from all the leading critics when it was published. A series of personal setbacks confronted her after the book was published and played a part in this talented novelist staying away from writing and publishing another book.

As far as I am concerned, and I assume this must hold true of other writers who have read this book and cherished it, *Sunlight on a Broken Column* has not only been a treasured companion over the years, but also served as a handbook to manage my aspirations when I sat down to pen the stories my context has given me. It is high time literature aficionados in this country woke up to this unsung masterpiece. Not just Laila, but all of her family and friends deserve much more. So does Indian writing in English that for the most part finds itself trapped in one of the two categories – the long-suffering martyrdom of the middle-class homemaker trapped in a loveless marriage or the poverty and deprivation of the nation – that find favour with publishers and readers from the West.

We owe it to Hosain for educating us that the great Indian novel is possible without either of these crutches.

READING *GODAAN*

Munshi Premchand's *Godaan*

SARA RAI

I first noticed *Godaan*, by Premchand, at the age of about eleven or twelve. It was a glossy, greenish volume that looked back at me at eye level from one of my father's bookshelves. Oddly enough, it was not in Hindi or Urdu, but in a strange language that I later found was Norwegian. This was the complimentary copy sent by the publisher to my father Sripat Rai, the eldest son of Munshi Premchand. The cover had the picture of an emaciated farmer and a cow with limpid eyes. I leafed through the pages, adrift on a sea of incomprehension in which the one word *Godaan* on the title page shone out like a beacon. Afterwards I came across the original Hindi version, first published in 1936, also an Urdu version, as well as Gordon Roadarmel's *The Gift of a Cow*, published by Allen and Unwin in 1968. But the only work of Premchand I read as a teenager were the short stories prescribed in the Hindi syllabus at the Catholic mission school I studied in, where everything else was taught in English by German nuns with a grim sense of purpose.

274

After all, Premchand was home turf and in my growing years, a nebulous feeling of having imbibed his writing through a sort of genetic osmosis persisted. So I came to *Godaan* only as an adult, by then at a comfortable distance from the complex mix of pride, awe and embarrassment involved in being a grandchild of the most famous name in modern Hindi and Urdu fiction.

Premchand wrote *Godaan* intermittently over a period of about three years, at a time when he had many things on his mind. There were niggling problems with his press and he was involved with bringing out a regional-languages magazine. In April 1934, he had been enthusiastically summoned to Bombay by Ajanta Cinetone. He signed a contract to write film scripts and had a minor role in the first of his stories made into a film, *Mill Mazdoor*. In addition to all of this, he was in frail health and there were other problems at home. It was not surprising then, that *Godaan* took so long to write, being published only a few months before he died in October 1936. It might also explain, to an extent, the uneven quality of the narrative and the fragmented structure of the novel as a whole.

Godaan, explained by Roadarmel in his glossary as the 'gift of a cow made by pious Hindus to a Brahmin at the time of death', does not really have much to do with the plot of the novel, except perhaps in the larger sense of providing a thematic ambience. The image of the cow, with its association of gentle resignation as well as religious ritual and its accompanying exploitation, may well be said to symbolize the theme of the novel. Exploitation at various levels is in fact Premchand's primary concern. The story revolves around the peasant Hori and his family's struggle for survival and dignity in the small village of Belari near Lucknow, in pre-Independence India. But it is not their story alone. Premchand presents a complex web of social relations through a range of characters, some of whom seem at different times to be both predator and prey. There is a blurring of boundaries between the wicked and the good; the hypocritical Rai Sahib and iniquitous Nokheram, Jhinguri Singh, Pandit Datadin and Lala Pateshwari the revenue collector are all parasites, but Premchand paints them with a compassionate brush and the reader comes away with the feeling that these villains are what they are not because of an intrinsic leaning to evil, but often because they have no other choice.

The smooth-talking, exploitative Rai Sahib, for instance, realizes that he is part of a system that not only ruins the poor but also destroys people like him who are imprisoned in 'the chains of wealth'. He wants to 'let go of worldly desires, but worldly desires would not let go of him'. 'Personal necessity' does not permit him to act in any other way than he does. Similarly, the bloodsucking Nokheram's culpability is mitigated somewhat; he has a huge family dependent on him and his paltry salary falls far short of his needs.

So what we have is a self-perpetuating system of exploitation there seems to be no getting away from. Even then there is room for hope, because no one is evil simply for the sake of it. No one is completely good either, not even the noble tradition-bound Hori, with his *maryada* or code of honour. After all, desperately poor as he is, honour is a luxury he can scarcely afford. Though Hori is a god-fearing man, 'constantly aware of the destructive side of God's nature', he thinks nothing of increasing the weight of jute by soaking it, or of cotton by leaving the seeds in. This is simply self-interest, not deceit and as such, is not antithetical to his maryada. Yet, he is a peasant who 'spends his whole life co-operating with nature' that is generous in its bounty. There is no room in Hori's life for petty selfishness. He has qualms about buying Bhola's cow at a time when the latter seems down on his luck. Seen through the prism of Premchand's vision, everyone, aggressor or victim, is caught in a vicious cycle of exploitation and indebtedness that only gathers momentum as one event spins off from the other.

There is a fissure running through the novel that seems to cleave it into two incongruent parts. On the one hand, there is the world of unrelenting hardship peopled by Hori, Dhaniya and their ilk, where interest on borrowed money keeps piling up and no matter what people do, they are 'still caught by the neck'. Premchand is masterly in his depiction of this world. Detail follows upon meticulous detail to articulate the unsentimental rigour of his social vision. In lurid contrast to this is the giddy domain of the urban rich, the likes of Khanna, Mehta, Miss Malti and Mirza Khurshed, rather unconvincing with its dreamlike hunting party, village feast and dramatic interludes. Premchand seems a little out of his depth here; he occasionally preaches, and threads are left hanging, some to be picked up later, seemingly as an afterthought.

Godaan is a political novel written at a time when the freedom struggle was in full swing and Premchand's failure to mention the British presence is ironic, if a little mystifying. His fascination with the figure of Gandhi as a moral and political force, capable of changing the destiny of the rural poor leading unimaginably wretched lives, if not immediately obvious, certainly infuses the spirit of the novel and the evolution of the characters. So with the progression of the novel, people seem to get transformed as if by magic, shedding the very qualities they had earlier been recognized by. After a lifetime of exploitation, the Rai Sahib's conscience now does not allow him to accept that 'cruelty, deceit, effrontery and oppression were the source of a zamindar's power and glory', Matadin, the erstwhile lecher, has his humanity 'cleansed and restored in the blazing sacrificial fire', filling him with love and respect for his 'goddess', the untouchable Siliya whom he had brutally discarded. Malti the social butterfly metamorphoses into an idealistic social reformer. Other characters, passing through various acid trials, undergo a similar mutation. We have here opposing threads of realism and idealism pulling in different directions. It is Hori's son Gobar, with his visits to the town, who straddles both worlds. Evolving from harsh, selfish defiance to industrious humanity, he is the harbinger of change and future turmoil.

The idealistic development of some of these characters places them in dynamic tension with those others whose minds are closely tied to their immediate needs. The daily struggle for survival occupies the mental space of the peasant characters, and it is in his portrayal of the cramped interior life consequent upon abject indigence that Premchand surpasses himself. Hori's greatest ambition in life is to possess a cow; his dream cannot extend further. Buying land or building a mansion are ideas his 'cramped mind cannot comprehend'. And after twenty years of marriage, Dhaniya realizes that 'however much she cut corners, skimped on food and clothes . . . it was still hard to pay the rent'. Yet she is unwilling to admit defeat and her rebellious outspokenness often lands her in trouble. As Hori dies in the end, destitute and defeated, his dream of possessing a cow unrealized, there is a moment of true inspiration in which Dhaniya, earthily intransigent, places on her dead husband's palm the few coins earned that morning. This becomes Hori's godaan and with Dhaniya's substitution of the cow with money, religious ritual is shown up for the farce that it is.

It can only be a tragedy of our time that *Godaan* remains still relevant, the village as bleakly despairing. 'A hundred men have to grow thin for one man to get fat. What happiness would that bring?' Hori asked, and his question resonates today with a desperate significance.

MAKING IT NEW, FOREVER

Fakir Mohan Senapati's
Six Acres and a Third

CHANDRAHAS CHOUDHURY

In a famous essay published in 1990, the poet and literary scholar A.K. Ramanujan asked the philosophical question, 'Is there an Indian way of thinking?' In the closing years of the nineteenth century, the Oriya writer Fakir Mohan Senapati appears to have asked himself the narrative question: 'Is there an Indian way of writing a novel?'

Senapati's brilliant answer took the form of a novel called *Chha Mana Atha Guntha*, published in serial form in an Oriya magazine from 1895 to 1897, then as a book in 1902, and at long last in an English translation adequate to its linguistic energy and narrative agility as late as 2006. Upon publication of *Six Acres and a Third*, as the English translation was called, it instantly became obvious that this was one of the greatest novels of the Indian pantheon, as revelatory and powerful today as in its own time.

What did Senapati do that was so remarkable? His novel tells the story of the rise and fall of a greedy zamindar, Ramachandra Mangaraj, as he plots to capture the verdant landholding – the eponymous six acres and a third – of a pair of humble weavers in his village in Orissa. But this in itself was not unique. All over India at this point of time, a generation of writers across the panoply of Indian languages was discovering the power of the novel as a tool to depict the realities and injustices of the world around them.

The crux of Senapati's achievement lies not so much in what he said, but in *how* he chose to say it. From the very beginning, Senapati's narrator uses a plural 'we' to bind himself and the reader with the world of the story, like a village storyteller sitting with an audience of friends and intimates by a lantern under a tree at night. At one point, the narrator, who often addresses the reader directly, remarks that 'unpleasant truths are better left unspoken; in other words, we are forced to forget half the truth and tell you the other half'.

These words might serve as a loose definition of satire, which tells the truth by denying the truth. When the narrator describes the greedy ways of his protagonist, the venal zamindar Ramachandra Mangaraj, defending him all the while by saying that he is really a 'kind and pious man' who is being slandered by his subjects, Mangaraj is exposed more effectively than a simple and uninflected chronicle of his evils could have managed. The narrator is, in effect, repaying Mangaraj with the same duplicity that Mangaraj himself practises on those around him – he has a friendly hand on Mangaraj's shoulder while simultaneously winking at the reader, confident that 'for intelligent people, hints usually suffice'.

This jaunty line of attack is Senapati's way of describing a cruel, exploitative order in a way that gives the reader pleasure. His work reveals not just a profoundly sceptical and germinal vision of Indian life and society but also a sophisticated understanding of how fiction has an autonomous existence, that a story is both a representation of some outward reality and also a kind of game.

'We're not absolutely sure what was meant by this,' says the narrator in the novel's opening paragraph, 'but our guess is that these men were slandering Mangaraj.' Reporting every story and slander that comes its way from multiple sources; making its own pronouncements on good and evil, human nature and history; and always keeping an entire field of meanings and implications in play with that ingenious 'we're not absolutely sure', Senapati's narration produces a fine weave of observation of character, family, village, society and colonial government, all of which we – the readers – are continuously decoding as we go along.

The plot of *Six Acres and a Third* revolves around Mangaraj's attempt to appropriate a village farmer's verdant smallholding, six-and-a-third acres in area, in his village Gobindapur. The plotline, however, is not linear – yet another respect in which Senapati seems ahead of his time. The reader finds in the book fascinating interludes on the place of the temple and the pond in village life, brilliant single-chapter character portraits such as the one of Mangaraj's shrewish maid Champa, and meditations upon human nature and Indian history.

The energy of Senapati's narration also owes much to its love of metaphorical play. Water lilies fold themselves up and hide during the day 'like young Hindu daughters-in-law'. Cows chew their cud 'like baishnavas, moving their mouths as if they were repeating the divine name'. Grand meanings suddenly emerge from metaphorical juxtapositions. At one point, speaking of the birds found near the village pond, the narrator notes how the cranes churn the mud 'like lowly farmhands' looking for fish all day long, while kingfishers appear suddenly, conduct swift raids, and gorge themselves on the stolen pickings. 'Oh, stupid Hindu cranes,' the narrator laments, 'look at these English kingfishers . . .'

Sly, salty, riddling and chirruping, the narrator of *Six Acres* appears not to inhabit a stable world of truth retailed to the reader from on high, in the manner of the classic nineteenth-century British novel. Rather, he is shunted between competing knowledge systems and ways of making meaning, such as the traditional village order, colonial modernity, and the flickers of his own nonconformist intelligence. There is no one target, whether person or system, for the novelist's satire. The narrator casts a searching ironic light upon the injustices of the zamindari system as well as the depredations of British colonialism, the suffocating hierarchies and prejudices of caste, and more generally on man's capacity for inhumanity towards other men.

The truth is — and this is what is most charming about Senapati — that the author was really an incorrigible ironist. His work is not dependent on the gross folly of the wicked but on the naturally crooked timber of humanity. In fact, if his novel persuades us of anything, it is the ubiquity of human vanity and frailty. The tone of his narrative is that of the village gossip — sly, garrulous, conspiratorial, brimming over with hints and winks and insinuations. At one point, the narrator describes the village priest, a respected man who runs the shrine of the village goddess, Budhi Mangala. 'The priest was very highly regarded in the village, particularly by the women,' says the narrator. 'The goddess frequently appeared to him in his dreams and talked to him about everything.' That 'about everything' — as if the goddess personally reports to the priest — is a damning phrase.

Elsewhere, the narrator makes fun of the assumptions of civilizational advancement held by the British. 'Today, in the nineteenth century, the sciences enjoy great prestige, for they form the basis of all progress,' he declares. 'See, the British are white-skinned, whereas Oriyas are dark in complexion. This is because the former have studied the sciences, whereas the latter have no knowledge of these.' Senapati is here equating scientific advancement, absurdly, with skin colour, as if to mock the easy British assumption of racial superiority. Once the Oriyas learn science and emerge from their benighted state of ignorance, they too will become white-skinned. At another juncture, the narrator mocks the slavish veneration of British culture by the newly emerging class of English-educated Indian intellectuals. 'Ask a new babu his grandfather's father's name,' he sniffs, 'and he will hem and haw, but the names of the ancestors of England's Charles the Third will readily roll off his tongue.'

In the years after the publication in English of *Six Acres and a Third*, the novel's place as a kind of foundation stone for the Indian novel has become ever clearer. The contributors to a recent book of essays on Senapati (*Colonialism, Modernity and Literature*, edited by Satya P. Mohanty and published by Orient Longman in 2011) demonstrate how Senapati Indianized the novel by seeding it with the communal intimacy and the scepticism of Indian oral storytelling traditions, creating in place of the 'descriptive realism' of contemporaries like Bankimchandra Chattopadhyay, a narrative voice as murky and as fertile as the village pond to which Senapati devotes one of his chapters.

For instance, in one essay, the critic Himansu Mohapatra explains how Senapati's 'complex and polyphonic realism' produces a more powerfully analytical world picture than even that of a novelist as socially conscious as Premchand, because Senapati works in such a way as to reveal the 'causal joints' of the world. Simultaneously, the 'links, nudges and dodges' of the narrator produce 'an active reader', one who discerns the sceptical and critical awareness required of him as a political subject. In another, the scholar of Telugu literature, Velcheru Narayana Rao, compares *Six Acres* with another late nineteenth-century work, Gurajada Apparao's play *Girls for Sale*, to show how both writers deserve to be seen as creators of an indigenous modernity that could see the faults and failings of the traditional Indian order without assenting wholesale to the values of Western modernity.

Even more interestingly, the critic Jennifer Harford Vargas links the magical realism of Gabriel Garcia Marquez not to Salman Rushdie but instead to Senapati. Both *One Hundred Years of Solitude* and *Six Acres* try to shake off the burden of the colonial gaze, Vargas notes, by employing 'underground types of storytelling – mainly oral, ironic, dialogic, and parodic ones – developed by those on the underside of power'.

Without raising the subject directly, Mohanty's anthology has something to say to the contemporary Indian novel in English. The great mass of novels in this domain today, whether popular novels written in an undemanding style or literary novels seeking a more complex awareness of language and character, remain intellectually lazy and formally unambitious, unthinkingly applying dozens of large and small narrative conventions to the act of storytelling.

Through the independence and energy of his example, Senapati serves as a rebuke to complacent, even consumerist, storytelling, and its demonization of formal innovation as something self-indulgent or pretentious. As *Six Acres and a Third* demonstrates, when someone works on the scale that Senapati did to think the novel anew, that book always remains new.

UNGODLY TALES

Saadat Hasan Manto's *Dastavez*

KISHWAR DESAI

Saadat Hasan Manto's short stories, which deal specifically with the Partition of India, remain embedded in my mind as possibly the most chilling, revelatory and mesmerizing account of our dark, unholy accoutrements. I first read them in Hindi in the five-volume anthology *Dastavez: Manto* (1993), which includes his essays, short stories and plays compiled and edited by Balraj Menra and Sharad Dutt (the collection faithfully follows the original Urdu – the language is the same, only the script differs. And to my mind, if you cannot access the Urdu version, this is the second best way to read them as no other translation does justice to Manto's writing). These are unforgettable stories, and every character in them can be recognized, even today, in the riots and oppression that take place anywhere in the world.

For me, as a north Indian, they bear special significance, because whenever I think of the Partition, I also remember the huge impact it has had on my parents' generation. It changed their lives forever and brought them face-to-face with a monstrous reality of human cruelty and greed. But while their innocence was ripped apart, the political patrons from all parties remained mostly unharmed. It was a bleak irony that certainly did not escape Manto.

With the burden of over six million deaths, many of which are still unaccounted for, no one who lived through the Partition can ever erase the memory, or indeed, should even attempt to do so. I feel I carry the Partition of India within me as a bloody memory, even though I did not see it myself. It is part of me; and when I read Manto, the pain and grief of it come alive before me, as do the sporadic spurts of kindness and heroism that also emerge in his writing. This is a powerful narration of what has made us what we are today, and when we face the other equally dysfunctional offspring of 1947, Pakistan, I can almost imagine a sardonic smile on Manto's face. His writing was, and is, prescient. He recorded events as only the greatest storyteller ever could, with anger, humour and compassion.

Manto, whose first well-known short story was about the Jallianwala Bagh massacre, wrote the Partition stories both as scathing satire and tragic happenstance. These are tales where good friends become assassins, where betrayal lurks behind a lover's lust, and where simplicity is raped. Many of the stories are so shocking that even rereading them sends a shiver down your spine. It was Manto's uniquely observant eye that could give a sudden twist to every story he wrote; the pathos behind every word in many of these tales — some of which are not even one page long — gets magnified upon the final paragraph. Sometimes the horror is so acute it can make you cry.

'Khol Do' is one such story; the impact of the initial reading remains with me till today. I first read it almost fifteen years ago: a father's search for his missing daughter during the Hindu-Muslim riots ends in the hospital. Sakina has been raped so brutally that she is in a coma, and her father thinks she is dead. The doctor who comes to examine her asks for a window to be opened in the airless room. He says, '*Khidki khol do* (open the window).' But the corpse-like, traumatized Sakina understands the command differently and her hands go automatically to her salwar and she pushes it down. The father rejoices that the daughter is alive. The doctor, however, realizes the enormity of the girl's gesture and is soaked in sweat.

Manto's style of writing in these stories is stark: the impact of violence is realized at different levels, but he dispenses of it in a few sentences. The descriptions of terror are equally laconic and terse. While describing the looting taking place in the short story 'Mazdoori' he says, 'From a window in a multi-storey house a roll of cloth came fluttering down. A flaming tongue licked it. It reached the ground as a heap of ash.' The entire story describes in a matter-of-fact fashion how people go about, guiltlessly and calmly, taking what they want from destroyed homes and shops. In the free-for-all, a few cops nab a poor Kashmiri trying to walk off with a stolen sack of rice. They force him to the police station, still carrying the sack. When they refuse to give him the rice, he says, with a brazen insouciance, 'Then at least pay me four annas for my labour of bringing the rice here.'

To be able to communicate a whole story in a few sentences is something that is becoming popular now among the 'Twitter' generation, but Manto's ability to do so is outstanding. Among the four-line haiku-style stories is 'Davate Amal' (which strangely resonates today in war-torn countries like Iraq and Afghanistan, where corruption has often overwhelmed the reconstruction efforts).

Manto also saw beyond the obvious normality maintained by many during the Partition. The false hopes, the hypocrisy. The desire to live. This satirical approach was best evidenced in the brilliant and well-known 'Toba Tek Singh', in which Manto used the allegory of the exchange of lunatics between the newly constructed India and Pakistan to convey his contempt of the Partition and its mindless devastation of lives. 'Toba Tek Singh' is not only among the best short stories ever written in the Asian subcontinent (at least in my opinion), but it also shows how humour and satire can make a point much more dramatically. Many people have linked the origin of the story to Manto's own incarceration in the lunatic asylum in Lahore to cure him of his alcoholism.

But in fact the story was rooted in Manto's bewilderment (also referred to in essays) over his own identity. Who was he? Was he Indian or was he Pakistani? And where did his loyalties lie?

The Partition had created a deep schism in his own psyche – and indeed in the psyche of all those who have lived through it. Today we have understood a great deal about immigration and the plight of refugees, as well as the burden of a migrant culture and the nature of multiple identities. However the Partition had created a whole generation of confused and rootless people both sides of the border, and there was very little done in terms of healing the wounds. On the contrary, people who had lost their homes and loved ones were simply expected to pick up the pieces and carry on – even though they had no control over their own circumstances. Nor had they been really able to decide where they should lead their lives. Suddenly, their religion, often something many had not really paid much attention to, became the identity that was most important.

For Manto, this deciding point was something he looked back on with bemusement. In many essays and short stories he would recollect the point when he took the decision to leave Bombay and board the ship leaving for Pakistan. In one essay he described how the anti-Muslim feeling had begun to invade the film studio he had worked in, expressed through worrying anonymous derogatory letters. In another he spoke of his fear when he drove through a predominantly Muslim area with Ashok Kumar, worried that something would happen to the film star, and he (Manto) would be held responsible. In his Partition stories too this unease crops up again and again.

In the almost autobiographical story 'Sahay', he writes about a rift between a Muslim and a Hindu friend when the latter confesses that if the circumstances demanded it, he could even kill the Muslim. At the beginning of the story Manto writes: 'Don't say that one lakh Hindus or one lakh Muslims were killed . . . say that two lakh human beings were killed. And the bigger tragedy is not that two lakh human beings died, but that these two lakhs will not be properly accounted for . . .'

This sharp, incisive and heartbreaking style, an ability to make you think even as his pen sears through your emotions, is one that Manto alone could bring to the Partition. It is that which makes these stories unforgettable, haunting and poignant. It is why I read them again and again. They are a reminder both of what we can aspire to be and the depths to which we can fall.

BEAUTY AND DREAD IN A BARSATI

Nirmal Verma's *A Rag Called Happiness*

ZAC O'YEAH

'Write what you see but what you see may not be right,' it says on the first page of the boy's diary, words written by his mother who died years ago. Now he is thirteen and ill with a persistent fever, and is sent from Allahabad to Delhi to recover.

He stays with his cousin Bitty. Some twenty years old, she lives in a barsati in Nizamuddin, on a rooftop behind the dargah, and is busy with daily rehearsals of a Strindberg play. As the boy's fever recedes, he studies Bitty and her upper-middle class friends: a couple of them are foreign-returned, from Oxford, from London, to an India of the 1970s; another is an idealistic university dropout who, during a stint in Bihar, saw genuine poverty and violence but didn't last there, and so came back to his parental home, a Lutyens bungalow, where he directs plays on the sprawling lawns. While out there is a world of real tragedies and deaths, here they are cocooned in their interpretations of foreign playwrights, each with his or her own sadness hidden underneath the everyday mask.

Despite their pursuit of freedom and creative lifestyles, ostensibly go-getting attitudes and artistic endeavours, they radiate insecurity, self-doubt, angst and despair – perhaps, the reader speculates, over being caught between cultures. The boy, however, can't always make sense of his observations: he sees everything so acutely it is often painful to read the descriptions of the theatrewallahs who, while partying on Bitty's rooftop, exert influences on each other via invisible social and mental laws akin to how gravity determines the mechanical movements of planets. 'At late night parties there always comes a moment when nobody seems aware of what is happening within or about him: the world at large sinks out of sight in the glittering stream of words. Voices swell through the air but what remains behind is the ubiquitous grey silt.'

It comes as a shocking realization to the boy that actors rehearsing a scene only pretend, no matter how genuine their emotions seem. This insight taints his perception of real life too: for what is it that people do as they enact their day-to-day lives, if not pretend and act much of the time? The question thus becomes, what is the self?

'As I read through my diary it occurs to me what a stupid little fellow I am. To tell you the truth, there is no end to my stupidity,' says the narrator (whose pronoun alters between 'he' and 'I') with the clarity and bitterness of hindsight, comparing his misunderstanding of things to watching a movie a second time and noticing all those small but significant things that shape events, the clues you missed when you first watched it because you were too engrossed in the film.

Every experience carries a potential disillusionment, but in the case of somebody who is thirteen, this disillusionment is part of the process of coming of age. The boy may be a mute witness, barely noticed by grown-ups, but he is an avid diarist and the key to the novel is this role of the authorial teenager, who once was 'he' but eventually becomes the 'I' of the novel – and who begins to catch on, with a child's talent for seeing through posturing.

Everything a reader experiences while reading a book is in fact already over; and yet, Verma suggests, the experience lives on. 'This is time past. I died a long time ago. And you who are alive follow me through my diary,' the boy/the I/Verma writes. In terms of narrative technique, the book is mostly linear and written in clipped prose, but with diary passages and occasional flashbacks that transpose the point of view. These occasional derailments telescope us a certain distance from 'actual' events, allowing Verma to drop his restraint and let the prose bloom out in hallucinatory segments, such as the central scene with the dwarf at a funfair sideshow who reveals the essence of happiness in a Steppenwolfian manner, planting the seeds of existential doubt that comes to unite the cousins.

Delicately slim but enormously intense, *Ek Chithra Sukh* (*A Rag Called Happiness*, 1979) is full of beauty and dread, one of those rare books that grow with every rereading and suddenly compel you to go back a page, rethink a just-finished sentence, merely for the enjoyment of letting an idea linger in the consciousness.

Credited with having pioneered Hindi literature's reaction against social realism – the Nai Kahani movement of the 1950s – it seems to me that Verma purposefully mined the depths of the self in order to depict changes in the protagonists' inner lives as they were outwardly faced with the onslaught of Indian urbanization, the breakdown of the joint-family system, and so on. Although Verma declared that he was able to only write fiction in his mother tongue, his attempts at breaking new literary ground were denounced early on as being derived from European influences and un-Indian. The progressives viewed him as an outsider. Yet despite this supposed un-Indianess he was, ironically, when he spoke of the importance of Indian traditions, labelled a conservative right-winger. But then again, it has never been easy to be a literary genius.

Verma's study was reached via a narrow staircase to the roof of his Delhi home, and it reminded me of the one-room barsati of the novel – although it was crammed with his books and had portraits of Virginia Woolf, Mahatma Gandhi and Ramana Maharshi prominently displayed on the wall. He was sixty-seven, I was a twenty-eight-year-old aspiring novelist, yet he took the time to chat for a long afternoon. 'The theme that runs through my novels, with some variations, is about our attempts to convey our identity to others and our failure. And the resulting sorrow. This loneliness is much greater than a mere lack of friends. It is our destiny. From my present position, my stories seem to be repeated attempts, again and again, to understand the meaning of that failure.'

And, I asked a trifle worried, *what is that meaning?* 'God, and the absence of God, and the meaning of a lack of meaning, the brevity of existence, the lack of morality, and death right in front of us . . .' Verma said and paused, searching for more words. 'To find a pattern or meaning in some kind of genetic belief in that there is no meaning. All that exists is chaos. Wishing to believe, but knowing that there's no permanent truth. So if you ask me for the themes I write about, I'll tell you that it is this: for me, art is a scream from the artist.'

I still recall the voice, feeble, just above a murmur, often drowned by city noises, but persistent – especially when speaking of words like 'loneliness' it was as if he pushed his utterances up some steep inner slope.

THE GRADUATE AS
WRITER-HERO

Siddharth Chowdhury's *Day Scholar*

PRADEEP SEBASTIAN

On a hot July afternoon in 1992, Hriday (BA English, Honours, Zakir Husain) returns to his hostel room to find a group of Delhi University students watching through a gap in the door their thuggish landlord indulging in torrid anal sex with his mistress, Mrs Midha, a section officer in Delhi University. The air is 'dank with sweat and Navy Cut smoke'. His buddy Pranjal, a fellow Bihari gallant, clues him in on the proceedings in a cool, matter-of-fact way: 'He has taken her once in the chut, then in her mouth, now he is doing her in the ass.' Jishnu da (MA Previous, English, Ramjas) as usual is watching, masturbating fervently. Jishnu da, Hriday tells us, is a compulsive masturbator ('making baingan bharta he called it') who never changes or washes his Bermuda shorts.

'In fact the shorts were so stiff with profligacy that the story was that once during an argument in the hostel over who was supposed to pay for the Old Monk khamba that Friday night, Jishnu da in anger had taken off his shorts and thrown them at Farid Ashraf's face. Though Farid managed to turn his face in time, he cut his fingers on the razor sharp edges of Jishnu da's shorts. The next day Farid (third year History Honours, KMC) had to take tetanus shots.'

Hriday Thakur, seventeen (just graduated from Patna Commerce College) has, along with his childhood buddy Pranjal, found strange digs in Delhi at the Shokeen Niwas hostel owned by Zorawar Singh, a small-time political broker and muscleman. The menacing Zorawar is the perfect foil against whom both violence and comedy erupts. One fine, unsuspecting day, the hostel boys get Hriday in a tight spot with this scary man. Zorawar's mistress, Mrs Midha, is searching for someone bright to teach English to her teenage daughter and Jishnu da, the de facto caretaker of Shokeen Niwas hostel, tells Zorawar that Hriday is the man because he is a merit student.

'Uncle, we ask him to come with us to Kamla Nagar, go out for a movie to Batra, but he has a standard answer to all that: "My parents have sent me to Delhi to study hard and do well. Crack the civil services."'

'That is all very well, Hriday, but I also do hope you will not try to suck the bachi's alphonsos once in a while.'

'Of course not, uncle. I do not like mango lassi. It upsets my stomach.'

'That is very sensible of you.'

Though the residents of Shokeen Niwas are not what Hriday bargained for when he left Patna to make it in Delhi, he is glad to be here for another reason. Hriday wants to be a writer, and amidst the shady goings-on at Shokeen Niwas, he wakes up early each morning to write. 'I loved the wanton amorality of the place. Its chanciness, its far remove from respectability. I wanted to be a writer. I had finally found my material, if not my voice.'

Meanwhile, at Zakir Husain College, he has begun lusting after his English senior, the ardent, erotic intellectual Anjali Nalwa.

As soon as the cinema theatre lights go off, Hriday and Anjali start kissing and fondling. 'Afterwards,' he tells us, 'I would light up a Gold Flake with pussy fingers. Fingering her pussy was like picking up a mango leaf drenched in the summer rain, feeling the well-defined ridges between one's forefingers and thumb . . . her smell would linger on my fingers for days and at unexpected moments would remind me of her passion.'

The sexual scenes are written with enough matter-of-fact graphicness to earn your respect at once for an Indian author willing to write with such brutal sexual candour. You know at once he isn't kidding around; this won't be another sentimental, cute or nostalgic account of college life. The tone is profane and darkly comic. Siddharth Chowdhury's *Day Scholar* (2010) is not only a finely realized college novel, it is also that rare thing in modern Indian fiction: the college novel with the graduate as writer-hero.

'The writer and his world is one of my abiding themes,' Chowdhury told me. 'I come back to it again and again. While *Patna Roughcut* is more about the provincial upper classes, *Day Scholar* is about the provincial middle class and lower-middle class. The banal but corrosive everyday prejudice of urban Indian life is one of the themes of the novel and which I felt had not been brought out in the Indian English novel earlier. The other theme which runs through Hriday's narrative is of course how to be good in a world where it is so easy and appropriate to be bad.'

I like to think of *Day Scholar* as R.K. Narayan meets Upamanyu Chatterjee; *The Bachelor of Arts* meets *English, August*. Chowdhury writes about young people with precision, honesty, affection, style, an accurate ear for dialogue centred around the themes of friendship, love, writing, girls, cinema, sex, rock music and college life. Literary writers seldom pick the college novel for a subject, and I am grateful to Chowdhury for taking the genre seriously and writing this modest masterpiece.

In Indian literature, the coming of age genre seems to lavish more attention (and respect) to the theme of childhood than to adolescence.* The college novel has suffered (it's even become a bit of a joke – though a good joke – ever since it fell into the hands of the IIT-IIM campus novel). When a college novel feels witty and honest, it seems to be lacking style and literary merit. When it has literary depth, it is never as honest or witty as it should be. The triumph of *Day Scholar* is that it is all of those things: witty, honest and finely written. It's unusual to find an Indian novelist who gives himself so fully to writing about young people. And I hope, like Salinger did, Chowdhury will never take his professional eyes off them. He writes about them with understanding, accuracy and cool style.

Chowdhury's novel actually seems to belong to an even smaller, funnier tradition within the genre: the hostel novel. Shokeen Niwas, not the college, is the set-piece of the novel and it works because it is like all the hostels we have known, full of cracked characters and philistines, and an intellectual like Hriday has to make sense of

---

* A lovely, strange and interesting parallel that seems to have gone unnoticed (and unremarked on) is between Satyajit Ray's Apu Trilogy and R.K. Narayan's first three (not counting *The Dark Room*) books. They form a trilogy of sorts (even though Narayan didn't mean them to be) and even resemble The Apu Trilogy. *Pather Panchali/Swami and Friends* – childhood; *Aparajito/The Bachelor of Arts* – adolescence; *Apur Sansar/The English Teacher* – adulthood. And as in *Apur Sansar*, the just married English teacher's wife dies young. And in both cases, it is the middle one about adolescence that is underrated – *Aparajito* and *The Bachelor of Arts*. (I felt gratified when I heard Adoor Gopalakrishnan once cited *Aparajito* as his favourite Ray film).

them. If Hriday had come to a place full of intellectuals and artists, there wouldn't have been any comedy or surprise. The sticky thing about writing about things that are so close to one's own growing up is to write without gushing and affectation.

In *Day Scholar*, there is a fine restrain with self-referential details. Chowdhury achieves this distance by making his hero-narrator self-effacing, keeping what happens to him in the background, while building up other characters and their desires. The spare, quiet prose, elegant in its economy, is note-perfect: sentence by sentence the novel is interesting. Nothing is wasted or thrown away: the writing is just so much, and not more. Every chapter is so carefully worked out that each feels self-contained and can stand alone as a short story in its own right.

The violent and sexually charged Delhi hostel chapters give way to charming accounts of the writer-hero and his 'fellow gallants' of Patna's Kadam Kuan, recounting the rituals of school-ending and college-beginning. I can think of only a few Indian authors who have used a real city and one of its actual neighbourhoods as fellow characters (or as Chowdhury would say, 'fellow gallants') with as much vivid recall, consistency and fondness. Patna and Kadam Kuan (a 'tough Bihari-Bengali neighbourhood') always form part of the action and background in Chowdhury's fiction. (His first book, *Disksha at St.Martins*, is fetchingly dedicated to Patna.)

'By staying faithful to the Kadam Kuan neighbourhood,' observes Amitava Kumar, 'Chowdhury manages to create an enduring portrait of a very specific community, the Bengali in Bihar.'

Hriday recalls his schooldays in the neighbourhood: 'Around 5.30, about three times a week on an average, Yamini Sahay, along with her elder sister Rukmini, would stroll in from Kadam Kuan for the chaat and gol-gappas sold near the market entrance. Time for the cigarettes to come out. Pranjal and I would stand in front of the bookstall, light our Gold Flakes and just stare at the Sahay sisters as they tucked in massive quantities of gol-gappas. The secret perhaps of their architecturally perfect behinds. After the gol-gappas, the sisters would take a leisurely stroll around Hathwa Market and we would follow them ten paces behind, passing a Gold Flake back and forth between us.'

In the evenings, Hriday and Pranjal would cruise Hathwa Market. He returns to a bookshop from his childhood.

'It was from that shop that I bought my first Tintin comic book for fifteen rupees on my seventh birthday. It was, I believe, *Prisoners of the Sun*, on which my mother later that evening put a cellophane cover so that it wouldn't get spoiled. It was from that shop that, while on one of my interminable cruises with Pranjal, I rescued *Vanity of Duluoz*, the bittersweet Jack Kerouac novel of his golden football-playing childhood, with twenty rupees. Pandey, the shop-assistant who earlier had sold me Amar Chitra Kathas and Commando comics, told me that the novel had been languishing in that shop for the past twenty years. So it was one rupee for each year spent in Patna. It has already spent more years in Patna than I. To this day it remains one of my favourite American novels and Kerouac an abiding influence.'

Characters recur from previous stories (like Ritwik Ray from his second novel), and we find them always going down the mean streets of Kadam Kuan. From their roots here, they move away later to other neighbourhoods in Delhi. The Patna-Delhi-Patna movement is a rock and roll anthem to the head-banging music of Kadam Kuan. The nostalgic references to the things of the late 1980s and 1990s are placed just right, sharply drawing a time and place without calling attention to itself: Vicky mopeds, Rajdoot/Yezdi bikes, North Star sneakers, Competition Success Guides/Brilliant Tutorials, Nataraj pencils, Golden Eagle beer, Binaca toothpaste, Navy Cut cigarettes, *Woman's Era*, Divya Bharti movies, Boney M, Charlie perfume, and Bata sandals.

The novel's background is equally gritty with references to the Mandal agitations, riots, caste conflict, and even a shadow of the Partition. The students in the story, whether in Patna or Delhi, are acutely conscious of caste, community and class. They are full of prejudices. Jishnu da is quick to express his distrust and distaste for dark-complexioned people. In an aside Hriday remarks, 'this was fairly rich coming from someone like Jishnu da, himself what we in Patna routinely called an IAS, Invisible After Sunset.' Jishnu da is also fond of saying, 'I do not like Bengalis. They think too much. You cannot trust such people.'

In daily conversation, students display a casual snobbishness.

'You do realize that he is a chutiya, don't you? You know what he had done?'

'Yes, I heard.'

'But then what can one expect from a bloody dhobi.'

Hriday himself, though sophisticated, isn't very different. Later in the novel he realizes with shame that though he had blamed Anjali for being a snob for moving away from him, it was he who had found excuses not to include her in his life fully — because she was, for all her erotic and writerly allure, beneath his class.

Hriday notes that Jaishankar Sharma's room is filled with civil service guides and public administration textbooks. 'For Jishnu da, like many other Bihari students in Delhi, whether in DU, Jamia or JNU, the white government Ambassador car with the red beacon light on top and all sirens blaring, was the ultimate achievement.' Though not a resident, associated to the hostel is another Bihari gallant, Satyabrat Ojha, a Mandal campaigner. His Mandal hero status has allowed him to stay on at the University, running a business supplying meals to students. For years now he has been working on an epic Sanskrit novel called 'Love in the Time of Mandal'.

It is the tough, crude and unpredictable environment of Shokeen

Niwas, full of danger and temptations that will teach Hriday to negotiate adolescence and make a tough-minded writer out of him.

'In Shokeen Niwas I would usually get up quite early in the morning and work on my stories. I would set the alarm for 5 a.m. and try to write for two hours before it was time to get ready for college . . . I would write on ruled A4 size spiral bound notebooks with pencil, so that I could erase and make new connections . . . I always wrote on the recto side so that on the verso I could write insertions and ideas for the next draft . . . I would sharpen three Nataraj pencils nestling in the chipped coffee cup, wherein I kept my pens and pencils, my writing tools.'

Siddharth Chowdhury doesn't make a big deal of this theme of the hero as reader-writer or how reading and writing become his salvation. But we sense that it is not only a cleansing act for Hriday but an affirming one, giving him identity, purpose and joy. And though reading and writing will not keep him pure, return his innocence, or ensure that he remains untouched by Shokeen Niwas, reading (*A House for Mr Biswas*, *A Movable Feast*) will keep him from totally identifying with this world, and writing (stories of the hostel and his college) will sustain him and lift him out of its parochial confines, like one of those zoom in, zoom out movie shots.

Chowdhury loves cinema. His work is strewn with references to film. For instance, I surely thought the eponymous story *Diksha at St. Martins* must refer to a character finding love in a convent school called St. Martins — turns out that he finds salvation in the movies of Martin Scorsese in a 'scabrous illegal video parlour'. In another story, a character says he considers Satyajit Ray's *Apur Sansar* 'the greatest love story', and it would be wonderful to have Hriday return in Chowdhury's own version of his 'Apur Sansar', grown up now, married, a published author looking for a way to explain and understand life.

Meanwhile, there is the promise of the closing lines of the book which never fail, every time I read the book again, to reassure me: 'The barsati was splendid . . . It was a good room. I would stay there for years. I wrote many stories there. Some published, some unpublished. But I wrote and kept myself alive.'

THE DANCE OF HOPEFULNESS
AND REALISM

Rohinton Mistry's *A Fine Balance*

PICO IYER

The second happiest experience for any reader of a great novel is to hand that novel over to someone and find her coming up to you, many sleepless nights later, in tears, and stammering her gratitude, as if you'd somehow conferred on her the key to the universe. And the happiest is to discover such an epiphany oneself. It is a happy experience in part because it is a rare one, and usually when I press *Mason & Dixon* or *Sabbath's Theatre* on friends, I'm used to seeing (too dramatically) how much their tastes differ from my own, or how novels have a small and particular province, as most art does, but cannot be guaranteed to speak to every reader in every mood or moment.

Yet the one novel I can count on giving to almost anyone, in any circumstance, is the life-changing book I read weeks before it officially came out in 1996. I've lost count of the number of people who have come up to me shaken, and said that it took them to a level of involvement and feeling that they'd forgotten, made them look on their fellow beings differently, or resolve to be a little more deliberate and compassionate in their actions. One film producer said to me, 'I can't believe I'd never heard of *A Fine Balance* until this year! And I thought Dickens was a master!' Rohinton Mistry's second book is the one novel of my life that I feel sure people of any culture will be reading, and learning from, and shedding tears over, long after I and the world I know are no longer around to commend it.

There's no need to dilate here on the richness of its texture, the care with which its images lock together or, what is most moving and transformative of all, the selflessness of its author, who gives himself over to his characters so entirely that you begin to feel for them as if they were your closest friends (the classic novelist's art, more and more forgotten, of not even trying to pontificate about cultures as a whole but simply plunging so deep into their people that larger conclusions come to us like tremors). I can still remember the avidity, pained but unstoppable, with which I turned over page after page, for hours on end, as I flew out of Bombay after a family wedding, a beloved uncle and aunt beside me, and felt that the city of my parents and my grandparents had been opened up to me as it had never been before.

The outline of the plot, of course, could hardly be more straightforward. Four characters, each with his own sorrows, find their lives intertwining in Bombay in 1975, during the time when Indira Gandhi has imposed her Emergency. Dina is a Parsi widow in her early forties, who's rented out a room in her small apartment to Maneck, a student from the mountains; Ishvar and Om are tailors from a village, uncle and nephew, who have come to the big city to make new lives for themselves and to try to rise up from their sorry status as Untouchables. As in Balzac or Hardy, or any of Mistry's great peers, these figures are indelibly formed by the city and country around them — and yet recognizable to those who've never been within 6,000 miles of Bombay.

In all of Mistry's novels, the sentences crackle with the lingo and chatter, the raucous scepticism of Bombay, as characters discuss how, for example, 'For politicians, passing laws is like passing water. It all ends down the drain.'

After leaving his hometown at the age of twenty-three, to settle in Toronto, Mistry has spent the past four decades meticulously recreating every last detail and cadence of the Bombay he remembers, whose sounds and streets he can perhaps see from afar as he could never see close-up. Yet underneath the shouting vividness is always the tragic sense that an official Emergency is only a metaphor for a world in which 'living each day is to face one emergency or another'. To that extent, the nightmare we are presented within the novel can never end. And the very precision and attention of Mistry's prose is a typically pointed, if gentle, rebuke to the 'bombast and rhetoric (that) infected the nation' and the flightiness of a world with 'a phobia about anything in slow motion'.

What I remember most, many years on, about my first encounter with the book are questions, so deep they extend far beyond the political circumstances of Mistry's novel: how much do we defer to injustice, and take it to be the unfathomable way of some Fate, even some Divine sense of order? How much do we rise up against it, and die, perhaps, in the struggle? Where does kindness end and weakness begin, and how do we ever begin to find the correct attitude — the right balance of hopefulness and realism — to treat life as a colleague? Can compassion itself at times be a form of hubris?

Lofty questions, to be sure, but they never begin to be abstract in this story of one wrong placed terribly against another. They prick us, and draw blood. They are set amidst painfully detailed and specific descriptions of how to load a dead buffalo onto a cart, and how to beg, or how to live by collecting human hairs. Why the professional beggar may look down on the blind, and how the legless help the hopeless. Unflinching descriptions of how women have acid thrown into their faces, and men are forced to eat excrement, or hanged from trees, because they were born into the wrong caste. And running against all this is the jokey warmth of those Mistry figures, who survey the scene like a Greek chorus. Part of the sophistication of the story is that it puts us all invisibly into a crooked, topsy-turvy world where you have to step around the law to survive: we learn to sympathize with murderers and to distrust philanthropists. The only villain in the book is abstraction, and any government or corporate institution or 'ism' that would take us away from the crying flesh and blood of real people in the streets.

In the years immediately before and after the book's publication, the West saw a great rush of books from India's city of dreams, which came to seem as much the centre of the literary landscape as New York had been in the twentieth century or London in the nineteenth. An unending stream of verbal, clever, richly coloured and very confident spirits seemed to leap onto the page to bewitch the far-off world with magical realist parables, or tales of forbidden love, with books that trafficked often in a world that will long seem exotic to London and New York. The stuff that might be commonplace to someone in Bandra or Juhu became almost irresistible to those who had never seen a sadhu, or a groom riding up to his wedding ceremony on an elephant.

But *A Fine Balance* has always struck me as one of the most enduring books I've read about India, in part because it is about something much deeper than just India. It doesn't trade in Orientalisms, and its revelations would be as shocking to someone living in Malabar Hill or Worli as to anyone in California or Melbourne (I know this from watching the shocked awe and admiration of my Bombay-born mother when she read it). For all the political outrage in Mistry's books, he refuses to traffic in easy prescriptions or slogans. Maybe that's why more and more books I come across remind me of his setting. Yet, few of his successors pose questions with the earnest detachment that gives Mistry his special air of clear sight and grievance all at once. How to hold on to patience and hope and dignity when reality seems to mock them? And how to learn to read with patience and attentiveness and care? Such issues would not seem strange, though they would seem very urgent, to those in Rio de Janeiro, the inner cities of America, or Abidjan.

I know Indians who complain that Mistry is taking his material from melodramatic newspaper headlines aimed at foreigners, or failing to keep up with a country that is rapidly changing. But to say this, as with R.K. Narayan, is to miss the point. *A Fine Balance* stands outside of time as much as place (perhaps because it was written two decades after the events it describes, on the far side of the world) even as it is deeply rooted in both. Rohinton Mistry's real domain, in all his work, is that place without names or addresses, where one soul is brought up against impossible pain and has to try to measure agony against faint possibility. In that regard, he might belong with Graham Greene or Beckett. His books are parables about the cost of being human.

To anyone who has not read the book, much of this may sound extravagant; to many who have, it will only seem inadequate. The thing that is most important about Mistry's novel, and that may be hardest of all for a critic or fellow writer or admirer to say is that, quite simply, it breaks your heart. Sixteen years after first reading it, I can still remember the effect it had on me, and the way in which it had me holding my breath as I all but prayed for Providence to smile down on its desperate, but constantly familiar, characters. A reader doesn't enter *A Fine Balance*, and then put the book down, moved and transported; more likely, *A Fine Balance* enters her, and she will never be quite the same again.

ACKNOWLEDGEMENTS

It is a pleasure to thank all the contributors — *50 Writers, 50 Books* would not have been possible without them, and so this is really their book. Nearly all but a few essays here were written for this anthology, and even those that first appeared elsewhere have been offered here in a different version by the authors. We are grateful for the way all our essayists gave themselves so fully to the project; a project that has been long in the making — over three years.

For their constant and gracious support through the making of the book we'd like to especially thank Amitava Kumar, Anita Roy, Shanta Gokhale, Kala Krishnan Ramesh, Ratheesh Radhakrishnan, Hartosh Singh Bal, Navaneetha Mokkil Maruthur, Dileep Raj, Nirmala Lakshman, Nilanjana Roy, Anjum Hasan, Zac O'Yeah, Lalita Rajan, Ira Pande, Pritham Chakravarthy, Charumathi Supraja, Vinaya Chaitanya, Padmaja Challakere, Rita Kothari and Pico Iyer.

Our deepest thanks to V.K. Karthika for nurturing the book at HarperCollins. And to our editor Neelini Sarkar for her enthusiasm, support and editorial counsel. Thanks and gratitude also to Pinaki De for the charming books-on-books cover design.

Suresh Paul for being such an ardent patron of the Arts, and for his very generous and warm support. Sumeet Shetty for his attention to writers and engagement with books. Kapu for conversation and steadfast friendship over the years. Nazarius for always making a meeting (and more conversation) possible. Anu Iyer for her unfailing generosity and warmth. And friends and family for being such a rich, supportive, nourishing presence in our lives.

ABOUT THE CONTRIBUTORS

EDITORS

Pradeep Sebastian is the author of *The Groaning Shelf*, a collection of bibliophilic essays on the book arts.

Chandra Siddan was born and raised in Bangalore where she studied English Literature. After a few years in New York, USA and Karlsruhe, Germany, where she studied filmmaking, Chandra moved to Toronto, Canada, where she currently lives, writes and makes films.

ABOUT THE CONTRIBUTORS

Aamer Hussein is the acclaimed author of five collections of short stories including *Insomnia*, the novella *Another Gulmohar Tree*, and the novel *The Cloud Messenger*. He has also edited an anthology of Pakistani short stories, *Kahani*. His fiction has been translated into many languages, including Italian, Arabic and Japanese. He is Professorial Writing Fellow at the University of Southampton, Senior Fellow at the Institute of English Studies (University of London) and was elected a Fellow of the Royal Society of Literature in 2004.

Abhijeet Ranadivé is a software professional who moonlights as a translator and writer. His articles have appeared in many Marathi periodicals. He has translated Sartre and Camus from French to Marathi. He is currently working on translations of essays on the visual arts.

Abhijit Gupta is Associate Professor of English at Jadavpur University and Director, Jadavpur University Press. He is co-editor, along with Swapan Chakravorty, of the Book History in India series: *Print Areas, Moveable Types* and *New Word Order*. He was associate editor for South Asia for the *Oxford Companion to the Book*. His most recent published works are two translations of Bengali stories for children, titled *Funny and Funnier* and *Mad and Madder*. His other research areas include science fiction and fandom, graphic novels, crime fiction and the nineteenth century.

Akshay Pathak loves a good story. Apart from teaching German he was and still is active in theatre. He has worked as a journalist for various German daily papers and cultural and trade journals like the *Boersenblatt, die Tageszeitung* and *Zeitschfrift fuer Kulturaustausch*, among others. He was most recently the Director of the German Book Office, New Delhi, an office of the Frankfurt Book Fair. He is currently an independent consultant and is also working on a book.

A former editor at Oxford University Press Pakistan, **Amina Azfar** is a freelance translator and book reviewer. Among the books she has translated are *The Oxford Book of Urdu Short Stories, The Light: A History of the Movement for Progressive Literature in the Indo-Pakistan Subcontinent* and *Courtesans' Quarter*. Azfar lives and works in Karachi, Pakistan.

Amitava Kumar is the author of *A Foreigner Carrying in the Crook of His Arm a Tiny Bomb* (judged the 'Best Non-Fiction Book of the Year' at the Page Turner Literary Award), *Husband of a Fanatic, Passport Photos* and the novel *Home Products*. In addition, he has edited five critical anthologies and serves on the advisory board of the Asian American Writers' Workshop as well as the Norman Mailer Center. The publications in which his work has appeared include *The Nation, The New Statesman, Boston Review, Harper's, Kenyon Review, The Caravan* and *Guernica*. He is Professor of English on the Helen D. Lockwood Chair at Vassar College.

Ananya Vajpeyi is an Associate Fellow with the Centre for the Study of Developing Societies, New Delhi, and a senior fellow with the American Institute of Indian Studies. Her first book, *Righteous Republic:*

The Political Foundations of Modern India, was published in 2012. She writes a monthly column for *The Telegraph* and contributes regularly to *The Caravan*. She guest-edited an issue of *Seminar* to mark the 150th birth anniversary of Rabindranath Tagore.

Ania Loomba is Catherine Bryson Professor of English at the University of Pennsylvania. She researches and teaches early modern studies, postcolonial studies, histories of race and colonialism, feminist theory, and contemporary Indian literature and society, often exploring the intersections between these fields. Her publications include *Gender, Race, Renaissance Drama*, *Colonialism/Postcolonialism* and *Shakespeare, Race and Colonialism*. She has co-edited several books and is editor of the Norton Critical Edition of Shakespeare's *Antony and Cleopatra*.

Anita Roy is senior editor with Zubaan, an independent, feminist publishing house based in New Delhi, and associate editor of *Geo* magazine. Her non-fiction writing has appeared in several anthologies and she is a regular reviewer, critic and freelance writer. She edited the short story collection *21 Under 40*, and is co-editor, with Urvashi Butalia, of the photography book *Women Changing India*.

Anjum Hasan is the author of a short fiction collection *Difficult Pleasures*, novels *Neti* and *Lunatic in My Head*, and a collection of poems, *Street on the Hill*. Anjum's works have been widely published in India and abroad. She works as books editor at *The Caravan*.

A.R. Venkatachalapathy is Professor at the Madras Institute of Development Studies, Chennai. He has published widely on the social, cultural and intellectual history of colonial Tamil Nadu. His publications in English include *The Province of the Book: Scholars, Scribes, and Scribblers in Colonial Tamilnadu* and *In Those Days There Was No Coffee: Writings in Cultural History*.

Arunava Sinha translates contemporary, modern and classic Bengali fiction into English. His translation of *Durgeshnandini* was published by Random House India in 2010.

Aruni Kashyap is the author of *The House With a Thousand Stories* (Viking, June 2013). He has also translated and introduced Indira Goswami's last work of fiction, *The Bronze Sword of Thengphakhri Tehsildar*, for Zubaan Books (January, 2013).

Ashutosh Potdar is a playwright, poet, translator and a critic writing in Marathi and English. He has worked with India Foundation for the Arts in Bangalore for five years and now teaches at Foundation for Liberal and Management Education (FLAME) in Pune.

Ashwin Kumar A.P. teaches in the Department of English, Tumkur University, Karnataka. He is a Doctoral Researcher at the Centre for the Study of Culture and Society, Bangalore. His current research is about the birth of linguistic identity and nationalism in India. Occasionally, he translates between English and Kannada.

Atreyee Gohain is a doctoral candidate in English at Ohio University, working on South Asian writing. She enjoys translating from Assamese to English and her translations have been published by Sahitya Akademi, Penguin India and Oxford University Press.

Bageshree Subbanna is a journalist with *The Hindu* in Bangalore. She has done translations between English and Kannada. Recently she published a collection of Kannada translations of Faiz Ahmed Faiz's poetry.

Ben Conisbee Baer is Associate Professor of Comparative Literature at Princeton University. His translation of Tarashankar Bandyopadhyay's *Hansuli Banker Upakatha* was published as *The Tale of Hansuli Turn* by Columbia University Press in 2011. He is completing a book on literary representations of indigenous vanguards in the colonial world between the 1920s and 1940s.

Chandrahas Choudhury is the author of a novel *Arzee the Dwarf* and the editor of an introduction to Indian fiction, *India: A Traveller's Literary Companion*. His book reviews appear in *The New York Times, The Washington Post* and *The Wall Street Journal*.

Charumathi Supraja has worked as a freelance journalist, teacher and communications consultant. After a sudden encounter with Theatre of the Oppressed, she started training in acting, theatre facilitation and Kalaripayattu. Her entry to a Humour Blog online contest was shortlisted and published by Penguin in an anthology, 'India Smiles.' She also wrote the script for a children's picture book on Mahatma Gandhi.

Hartosh Singh Bal is political editor of *Open* magazine and co-author of *A Certain Ambiguity*. His travelogue set along the Narmada will be published by HarperCollins in 2013.

Kala Krishnan Ramesh lives with her family in Bengaluru, where she teaches and writes in English and uses Malayalam with her mad-hatter parents whose insistence on a thread of fiction in daily life made her childhood a magical and playful time and was probably the foundation for her fascination with stories.

Kishwar Desai is the author of *Witness the Night* which won the Costa First Novel Award. She is also the author of *Origins of Love* and *Darlingji: The True Love Story of Nargis and Sunil Dutt*. She is a columnist for *The Asian Age*, *The Week* and *The Tribune* and has published articles in *The Guardian* as well as *The Daily Mail*, among other international newspapers.

Meghnad Desai is the author of several books including *The Rediscovery of India*. He writes a weekly column in *The Sunday Express*. He is Professor Emeritus at LSE and was made Lord Desai of St. Clement Danes in 1991.

Mita Kapur is a freelance journalist and the author of *The F-Word*. She is the founder and CEO of Siyahi, a literary consultancy where she doubles up as a literary agent along with conceptualizing and directing literary events. She co-directed and directed the Jaipur Literature Festival in 2006 and 2007.

Mitra Phukan is a writer, translator, columnist and classical vocalist. Her published literary works include four children's books, a biography and two novels, *The Collector's Wife* and *A Monsoon of Music*. Her works have been translated into several languages.

Mrinalini Sebastian worked for many years as Fellow at the Centre for the Study of Culture and Society. She was centrally involved in the Educational Initiatives Programme of CSCS. She is currently Adjunct Faculty at the Lutheran Theological Seminary, Philadelphia. She is interested in postcolonial theory and literary studies, a critical history of higher education in India, and feminist interpretations of minority rights.

N. Kalyan Raman is a Chennai-based translator of contemporary Tamil fiction and poetry. His translation of Ashokamitran's *Manasarovar* was shortlisted for the Vodafone-Crossword Translation Award 2010.

N. Manohar Reddy has worked as lecturer in English in India and Saudi Arabia, and is currently Guest Faculty at the Centre for Comparative Literature, University of Hyderabad.

Navaneetha Mokkil Maruthur is an assistant professor at the School of Language, Literature and Culture Studies, Central University of Gujarat. She received her PhD in English and Women's Studies from the University of Michigan and has published on Indian cinema, sexuality and cultural studies.

Nilanjana S. Roy is the author of *The Wildings*, a first novel that stars a clan of cats in Nizamuddin. A collection of literary journalism, *How To Read In Indian*, will be published by HarperCollins in 2013. Her column on the reading life for the Business Standard has run for over 15 years. She started India's first literary blog. Her fiction and journalism have appeared in *International Herald Tribune*, *The New York Times' India blog*, *The Hindu* and *Biblio*. She also edited the anthology *A Matter of Taste: The Penguin Book of Indian Food Writing*. She lives in Delhi with her husband; they are jointly owned by two cats.

Nirmala Lakshman, formerly Joint Editor of *The Hindu*, is the Director of The Hindu group of publications. She is the author of an anthology of contemporary Indian journalism titled *Writing a Nation*, published in 2007. Recently she conceptualized and curated a literary festival called Lit for Life for *The Hindu*, and also formulated the now annual Hindu Literary Prize. She is currently working on a novel and has been commissioned to write a book on Chennai.

P. Radhika is a Postdoctoral Researcher in the Department of Psychiatry, National Institute of Mental Health and Neuro Sciences (NIMHANS), Bangalore. She is involved in the assembling of a database of the NIMHANS archive and is currently working on a project that looks at how the 'mad woman' was thought of in early psychiatric/asylum discourse at NIMHANS. Her doctoral work examined the configuration of 'self' and 'modernity' in post-independence Kannada women's writing.

Padmaja Challakere has written articles on topics such as the war on Afghanistan, neoliberalism and culture, and published essays on the writings of Mukul Kesavan, Pankaj Mishra, Noam Chomsky and Arundhati Roy. Her interests include Hindustani classical music and she has written about the music of Ustad Nusrat Fateh Ali Khan and Kishori Amonkar.

Pankaj Mishra is the author of several books, most recently *From the Ruins of Empire: The Revolt Against the West and the Remaking of Asia*.

Pico Iyer is the author of two novels, *Cuba and the Night* and *Abandon*, and eight works of non-fiction, including books on globalism, Japan, forgotten places, multicultural fiction, the subconscious and the Fourteenth Dalai Lama. His most recent work, *The Man Within My Head*, addresses Graham Greene, fatherhood and his abiding theme of how to act with conscience and clarity in a conflicted world on the move.

Rana Nayar is Professor, Department of English & Cultural Studies, Punjab University, Chandigarh. As a translator, he has rendered around ten modern classics of Punjabi into English. Apart from some sixty-odd papers in national and international journals, he is also the editor of *Inter-sections: Essays on Indian Literatures, Translations and Popular Consciousness.* A committed theatre lover, he has directed over twenty major, full-length productions, and has acted in almost as many.

Rimi B. Chatterjee is a novelist and academic. She is the author of *Empires of the Mind* and three novels, *Black Light, The City of Love* which was shortlisted for the Vodafone Crossword Book Award 2008 and *Signal Red. Empires of the Mind*, her academic history of Oxford University Press's relations with India before 1947, won the SHARP DeLong Book Prize. She teaches English at Jadavpur University.

Rita Kothari is currently with the Humanities and Social Sciences Department at the Indian Institute of Technology Gandhinagar. She is the author of *Translating India: The Cultural Politics of English, The Burden of Refuge: Sindh, Gujarat, Partition* and *Memories and Movements: Borders and Communities in Banni, Kutch* (Orient Blackswan, 2013). She has edited and translated several books including *Decentering Translation Studies: India and Beyond, Chutnefying English: The Phenomenon of Hinglish, Speech and Silence: Literary Journeys by Gujarati Women* and *Unbordered Memories: Partition Stories from Sindh.*

S. Theodore Baskaran's *The Message Bearers: Entertainment Media and Nationalistic Politics* is considered a pioneering book in the area of popular culture. His *The Eye of the Serpent: An Introduction to Tamil Cinema* won him the National award, Swarnakamal in 1997. He writes both in English and Tamil on cinema and on conservation.

Sampurna Chattarji is a poet, novelist and translator. Her ten published books include three poetry collections – *Absent Muses, The Fried Frog* and *Sight May Strike You Blind*; and two novels – *Rupture* and *Land of the Well.* Her translation of Sukumar Ray's *Abol Tabol* is a Puffin Classic titled *Wordygurdyboom!.* Her latest book, *Dirty Love*, is a collection of stories about Bombay/Mumbai. More about her writing can be found at sampurnachattarji.wordpress.com.

Sara Rai is a writer and translator working in Hindi, Urdu and English. She has written two short story collections *Ababeel ki Uraan*, *Biyabaan Mein* and a novel *Cheel Wali Kothi*. Her translations include *The Golden Waist-Chain*, *Imaging the Other* and *Hindi Handpicked Fictions*.

Siddharth Chowdhury is the author of *Day Scholar*, *Patna Roughcut* and *Diksha At St Martin's*. He lives in Delhi and works as an editorial consultant with the House Of Manohar.

Utkal Mohanty is creative head of an advertising agency based in Bangalore. His translations from writings in Odia and Bengali have been published in various magazines. He has also translated Arun Mukhopadhyay's Bengali play *Mareech Sambad*.

Vidya Pai has translated four Konkani novels: Pundalik Naik's *Acchev*, Mahabaleshwar Sail's *Kali Ganga* and *Havthan*, and Damodar Mauzo's *Karmelin*. *Kaleidoscope*, her translation of Konkani essays by Ravindra Kelekar forms the first volume of the World Konkani Literature series of the Konkani Language and Cultural Foundation. Her translated short stories have appeared in several anthologies.

Vijay Nair is a writer and writing coach based in Bangalore. His books include *The Gloomy Rabbit and Other Plays*, *Master of Life Skills*, *The Boss Is Not Your Friend* and *Let her Rest Now*. His essays have been published in international anthologies. He is a recipient of the British Council Charles Wallace Award.

Zac O'Yeah is a novelist and book critic. He has written twelve books in Swedish, including the Gandhi-biography *Mahatma!* which was shortlisted for the August Prize 2008 for best nonfiction book of the year. He is the author of two detective novels, *Once Upon a Time in Scandinavistan* and most recently, *Mr Majestic: The Tout of Bengaluru*.

LIST OF BOOKS

The editions referred to indicate those used by the contributors and do not necessarily indicate the first edition/year of publication.

Bankimchandra Chattapadhyay, *Durgeshnandini,* translated by Arunava Sinha (Random House India, 2010)

Ambai, *In a Forest, a Deer*, translated by Lakshmi Holmström (Oxford University Press, 2006)

Amitav Ghosh, *The Shadow Lines* (Penguin Books India, 2009)

Amrita Pritam, *Pinjar* (Darbar Publishing House, 1998)

Arundhati Roy, *The God of Small Things* (Penguin Books India, 1997)

Ashokamitran, *Thanneer* (New Horizon Media, 2006)

Attia Hosain, *Sunlight on a Broken Column* (Chatto and Windus, 1961)

Bama Faustina Soosairaj, *Karukku*, translated by Lakshmi Holmström (Oxford University Press, 2011)

Bhalchandra Nemade, *Kosala* (Popular Prakashan, 1997)

Birendra Kumar Bhattacharya, *Mrityunjoy* (1970)

Charu Nivedita, *Zero Degree* (Blaft Publications, 1998)

Fakir Mohan Senapati, *Six Acres and a Third* (Penguin Books India, 2006)

G. Kalyan Rao, *Antarani Vasantham*, translated as *Untouchable Spring* by Alladi Umar and M. Sridhar (Orient Blackswan, 2000)

G.V. Desani, *All About H. Hatterr* (1948)

Gopinath Mohanty, *Paraja*, translated by Bikram Das (Oxford Univerity Press, 1987)

Gurdial Singh, *Parsa* (National Book Trust, 1999)

I. Allan Sealy, *The Trotter-Nama* (Roli Books, 1999)

Indira Goswami, *The Moth Eaten Howdah of the Tusker* (Publication Board of Assam, 1981); translated by A.J. Thomas (Rupa, 2004)

Ismat Chughtai, *Terhi Lakir* (Rajkamal Prakashan, 2004); translated as *The Crooked Line* (Kali for Women, 1995)

Joseph Macwan, *Angaliyat*, translated as *The Stepchild* (Oxford University Press, 2004)

K.M. Munshi, *Gujarat No Nath* (1920)

Kamala Das, *Pakshiyude Manam* (DC Books, 1964)

Krishna Sobti, *Dil-O-Danish*, translated as *The Heart Has Its Reasons* by Reema Anand and Meenakshi Swami (Katha, 2005)

Lummer Dai, *Prithibir Hanhi* (1963)

Mahabaleshwar Sail, *Yug Sanvaar* (2004)

Mahasweta Devi, *Aranyer Adhikar* (1977)

Munshi Premchand, *Godaan*, translated as *Gift of a Cow* (Permanent Black, 2007)

Nabarun Bhattacharya, *Harbart*, translated by Arunava Sinha (Tranquebar Press, 2011)

Nirmala Verma, *Ek Chithra Sukh*, translated as *A Rag Called Happiness* by Kuldip Singh (Penguin Books India, 1979)

O.V. Vijayan, *Khasakinte Ithihasam*, translated as *The Legends of Khasak* (Penguin Books India, 2008)

Poornachandra Tejaswi, *Carvalho*, translated by D.A. Shankar (Allied Publishers, 1990)

Pudumaippithan, *Pudumaippithan Kathaigal* (Navayuga Prasuralayam Ltd, 1940)

Qurratulain Hyder, *River of Fire* (Aakar Books, 2011)

R.K. Narayan, *The Guide* (Penguin Books India, 2012)

Rabindranath Tagore, *Ghare Baire*, translated as *The Home and the World* (Penguin Books India, 2005)

Raja Rao, *The Chessmaster and His Moves* (Vision Books, 1988)

Rohinton Mistry, *A Fine Balance* (Faber and Faber, 2006)

Saadat Hasan Manto, *Dastavez*, Vol. 2 (Rajkamal Prakashan, 1993)

Salman Rushdie, *Midnight's Children* (Random House India, 1980)

Shivaram Karanth, *Marali Mannige* (Sapna Book House, 2009)

Siddharth Chowdhury, *Day Scholar* (Picador India, 2010)

Tarashankar Bandyapadhyay, *Hansuli Banker Upakatha*, translated as *The Tale of Hansuli Turn* by Benjamin Conisbee Baer (Columbia University Press, 2011)

Triveni, *Sharapanjara*, translated as *Cage of Arrows* by C. Vimala Rao (1997)

U.R. Ananthamurthy, *Suryana Kudure*, translated as *Stallion of the Sun* (Penguin Books India, 2000)

Uddhav Shelke, *Dhag*, translated as *Embers* by Shanta Gokhale and edited by Mini Krishnan (Macmillan India, 2001)

Upamanyu Chatterjee, *English, August* (Faber and Faber, 2011)

V.S. Naipaul, *A House for Mr Biswas* (Picador, 2011)

Vaikkom Muhammad Basheer, *Poovan Banana and Other Stories* (Orient Blackswan, 1994)

Vijaydan Detha, *Rachna Sanchayan* (Sahitya Akademi, 2009)

Vikram Seth, *A Suitable Boy* (Penguin Books India, 1993)